T0333783

WANDERINGS

IN

NORTH AFRICA.

BY

JAMES HAMILTON.

LONDON
DARF PUBLISHERS LIMITED
1985

First Published 1856

New Impression 1985

ISBN 1 85077 024 7

Reprinted by A. Wheaton & Co. Ltd, Exeter

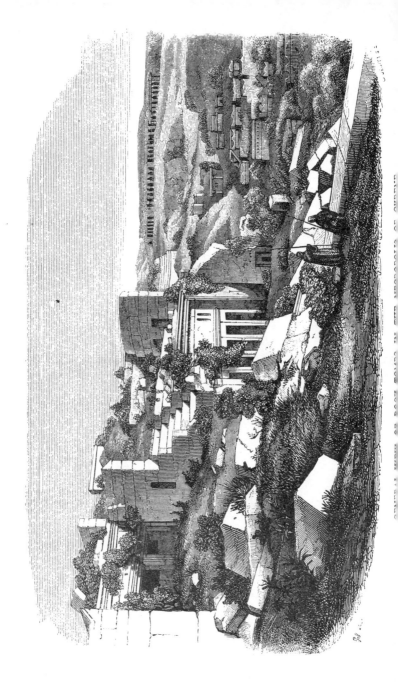

GENERAL VIEW OF ROCK TOMBS IN THE NECROPOLIS OF SIOOT.

LIST OF ILLUSTRATIONS.

CONTENTS.

CHAPTER V.

CHAPTER VI.

CHAPTER VII.

CHAPTER VIII.

CHAPTER IX.

CHAPTER X.

CHAPTER XI.

CHAPTER XVIII.

CHAPTER XIX.

CHAPTER XX.

INTRODUCTION.

A FEW words of preface concerning a country so little known as that in which these pages were written may, perhaps, be useful to the reader. For the sake of those who may be interested in its past history or present condition, I shall indicate the sources which will supply further information.

Cyrenaica, or, as it was called under the Ptolemys, Pentapolis, is situated on the northern coast of Africa, between Carthage and Egypt. In its commercial importance it once almost rivalled the former, and in the fertility of its soil, the latter. Its early political vicissitudes are little known in detail, nearly all the works which were specially dedicated to its history having disappeared in the wreck of ages, among which the most to be regretted is the Book on the Republic of Cyrene, which Aristotle inserted in his Politics.

The Cyrenaica presents a succession of hills and table-lands, bounded on the east by the barren plains of Marmarica ; to the south it is separated from the Great Desert of Libya by the hills of Hercules and the Velpa Mountains ; on the north and west it is washed by the Mediterranean. Its insular position amidst water and sands afforded considerable security as well as great facilities for commerce. In contrast with the countries on either hand, it was well watered with frequent rains and perennial springs, so that it seemed an earthly Paradise, well fitted to be the site of the Garden of the Hesperides, or the abode of the Lotos-eaters.

Cyrene, the capital of the country, was founded by a colony of Theræans, who quitted their native island in the Ægean Sea in the latter half of the seventh century B.C., under the conduct of Battus the Dorian. He was said to derive his origin from the Minyæ, the descendants of the Argonauts, and was pointed out by the Pythian Oracle to be the founder, with his countrymen, of a colony in Libya. The inhabitants of Thera, says the story, did not even know where Libya was situated, and, returning home, neglected to comply with the orders of the god. At length, admonished by a severe calamity—the total cessation of rain for seven years, and the consequent destruction of all the trees in the island excepting one—they sent one of their number into Crete, whose inhabitants were of kin to them, to inquire if any one there had ever heard of Libya. One Corobius undertook to be their guide. With him they sailed to the island of Platæa, in the Gulf of Bomba and (after taking possession of it) returned home with the news. Thereupon, Battus, " alike distinguished by nobility of birth and genius," was despatched, with two fifty-oar galleys, as king, to the new colony.

The situation thus chosen was an unfavourable one, for the island was small and barren. After suffering great privations, its inhabitants left it for the main-land, and at length, under conduct of the Galigammæ, one of the Libyan tribes, (who were tired of the new comers, and in return had proved themselves trouble-some neighbours,) they settled around the fountain of Cyre, which issues from a cave in the side of a hill about twelve miles from the sea-shore; and returned thanks to the god under whose auspices they had found at length a new home in the midst of a fertile country, " under an open heaven."

Cyre was a daughter of the king of the Lapithæ, and displayed her courage in combats with the wild beasts, which attacked her father's herds. One day being seen by Apollo, when, in the fastnesses of Pelion, she wrestled with a lion, he became enamoured of her. Counselled by Chiron, he carried her off in a golden chariot into Libya. They were there kindly received by Venus, their nuptials were celebrated, and the god gave her the country as a kingdom. Of the other fables which connect the origin of Cyrene with the gods of Greece; of the Grecian Hercules, who wrestled and overthrew Antæus, the son of the Earth (the native Libyans); of the Garden of the Hesperides, which bloomed with golden apples, inaccessible on the western shore,—I need say nothing. The hidden meaning of the myths, with which a patriotic religion was not long in enrolling the obscure origin of a Grecian colony, perpetuates the story of its early struggles, throwing a poetic gauze over facts too humbling for its full-grown pride.

The new city was built on the table-land above the hill, from whose side the fountain issues. The lofty walls which inclosed it, and the temples and palaces which adorned it, arose a landmark for the mariner. Seven descendants of its founder reigned in it successively until about 450 B.C., probably invested with a sort of patriarchal authority, such as the early kings of Athens exercised. This was followed by a hundred and thirty years of liberty or licence, succeeded by a strict monarchical government under the Egyptian Ptolemys, the last of whose kings bequeathed his country to the Roman Senate.

The history, as it has come down to us, begins with

a period of profound obscurity, which clouds the reigns of Battus and his son Arcesilaus. To the latter succeeded Battus II., Eudaimon, Felix the Happy. His reign was the golden age of Cyrenæan tradition. Fresh settlers from the mother country brought increased prosperity to the colony. Their territory became too narrow for its inhabitants, who, gradually spreading over the surrounding country, drove out the Libyan nomads; and thus the foundations of a power were securely laid, which soon gave (with the possession of a sea-port, Apollonia) a new impulse to enterprise. Teuchira and Hesperides were afterwards founded to the westward, and Barce—long the most flourishing of the daughter-cities, and at one time the rival of the metropolis—whose name is still perpetuated in the Turkish province of Barka. The native nomads did not, however, relinquish their pasture grounds without a struggle; they implored the assistance of the Egyptian king Apries, and the surname of Happy was, perhaps, earned at the fountain of Theste (Kubbeh?), where Battus defeated his troops. The Libyans were now subdued; the victors intermarried with the daughters of the soil; Greek genius was not long in adopting some, at least, of the mythology of their subjects; and thus a permanent dominion, supported by force, consanguinity, and religion, was established by the conqueror.

But it was not long before the monarchy was weakened by the defection of the brothers of Arcesilaus II.,
son of Battus Felix, who, retiring from their brother's
capital, founded Barce, and soon formed around it an
independent territory, peopled, like the new city itself,
for the most part by Libyans. Civil discord now
divided the colony, and bloody feuds stained the royal
house. The constitution, thus undermined by popular
tumults and by regal encroachments, or weakness,
threatened to involve in its ruin the material prosperity of the colony. In this conjuncture, the Cyrenæans again applied to the Pythian Oracle for advice,
and Demonax, the Mantinean, was deputed by the
god to restore order; he gained the good-will of all
parties, and established new institutions, which greatly
curtailed the royal power, but which were maintained
during the reign of the third Battus. His son and
successor, Arcesilaus III., not content to follow in his
father's steps, and impatient of restraint, was driven
into exile by the insurrection which his arbitrary conduct had aroused; but soon returning, with Samian
reinforcements, he repossessed himself of a power
which he now used with uncurbed barbarity.

Such was the situation of affairs, when the Persian
conquest of Egypt threatened to destroy the political
independence of Cyrene. The king, not daring to
trust his disaffected subjects (after promising tribute

to his new neighbour), retired to Barce, where he continued the cruelties which had rendered him odious in his own dominions. He and his father-in-law, the king of Barce, were soon afterwards murdered. His mother fled to Egypt, and claimed the protection of the Persian Suzerain, with whose troops returning she laid siege to Barce, and savagely revenged the assassination of her son. Cyrene, by timely concessions, escaped uninjured from the Persian raid. Another Battus and a fourth Arcesilaus reigned in it with mingled feebleness and severity; in their hands the royal power lost all consideration, and on the death of the last, royalty was abolished. A free republic, aristocratic rather than democratic, now took its place, accompanied by all the party contests and all the civil seditions of which the history of the mother-country shows so many examples. To this unsettled condition of its government must be ascribed the fact, that, notwithstanding its situation—equally favourable to commerce as that of Carthage — and its infinitely more fertile soil, Cyrene never, either in the arts of war or in the arts of peace, rivalled the city of Dido. A love of turbulence and feuds seems to have formed an essential feature of the Greek character; all the efforts which, from time to time, were made by her wiser citizens to introduce better order into the republic, were vain. At last they applied to the divine

Plato, requesting him to furnish them with a code of laws; and posterity regrets that he was too prudent to compromise his reputation, by legislating for so turbulent a community.

Alexander's apparition in Egypt was followed by a treaty which seemed to guarantee the independence of Cyrene; but after his death intestine troubles and the solicitations of exiles (who, for whatever cause expelled their country, are ever its worst enemies) attracted armed bands into their fertile provinces. These marauders seized the ports, twice besieged the capital, and filled the country with rapine and ruin, which neither the aid of Carthage nor of the Libyan nomads could stay. At last, one stronger than either party, Ptolemy, who had succeeded to Alexander in Egypt, sent a fleet and troops and re-established tranquillity, B.C. 322—a service which he turned to his own profit, so that Cyrene became thereafter for many years a province of Egypt, under the name of Pentapolis.

Unaccustomed to a regular government, the turbulent Cyrenæans bore the yoke impatiently. Revolt followed revolt, and the Egyptian viceroy himself rebelled against his master. But these vain attempts at forming an independent government only sunk the Pentapolis in deeper misery. It was about the time that the first Jewish colonies were introduced, in conformity with the general policy of Ptolemy; and they soon became so numerous here, that, at length, no other country besides Palestine, contained so many individuals of their nation.   Enjoying equal rights with the Greeks and the special favour of the king, they formed in the end a fourth order in the State, and were governed by municipal magistrates of their own. That they had a separate synagogue at Jerusalem, we learn from the Acts of the Apostles, vi. 9; and their frequent mention in the New Testament proves how important a part of the Jewish nation they constituted. They distinguished themselves under Trajan by a rebellion, in which they exhibited great ferocity; this rebellion was only suppressed after immense slaughter had taken place on both sides.

The reign of the third Ptolemy was a remarkable era for Cyrene. The original laws delivered by De-monax the Arcadian had been retained (with what corruption or modifications we know not) up to this time; but now, with the king's consent, the people called in two distinguished natives of Megalopolis in the same province, Ecdemus and Demophanes—disci-ples of the philosopher Arcesilaus—to revise them. These two, as the historian informs us, " restored the public peace and the safety of the citizens." The history of the following years is generally obscure; but enough remains to show, that this tranquillity was not of long duration, and tumults and rebellions continued to weaken the country till Ptolemy Apion, on his death, B.C. 96, bequeathed it to the Roman Senate. About twenty years later, after a vain attempt had been made to leave it in the enjoyment of self-government, it was merged into a Roman province in conjunction with Crete. It was, perhaps, in his administration of this quæstorship, that Vespasian first came in contact with the Jews. In the division of the empire, it fell to the share of Constantinople, and was exempt from none of the miseries which afflicted the distant provinces of the empire in its decay. The subsequent desolation of the country is described in the inflated eloquence of his time by the rhetorician Synesius, the Platonist bishop of Ptolemaïs, who, in espousing his church, refused to part with his wife. The nomad tribes gradually regained the ascendancy, driving out the more civilised inhabitants; and from the date of the Arab occupation, which immediately followed the conquest of Egypt, we hear no more of the Cyrenaica, excepting what is given of it in the short notice, which Abulfida has inserted in his Geography, under the head of Barka. It now forms the eastern part of the Turkish pachalik of Tripoli, divided into two prefectures, Benghazi and Derna, which are the only inhabited towns remaining in its whole extent.

The sources of wealth which the Cyrenaica presented

were many and valuable. Its trade with the interior
of Africa, by way of Angila, furnished for exportation
ivory, gold, precious stones, ostrich feathers, and slaves
—the same products which the triennial caravan from
Waday, at the present day, brings to Benghazi. Judging, however, from the accounts of the ancients, from
the remains of the splendid caravanserais which we
meet with on this route, the trade must have been
conducted on a far greater scale than at the present
time.   Pindar refers to the commercial navy of Cyrene,
by means of which an active commerce was carried on
with the main land, the islands of Greece, and the
coasts of Asia Minor.   Of the indigenous produce of
this country, the first in rank, both for value and
utility, was derived from the silphium, which yielded a
gummy juice, the laserpitium, esteemed by the ancients
as a remedy for almost every disease.   So universal
was its fame that it gave a common epithet to the
country ; and the "Silphium of Battus" is used by
Aristophanes as a synonym for exceeding wealth.   It
was a government monopoly, and in Rome was sold
for an equal weight of silver.   It is mentioned, if I
mistake not, among the treasures which Cæsar laid
hold of at the commencement of the civil wars.   Theophrastus and Pliny describe the method of its cultivation, though, from the expressions used by other

authors, it seems to have grown wild in the desert places; but, however obtained, it undoubtedly yielded a large revenue to the country.

The olive flourished with remarkable fruitfulness in its soil; and the immense tracts which are at the present day still covered with it, proves how extensive its cultivation must once have been, and how congenial to it is the soil in which, after ages of neglect, it still flourishes. Its crops of grain were as abundant as those of Mauritius and Sicily, and furnished large exports. During four months of my stay in the country I ate ripe grapes, and in one place I left the half-formed fruit hanging in rich clusters from the vines; so true is the ancient description which, speaking of the various climates of the Cyrenaica, says, that the harvest lasted nine months, beginning in the low grounds, then ascending to the table-lands, and ending in the hills. The flowers of the Cyrenaica were also celebrated, and the ground is still enamelled with a rich flora; the crocus officinalis furnished a considerable article of export, and its roses yielded the finest attar distilled for its Egyptian Queen. The honey almost vied with that of Hymettus, and in some places it is still gathered by the Arabs, who send it in presents to their distant friends. The herds and flocks which Pindar celebrates are still the wealth of its nomad inhabitants. The breed of horses was remarkable for fleetness and endurance; and the war-chariots in which they were harnessed were as celebrated as the skill of the drivers who conducted them.

But the ancients do not confine their praises to the natural productions of the soil. Cyrene was fruitful, also, in men distinguished in the arts and sciences. Architecture and the engraving of precious stones were both carried to great perfection by the Cyrenæans. Of their skill in painting and sculpture few evidences have reached us. It was in the liberal arts that they especially shone; and a long list might be produced of men of letters and science who adorned their birth-place or spread its fame in other lands. The poems of Callimachus, a Cyrenæan of noble birth, prove that the noblest exercise of genius was not neglected. But the brightest lustre is shed upon the African Doria by its mathematicians, physicians, and philosophers. Eratosthenes, the poet, philosopher, and geometer, may also be called the Father of Geography. But all are eclipsed by the fame of Aristippus, his daughter Arete, and her son Aristippus (the mother-taught), who founded, and to the third generation sustained, the glory of the Cyrenæan School of Philosophy—a rare, perhaps a singular instance of such mental gifts descending, as it were, by inheritance.

We know the doctrines of this school only by the writings of its adversaries ; we are not, therefore, qualified to pronounce judgment upon them. In the original teaching it seems rather to have been a contradiction to the stoic and cynical doctrines, establishing enjoyment as the chief end of man, allied to moral freedom—a philosophical enjoyment, which consists in using all the good things which Providence has showered upon us. This was a doctrine not discordant with the habits and genius of the people with whom it originated. If later disciples of this school contended that the true philosophy of life consists in the pursuits of voluptuousness, or, exaggerating even this doctrine, taught that virtue for itself is despicable, that no Deity exists, and that, since pain cannot be entirely avoided, life itself is detestable—we may regard such aberrations as the declamatory sophistries of ill-regulated genius, not as the real opinions of a school whose first teacher sat at the feet of Socrates.

I shall conclude by mentioning the authors who in modern times have called attention to this country. Our guide in all that relates to its ancient condition is the learned Dane Thrige, who, in his work " Res Cyrenensium," has exhausted all the information that the most ingenious acuteness could extract from the writers of antiquity. Of modern observers, the first in

point of time is Leo Africanus, who, with naïve simplicity, describes the Desert of Barka as a hideous
waste, peopled only by barbarians sunk in the most
abject poverty.   Early in the eighteenth century, Lemaire, quoted by Paul Lucas, was sent to explore the
ruins which it was reported to contain, by Louis XIV.
After him, Shaw and Bruce visited some parts of the
province ; but the first work which treated in detail
of its antiquities was that of the French artist Pacho,
whose untimely end prevented his reaping the laurels
which his enterprising genius had planted.   He may
be regarded as the re-discoverer of the remains of
Greek civilisation in this part of Africa.   The work
which he produced under incredible difficulties is remarkable among modern books of travel as a monument of industry and daring ; and I here gratefully
acknowledge the amount of enjoyment for which I
was indebted to it during my tour.   To his name it is
only just to add that of Beechey, whose accounts and
scientific labours have deprived future authors of the
right to intrude upon their readers the results of
geographical observations.   The plans and map which
accompany his work are of great value.   Two Italian
travellers, anterior in point of time to the last-men-
tioned, must not be forgotten, viz. Della Cella, a
Genoese physician, who in the suite of the Bey of Benghazi, visited this country in 1819, and published an

account of his travels, which, though not without merit, leave much to be desired in accuracy; and a merchant Crevelli, whose meagre journal was published by the French Society of Geography. The last of the few travellers who have penetrated into these almost unknown regions is Dr. Barth, on whose hazardous attempt to reach the central kingdoms of Africa the eyes of Europe are now turned with equal hope and admiration. May the desert which has devoured so many valuable lives, spare his to the advancement of science and civilisation!

J. H.

Cairo.
September 1, 1853.

WANDERINGS

IN

NORTH AFRICA.

CHAPTER I.

Malta to Benghazi.—Benghazi.—Aspect of the Town.—Population.
—Diseases.—Government.—Antiquities.—Dress of the Inhabitants.—Trade.—Artisans.—Jews.

THE journey which the following pages describe had
been for many years the object of my wishes, although
it was only in 1852 that I was able to put my design
in execution. The experience of several tours in
Syria had taught me the necessity of knowing the
language of the country, for the sake of personal
safety, as well as for gaining information ; I therefore
lost no opportunity of making myself acquainted with
the colloquial, which differs so much from the classical,
Arabic. The study of this language is, indeed, very
difficult, but it has been to me a most charming

employment, and I have never regretted the many long hours which I have devoted to the acquisition of it. Before leaving Europe I had carefully studied all that ancient or modern authors have written upon the old Pentapolis; and I came to this country provided with the necessary instruments for measuring heights and ascertaining the positions of the several points I should visit. I do not, however, pretend to write a book full of antiquarian lore or geographical details— on this head, my predecessors have left little to be gleaned. Thrige, in his " Res Cyrenensium," offers an ample repertory for those who are desirous of knowing every fact that classical antiquity has handed down to us, concerning the ancient wealth and arts of the Cyreneans; and Beechey has given, with the utmost accuracy, the position of the principal points of in- terest. Pacho gives us many interesting details in his work, though, perhaps, he has too highly coloured his descriptions; his drawings of the remaining ruins are full of errors. Pacho has the merit of having alone traversed this country at a time when it required no little enterprise to risk a passage through it. I disclaim all merit on the score of enterprise or remarkable discoveries; and if the narrative of my visit to this lovely region should induce others of my countrymen to vary their Egyptian and Syrian tours by a visit to the Pentapolis, the object of my ambition

will be gained. I shall have conferred upon them the
benefit of calling their attention to this forgotten land,
and on the inhabitants the still greater advantage of
a more frequent contact with European civilisation.
There is no country, excepting Morocco, where the
Moslem has so little felt the influence of modern
civilisation, or where his fanaticism is more offensive.
Here, we are still in the sixteenth century; the pages of
Shaw and other old travellers are recalled in our daily
dealings with the Arabs, whose most offensive charac-
teristics are only mitigated by the vicinity of Malta,
and through a certain traditionary fear of British
power.

Without further preamble, I shall state that my
point of departure was Malta, from whence I sailed for
Benghazi, now the principal town in the district, and
the seat of Government. I took my passage on board
a brigantine of 150 tons, the *Pace*, the largest vessel
which trades between Malta and Benghazi. The depth
of water in the small part of the ancient harbour, which
is not yet sanded up, admits no vessel which draws
more than ten feet of water; after September the
passage is so insecure, that all direct intercourse
ceases, and letters then can only be conveyed from
Malta by Tripoli, whence there is a weekly courier
who comes in thirteen days. I stowed myself on the
deck of the brigantine, in a box ten feet by five, and

about three and a half high, which, when washed and carpeted, formed no inconvenient cabin, and saved me in great part from the attacks of those creeping and jumping fellow-passengers from which no Mediterranean merchant-vessel is free. Being well supplied with new books, I managed to kill time pleasantly enough during the six days that the passage lasted. In the evening, after sunset, I used to take a seat upon the deck, to chat with the captain and the scrivano,—a sort of mate,—and thus learnt from them all they could tell me of the trade between Europe and the regency of Tripoli, and of the wonders of the unknown land I was going to visit. In their gossip I sometimes caught a faint echo of old Herodotus. I much enjoyed one of their stories, which they told with the greatest gravity, assuring me that they had heard it from the most respectable natives. In the interior of Africa, beyond the black hills, is a race of people whose men are dogs, their women being like those of other nations. The husbands spend their days in hunting, and at night bring home to their wives the game they have killed; these cook and eat the meat, and give the bones to their dog-husbands. They were both intelligent men, able to give a satisfactory account of their trade; but they made no difficulty in believing this story, and other tales not less marvellous. The profits of the trading vessels are principally made on the return

voyage, when the cargo consists of cattle for the consumption of the island, and bales of coarse wool,
which is principally destined for Leghorn. Paper and
glass from this place, plain and printed cottons from
England and Switzerland, with planks from Trieste,
form nearly all the imports to Benghazi. The approach
to the town is not promising; the long, flat line of
sand, broken here and there by groups of palm-trees,
becomes visible only at a very short distance from the
shore.   On nearing it, two insignificant white-washed
marābuts, and the castle—a square building, flanked
with round towers, standing on the sea-shore, and
conspicuous only from its whiteness—are the first
objects which strike the eye. The town itself is not
seen until the traveller is close to it; it looks like
a large collection of mud huts, unrelieved by a single
minaret, or even by the dove-cots, which render many
of the mud villages on the Nile so picturesque.
Closer inspection confirms this first impression of the
town.   The houses are indeed built of stone, badly
cemented with crumbling lime; but in the whole town
not more than a dozen have the convenience of a room
raised above the ground-floor (ghorfa).   They are
built round an oblong court, with no attempt at architectural ornament, the walls not exceeding fourteen
feet in height, and almost in no case are the rooms
more than ten feet in breadth, though frequently thirty

or forty feet long. They are lighted from the door; and, in the better houses, one, or perhaps two, rooms have the additional convenience of small windows, which are closed by wooden shutters. The flooring is sometimes of flag-stones, generally of mud; and the flat roofs, formed with the undressed trunks of the juniper trees, laid side by side across the walls, covered with mats and plaster, are not impervious to the winter rains. This is no unfavourable account of the houses of Benghazi; and when I add, that the streets, filled with loose sea-sand, are kept tolerably clean—remarkably so for an Oriental town—I have done ample justice to its merits. The water for drinking is brought from wells at a distance, in barrels or skins; and every house has in its court-yard a well of brackish water, which in many places is found at a depth of six feet. There are near the shore two public wells— one due to a former English consul—which are used for watering the cattle, but the essential luxury of a fountain, or the convenience of a walk where the sand does not reach the ankles, has not been thought of. The sanitary inspection, under a talented German doctor, is very strict, and in some cases might, perhaps, be adopted with advantage at home. His word is law in all such matters as cleaning the streets, or removing nuisances; no meat can be exposed for sale in the market, which has not been offered for his in-

spection before going to the slaughter-house; no
burial takes place without his certificate, though he
only examines the body when death is suspected to
result from plague or other infectious disease.   He
has not only the right to examine the bodies of
females, but he can have them disinterred if buried
without his certificate.   Proceedings so contrary to
Moslem prejudice, and even to Moslem law, afford
perhaps the strongest proof that can be adduced
of the utter disregard which the powers at Constantinople show to the religious laws of the Koran, as
well as of the slavish submission of the people to the
Government.

The census just completed gives 1200 for the number of houses in Benghazi, which, in this country,
represents a population of 10,000 to 12,000 souls; the
deaths in the last year were 333, and seem to favour
the higher number, but they were above the annual
average, in consequence of epidemic measles having
carried off 57 children.   In general, Benghazi may be
considered the most healthy town in North Africa;
neither fever nor dysentery are endemic here, nor is any
other form of disease frequent, except ophthalmia, the
prevalence of which may be ascribed to the general
filthiness, and to the habit which the people have at
night of sleeping exposed on the terraces, or in the
damp court-yards.   It is disgusting to see the little

children, round whose inflamed eyes swarms of flies
cluster, no one taking the trouble to drive them away.
The markets are abundantly supplied with mutton;
occasionally beef is offered for sale; but vegetables
and fruit are very rare, and, till the last six years, nothing but onions were to be had. Though the sea
abounds in excellent fish, the quantity taken is very
small. Wine, potatoes, and fruit are sometimes to be
had, brought from Malta or Canea, from whence the
European and wealthier Turkish residents obtain their
few luxuries. When I speak of wealth, it is in a
comparative sense; probably no one, either native
or foreigner, has a capital of 4000l.; but there is no
absolute poverty among the people, for the cultivation
of the land is open to all, on paying a tax of one-tenth
of the produce; and, excepting the Morocco or Tunis
Hajji, who pass through on their way to Mecca, I
have never seen a beggar in Benghazi.

The government of the province is in the hands of
a Bey, sometimes sent from Constantinople, sometimes nominated by the Pacha of Tripoli, to whom
he is subordinate. Soliman Agha, the present Kaimakan, formerly in a domestic situation in his household, was long Kehin to the present Pacha of Tripoli
(Izzet Pacha), and by him was appointed to Benghazi. His inability to read or write is considered no
obstacle to his being an efficient Governor of an ex-

tensive district; and in the visits I paid him I must
acknowledge that he seemed to be well-informed regarding the affairs of his government, and to have
an excellent memory. The object of such an appointment is, of course, that the Pacha may have in
Benghazi a dependant who will not interfere with his
peculations. The Kaimakan, or Bey, is assisted by
a Medjlis, or council, composed of the Cadi, Mufti,
and some ten members chosen from among the
principal persons of the place; and his consideration
is sustained by part of a regiment which is stationed
here—the rest of it doing duty at the castles newly
erected for the purpose of keeping the Arabs of the
interior in subjection. The Consular body consists of
an English Vice-Consul, a French Consular Agent,
and Vice-Consuls—or calling themselves such—for
Tuscany and Sardinia. All of them, excepting the
Englishman, are merchants, and it may be questioned
if their action is consequently as independent as it
should be, when we remember the monetary transac-
tions which they have with the customs, which are
here administered by the local Government. I can
personally bear testimony to the cordial hospitality of
the French Consular Agent, M. Brest, and of his family; and to the unceasing attentions of M. Xerri,
a young Maltese merchant, whom I found acting as
Vice-Consul in the interim between the departure of the

last Consul and the arrival of his successor. Although the climate of Benghazi is perfectly wholesome, I should not recommend it to any one as a residence : there are few of the necessaries, and none of the luxuries, of life to be found there; above all, there is no kind of society. Its antiquities afford at most two days' employment. They consist of large squared blocks of stone scattered along the sea-shore, foundations of ancient buildings in the sea, between the reef, which probably formed the old mole, and the shore, with a flight of steps at the extremity of the former. The shore has sunk considerably in this part of the coast, as the foundations of buildings now beneath the water testify; and often, after a winter storm, gems and medals are picked up on the beach. On the land side of the town, the sea has also made an irruption, forming a shallow lake in winter, which dries up in summer, and leaves the surface glittering with salt, if the winds are not high : hence Benghazi may be said to be built on a narrow tongue of sand. On the opposite side of this lake, the summits of the hills to the south-east of the town are covered with old tombs, many of which are rifled, but not a few still yield vases and stalactites of *terra cotta.* It was from here that M. de Bourville obtained the splendid Panathenaic vases which adorn the Museum of the Louvre ; but such good fortune is hardly to be looked for again. The existence of

the tombs is not indicated by monuments or other
external marks,—a circumstance to which, perhaps,
they owe their preservation. Some are grottoes cut
in the rock, beneath its surface, and have long been
sanded up ; the more common are rectangular excavations, about five feet by two feet, cut in the rock,
and covered by rough flattish stones. These also
are always found completely choked with sand ; they
contain vases generally of a coarse quality, really fine
vases being rare. The statuettes are, generally, much
more beautiful; and nothing can exceed the grace
of some which I saw in Paris, derived from M. de
Bourville's collection. Though this country is named
by ancient writers as famed for its engravers, I have
not seen a single fine intaglio or cameo found here.

The modern costume of the Benghazini is simple,
but not ungraceful, and, like that of all countries which
have not yet adopted the tight-fitting fashions of
Europe, is admirably adapted to the climate.   The
red cap (tarboush or takyeh), with which a cotton
skull-cap (ma'raka) is generally worn, without the tur-
ban. The under-garment consists of blue or white cotton drawers (serwàl), generally reaching to the ankles,
and rather tight from the knee, exactly like those which
one sees on the Roman statues of barbarian prisoners ;
a shirt, with wide sleeves (sourieh), and a waistcoat
without sleeves (fermleh), or with sleeves (reboun),

but this is not always worn. A long, narrow, woollen
sash (hhezàm) is wound several times round the body,
and the whole is covered by the barracan (jerd), the
simplest and most graceful, as it probably was the
earliest, article of dress ever invented. It is of white or
gray, sometimes of red wool, heavy or light, according
to the season ; very like the Scotch plaid, though rather
longer, but differently worn. One corner is looped to
the edge, about a yard and a half from the end; the
right arm and head are passed through the aperture
thus formed, the loop resting on the left shoulder; the
long end is next passed under the left elbow, and is
then thrown across the right arm and shoulder. This
is the usual way of wearing it in the town; but in the
country, or where exposed to the sun, a part of the
breadth is passed over the head, and the end is brought
over the left shoulder in front. Thus worn, it is
exactly the costume of the antique statue of the sacri-
ficator, which one sees in many museums. The apparent cleanliness of this costume, entirely white in
summer, and its graceful folds, render it one of the
most elegant I have ever seen. These barracans are,
for the most part, the manufacture of Jerbel, in the
regency of Tunis, and the finer have stripes of silk in-
terwoven in the breadth. Socks or stockings (to complete my fashions of Benghazi) are seldom seen ; the
yellow under-shoe (mest) more frequently. There are

three kinds of slippers worn : the red Egyptian (mar-koub) ; a yellow slipper, with no heel, and a red shoe, which leaves the instep quite uncovered, both called sebàt.

The barracan forms, also, the principal dress of the women ; but they wear it in a different way, making a petticoat of it, and a bag behind, in which they carry their children, or any other *impedimenta* they may have ; and they bring it in such a way over the face as to form a very effectual veil. I have seen none on whom this dress sat gracefully, and all seem frightfully dirty. Some of the children whom one sees rolling naked in the sand of the street would, if washed, be pretty, but the filth in which they are reared soon destroys all vestige of good looks. Both women and children wear immense hoop ear-rings, three and four inches in diameter, and sometimes four or five in each ear, inserted one above the other in the cartilage. The silver bracelets and anklets which complete their adornment are sometimes of great weight. A Jewess in Benghazi wears a pair of anklets which weigh five pounds.

The flies form a remarkable feature, which must not be omitted in describing Benghazi. None of the plagues of Egypt could exceed them, and they often during the day render writing, or any occupation which does not leave one hand free for the fan, utterly impossible. They exist in myriads ; hence, the Turks call

Benghazi the fly kingdom ; and the flies by their perti-
nacity and voracity evidently show that this is their
own opinion. Nothing but continual fanning can keep
them off; even the musquitoe-net being unavailing
against plagues which creep as well as fly. When very
thirsty they draw blood, even through one's stockings,
their bite resembling the sharp pricking of a leech ;
and wafers left upon a table entirely disappear under
their attacks in a very short time. In the evening, if
disturbed on the curtains, they rise in hundreds, making a rushing noise like pheasants when a well-stocked
cover is beaten. In addition to the plague of flies, the
shrill trumpet of musquitoes keeps one constantly on
the *qui vive*, but their bite is not venomous like that of
the musquitoes of Syria, Egypt, or even Italy ; and it
is rather the association of ideas which renders them
harassing, than any actual injury they inflict. Other insects, though not unknown, are seldom seen, or with a
little care may be entirely avoided. The first day I was
in Benghazi my servant killed a tarantula, a hideous,
rough-backed, flat-headed lizard, in the room I was
put up in; but I have not seen a second. Nor have I
met with any scorpions, though they are sometimes
found ; their bite is hardly to be called venomous. So
insensible is the Arab epidermis to pain, that a native
hardly takes the trouble to apply even a little butter
or honey to the wound.

Scarcely any trades, beyond those of the most necessary description, are exercised at Benghazi. The
French Consul, during my stay there, was unable to
have a pane of glass put into a window; the Tunisian
who formerly performed such feats having allowed
himself to die. The glass was there, but no one could
cut it to the size of the window. There are Jews here,
into whose hands most of the less laborious trades
have fallen, as is usual in all countries, especially in
the East. They can sew a covering for your divan, or
make up the cushions; they will repair, in a certain
fashion, any article of silver or gold, or make you a
saddle-cloth, or a sabre belt. They are ready to turn
their hands to anything; but after showing themselves
serviceable as may be, ask prices equal to about ten
times what would be demanded in Bond Street. A
few days before starting for the interior, I wished to
have some balls cast, and I soon saw the same Jews
at work who a few days before had come to repair a
silver nargilih, which had passed through an Arab
servant's hands. They worked in the court of my
house; the casting of balls being a highly prohibited
operation. I was amused at the way in which they
set to work. Two commenced, but before the end of
the performance a third came to their aid, and then two
more, apparently to lighten the labour by the charms of
their conversation. My Jews sat down opposite to each

other, and scraped a hole in the ground between them. In this they placed some lead, and covered it with charcoal, which they soon blew into a bright heat by means of a pair of bellows made of an entire goat's skin, one end of which was fitted with a nozzle, while the edges of the other extremity were sewed to two flat sticks, so as to open or close by the pressure of the hand. The lead was now melted, and to extract it from its primitive crucible a little bit of tin, which was lying on the ground, the lining of an old packing-case, was slipped and fashioned into something like the bowl of a ladle, and this, held by a pair of pincers, was all the apparatus required. It was highly simple, but the quantity of wood and charcoal consumed was enormous, and it took nearly five hours to cast little more than a hundred balls. It must be confessed, in favour of the Jews, that if their filth and ignorance equal those of their brethren in all these countries, they are not behind them in industry. They are the only hard workers in the place: other tradesmen, whether Moslem or Maltese, seeming utterly indifferent to obtaining custom. I required a framework for a divan, and the Maltese carpenter whom I had sent for, after keeping me two days waiting, send word on the Monday that he would come next week. I therefore found a couple of Jews, who knocked together a very creditable divan in two hours. One of the community, who by a series of most ingenious manœuvres has contrived to obtain English protection, and is now broker to the Vice-Consulate, was hardly ever out of my house during my stay in Benghazi. His voice was generally the first I heard in full exercise about sunrise, and from time to time during the entire day, his tongue seemed never to tire of discharging bad Arabic and worse Italian. Such cleverness, such industry, never were employed for smaller ends, for his profits must be inconsiderable. He knows, I believe, every article in every house in the town, as well as if he had taken an inventory of their contents, and when he pronounces some longed-for object unattainable, it is certain that neither money, diplomacy, nor address have been able to discover its existence.

There is nothing to be said of the domestic habits of the Moslem inhabitants. Their life is less luxurious, their feasts are less frequent and less gay than those of richer places; they have few or no amusements, and there is no bath in the town, excepting in the castle, where there is one capable of containing a single person. I have nowhere seen Moslemin so dirty in person.

CHAPTER II.

I WAS detained in Benghazi much longer than I could
have wished by the non-arrival of a vessel containing a
part of my luggage, and by the beginning of Ramadhan,
during which time it is next to impossible to travel.

Servants who are fasting all day cannot be expected
to be much inclined for exertion, and as at night they
sit up to gossip, or to sing, waiting till it is time to
take the last meal before the dawn, it is hopeless in a
tent to look for sleep. I made up my mind, therefore,
to wait till this month was over, and gave orders for a
start on the morrow of the Bairam. This, however,
happened to be Wednesday, and my guide represented
to me that Wednesday is the most unlucky of days to
start on a journey, and the argument was too sound
for me to think of opposing it. Thursday afternoon
was, therefore, fixed on, but so little notion have the

Arabs of punctuality, and so little are Arab servants
of use in preparing for a journey, that everything had
to be done by my European servant, and it was Saturday morning before I left the town.   An Arab merchant, who was frequently in the habit of visiting me,
gave me, however, some consolation for the delay, by
explaining that the seventh is the luckiest day in the
month, and as Saturday was the seventh, I had only
gained by the change of day.   This is, perhaps, the
place to describe my equipment for the journey, and
my companions.   I bought two wretched horses for
myself and servant, hired a quick stepping camel to
carry a light tent, carpets, and other articles required
during the day (which was ridden by a young Arab
servant, who acts as coffee-maker and pipe-filler), and
other camels for carrying the rest of the baggage, including a larger tent, crowbars and pickaxes for excavations, with water-skins and barley for six days for
the horses.   My guide, an immense man, one Mohammed El Adouly, provided his own horse, rather a
showy white mare, and one of the best I had seen in
the country; mounted upon this, and enveloped in his
white barracan, new yellow and red shoes on his feet,
which rested in the broad shovel-shaped brass stirrups;
his long gun slung over his shoulders, with a blunder-
buss at his saddle bow; a pair of pistols slung under
the left arm, and a Koran and a white bundle of talis-

mans under the right—he presented a very majestic figure, and evidently thought so himself.   He was re-commended to me as an indispensable guide for such a journey, as he is well known to all the Bedawin in the country, and his last wife was from the neighbour-hood of Grennah ; he had accompanied M. de Bour-ville and one or two English Vice-Consuls in their ex-cursions through this country.   I am, in general, averse to taking into my service such necessary personages, as they invariably endeavour to become the masters ; but as the written information concerning the places I was to visit is very scanty, and no trust can be placed in the oral communication of the natives, I submitted to the infliction.   I was determined, however, to have my own way, in which I succeeded very well, retrenching myself in my English coldness, while listening to his reasons why I should not do as I proposed, and then simply repeating the order ; this being somewhat the Turkish fashion, he soon understood my method, and for some time obeyed my orders without opposition. In addition to Mohammed and the pipe-boy, I had with me a tall thin man, who fancied himself a cook, and an inexpressibly dirty fellow who was to groom the horses, and also make himself generally useful.   The breed of horses in the Pentapolitan is sadly degenerated from its renown in former times ; they are small and ill made, with no appearance of Arab blood ; but there

are a few in the interior which have great powers of
endurance.   My servant's horse, of the Dongola breed,
which had been reduced to a skeleton by a thirty-five
days' journey, during which his only food was what he
could pick up on the road, promises to turn out a
better horse than is usually met with in the country;
he delights me by the very knowing look, which he
owes to his ears being slit at the top—a sign that
he was foaled at night.

After much screaming and scolding among the
drivers, and the usual amount of growling on the part
of the camels, everything was got into marching order,
and, accompanied by some of my acquaintance, who
escorted me for an hour out of the town, I quitted
Benghazi.   We stopped in about an hour and a half to
fill the water-skins, at a deep well of cool and sweet
water, as we were to find none till the next day, at
Labiar.   Our route was in a south-easterly direction,
across the hills, which bound the plain of Benghazi,
and while my luggage made directly for the spot
where we were to spend the night, I made a long *dè-
tour* to visit a ruin called Kasa Tawileh, through an
uninteresting country, and without finding anything
to reward my exertion.   At about six hours and a
half from Benghazi we reached the foot of the hills,
and entered a beautiful ravine clothed with bushes and
underwood ; here we saw some coveys of partridges,

a few hares, and flights of wood-pigeons; but the
Arabs galloping about frightened them, so that it was
impossible to get a shot. They never think of firing
except when the game is on the ground, having never
dreamt of a flying shot; but their flint-locks generally missing fire, their poaching does not do much
harm to the game. We slept in an open space towards
the end of the ravine. The hills around it are called
Bu Miriam, and from them we descended the next
morning to the great plain called Ghat-es-Sultan, which
stretches away to the right; we crossed it in a south-
east direction to Labiar. The country to the edge of
the hill, at the foot of which lies the valley of Labiar,
is covered with low underwood, juniper trees occasionally rising amidst it.

From Benghazi to Labiar is fourteen hours of camel
travelling.

Labiar presents a strange appearance; a marābut on
a slight eminence looks down upon a long stony vale,
in which are several wells, but not a trace of vegetation. These were surrounded by Bedawin busily employed in drawing water in goat-skins, while their
flocks and herds covered the bare rocky sides of the
surrounding hills, patiently waiting their turn to
approach the watering-place. From constant agita-
tion the water in these wells is always muddy, and
even of this the cattle only have a drink once in two

or three days, as many are driven from pasture grounds at a great distance. Here we were visited by hosts of Bedawin, who formed a circle round the small day-tent in which I was resting until the camels should come up. Nothing was to be learned from their conversation, but they left behind them many lively reminiscences of their visit, and as this was the case every time a Bedawy visited me, I soon came to the resolution of forbidding their reception. The genuine Bedawy, of this country at least, is one of the dirtiest animals on the earth; their dress is often nothing but a brown barracan, which is a mass of rags, and a dirty, very dirty, skull-cap. There is one of them in this neighbourhood, who boasts of not having used water for forty years, and it is only rarely that any of them make external use of this precious commodity. The sheikh of Labiar brought me a small skin of milk, and I bought of him a sheep for the evening's meal, which he made me pay dear for, though he refused money for his milk, as to take money for it would be, as he said, ('aib,) " a shame."

Beyond Labiar, the country becomes less barren, being covered with short grass, which, even when quite dry, has a greenish yellow tone ; it is thickly dotted with thorny plants, some of which were just bursting into fresh leaf, and were most gaily green.

In four and a half hours from Labiar, our route

taking a direction east by north, we reached Sanct Bella Ghür, where we stopped near a well ill supplied with water. From this vast plain five hours' travelling over a beautiful range of hills called Jebel Fawaid, through gorges clothed with the juniper—here almost a stately tree—brought us to the wells of Elbenish, which presented a very similar appearance to those of Labiar, though the country round the Wadi, in which they lie, is less bare. While my tent was being pitched for the mid-day repose, I rode to a distance of twenty minutes to the north to see the remains of a ruined castle, called by the Arabs Kasr Jbilla. It is a square building, with towers at the corners, built of oblong blocks of wrought stone, of which, in some parts, several courses still exist, devoid of ornament; it may belong to Roman, or still earlier times. Placed on the summit of a conical hill, it commands an extensive view, and may have been destined to serve as a place of refuge from the attacks of the nomad tribes. With every care I could discover no trace of the inscriptions of which Della Cella speaks, and am inclined to think he mistook for characters the effect of the weather on the worn surface of the stones. The Arabs of the neighbourhood (they are Anaghir) bury their dead round the walls, and I saw several recent graves.

From Elbenich we entered the Jebel el Abid, inhabited by Arabs of the same name, and in four hours reached Zardes, where we slept, keeping, however, a good watch, as the Abid have a villanous reputation for thieving, and during the night gave us more than one *alerte*. Zardes is a valley containing wells, and surrounded by hills, in the protruding summits of which are many crevices, wherein grow the juniper and wild thyme, whose perfume fills the air; the ground around glittering with white flowers. This country, towards evening, when a pink tinge covers it, reminded me frequently of a Scotch moor. The next day was a fatiguing one; there being no suitable place for resting in the middle of the journey, I rode six hours before I halted my party. I generally left the camels with my servant, to prevent loitering, and rode on ahead with a guide and some Arab attendants. At the leisurely pace of an Arab traveller I gained upon the luggage fifteen or twenty minutes in every hour. I have noted the distances, for convenience' sake, by the times of the departure and arrival of the camels, (at which I was always present,) their pace being uniform. I rode on or loitered on the road. Mohammed, in all his magnificence, led the way; the servants, equally well armed, being generally with him, and any chance traveller who might have joined the caravan; I usually followed a little in the rear. My guide and the other Arabs from time to time solaced themselves with song. They have two or three airs, all equally unmusical and strange, which is remarkable, as the music of the countries on either side—Egypt and Tunis—is very pretty. The leader sings a couple of lines, which he constantly repeats with slight variations, while the rest join in a strange howling chorus. The verse is generally extempore, containing little rhyme and still less reason, and the best idea I can give of its import and style is by recalling the nursery ditty,—

> Here we go up, up, up,
> Now we go down, down.
>
> *Chorus*—How, wow, how.

as like bow wow wow as can be.

In leaving Zardes our road lay for three hours over hills covered with large junipers and other trees of the cypress tribe. This species of juniper is indigenous to the Cyrenaica; it is the *Thuya* of Pliny, and though it now only furnishes the small rough beams of which the roofing of the Benghazi houses is formed, it was in ancient times extensively used in upholstery, and furnished the precious citrian tables to the luxury of Greece and Rome. The wood has a bright yellow colour, and might, I should think, become again fashionable if introduced into Europe.*

* In the morning it emits a perfume, which is delicious in the open air, but in a closed space I should think stupifying, like the

We now came to an extensive plain called El-Hhiah, and further on to Sharb Tawalun, which was entirely burnt up, though the camels still found ample amusement, as they stragglingly loitered along, in plucking on this side and on that the half-dried tufts of thorny shrubs with which it is overgrown. Merawah, eleven hours distant, was our next halting-place; near it we started numbers of gazelles, which I could not get within shot of, though I had murdering intentions, our stock of provisions being very low. Here the camel drivers were busy, all the evening, preparing muzzles for the camels, to prevent them eating the *Driâs*, with which the country between here and Cyrene is covered. Most authors consider this plant to be the old *Silphium*, though its medicinal virtues are forgotten, and it is only known as the dreaded poison which threatens the lives of camels which are not reared in this tract of country. It is from no partiality for its flavour that they eat it, for they refuse it when offered to them. They crop it as they pass along, tempted by the long stem, which brings it so near their noses. It is at the present season, when in seed, that it is considered most deadly; I am told that in spring it is unnecessary to take precautions against it. If not the real *Silphium,* it certainly answers to the description given

Circean enchantments; it is said to be that with which Circe fumigated her grotto.

of the plant by Theophrastus, and I cannot think the objection to its identity urged by the learned M. Duchalais, from the form of the seed on the medals, is of much weight. I have seen seeds which nearly enough resemble the *Magydaris* on the medals, though they certainly are not heart-shaped, but the plant itself, as represented on them, is evidently what Mr. Pugin would call a conventional Silphium, for no plant of this species has the stem so thick in proportion to its height and flower. The seeds are highly medicinal, but I was unfortunately too late to ascertain if it yields a juice corresponding to the ancient Opos.

The next day our travelling from Merawah to Sireh, nine hours, and thence to Slŭnt, two hours, was very slow, for the camels, with their mouths tied up, were in a very bad humour, and could hardly be made to move. The appearance of the country was now varied by a number of caroub trees, which, contrasted with the duller juniper, looked of a bright green, and afforded a most grateful shade. Half-way between Merawah and Sireh is a large reservoir of ancient construction. It had been supported on six columns, and in many places the cement still adheres to the walls. There being no well in this neighbourhood, it was constructed to collect the rain-water from the hill at whose base it lies; its presence denotes, I presume, the site of some old town or village; but I observed no other remains of antiquity in its neighbourhood. It is true that the morning was very hot, and I, perhaps, gave myself little trouble in looking for them.*   At Sireh are remains of a square castle, like that which I visited at Elbenich, but not so well preserved nor in so commanding a situation.   Many similar remains of castles, which probably formed a line of defence against the border tribes, are to be seen on the summits of the hills.   In the face of the rocks at Sireh are many excavations, devoid of ornament, and evidently intended as sepulchres, though the Arabs, of course, assert that they were the abodes of the ancient inhabitants.   At Slŭnt the rock is burrowed with such excavations, each with a fore-court cut in the rock, having one or three entrances to the sepulchral chambers, some of which are most extensive, and supported by rude columns.   I found one occupied by Arab ladies, who did not welcome my

* At all the wells many Arabs were to be seen; and occasionally horsemen were met with, but generally two or three together; for though the country is now peaceful enough, the associations of other days seemed to deter them from venturing out singly.   In no part of the road did we see a trace of an encampment, and the whole country seemed deserted excepting in the neighbourhood of the wells.   On my remarking this to my guide, he said that the country was filled with inhabitants, but that they pitch their tents in the places least likely to be visited by passers by, to avoid too frequent calls on their hospitality.   The Arabs here have a great reputation for this virtue, but it appears that they are not ambitious of exercising it.

visit ; probably thinking I had sinister intentions on
their grain, for which it served as a magazine.   It was
certainly from no Oriental idea of the sacredness of
the Hareem that they seemed so relieved when I
turned my horse's head.   The Bedawin women, dirty
and tattooed, have no difficulty in showing their bare
faces to strangers ; and, notwithstanding the stories of
Herodotus, I think there is no risk in their doing so.
They wear leather leggings up to the knee; in other
respects their dress differs little, except in its darker
colour, from that of the Benghazi women.

The next morning a ride of two hours and a quarter
through an interesting country brought us to the Marābut Sidi Mohammed el Himary, where there is an ill-
supplied well, and a rock, under which a shade may be
obtained without the trouble of pitching a tent.   Barth,
I think, gives this as the site of the ancient Balaerai,
whose distance was twelve miles from Cyrene; but it
took my camels seven hours and a half from here to
Grennah, which, at the slowest rate of travelling, must
give fifteen miles, and from the length of time I was
on horseback I should judge the distance nearer
eighteen.   The ride from here to Grennah is worth
a journey from Europe.   About half-way, after passing through a valley containing many splendid old
junipers, under which goats, flocked together, were
enjoying the shade, we came to a spring of living

water, called Menezzah Wad Fairyeh.   The rest of the
journey was over a range of low undulating hills,
offering, perhaps, the most lovely sylvan scenery in
the world.   The country is like a most beautifully arranged *Jardin Anglais*, covered with pyramidal clumps
of evergreens, variously disposed, as if by the hand
of the most refined taste; while *bosquets* of junipers
and cedars, relieved by the pale olive and the bright
green of the tall arbutus tree, afford a most grateful
shade from the mid-day sun.   In one of these bowers
I had my carpet spread for luncheon; some singing
birds joined their voices to the lively chirping of the
grasshoppers, and around fluttered many a gaily-
painted butterfly.   The old capital of the Pentapolis
was before me, yet I was strongly tempted to pitch my
tent for a time in this fairy scene.

> " Nunc viridi membra sub arbuto
>   Stratus, nunc ad aquæ lene caput sacræ."

Whoever has traversed these fresh groves in the
parching heat of an African July can understand
the enthusiastic praises of the older writers, and
why the Arabs, coming from the Desert, called the
country the Green Mountain.   As we approached
Cyrene, this exuberant vegetation disappeared, and in
its place we passed through long avenues of tombs,
hewn in the rock, or out of it; next we came in sight

of the ruined towers of the old city walls; and then, through a long line of ruins, we reached the street of Battus, where a narrow gorge opens upon a magnificent view over plains and hills to the blue Mediterranean. I rode on to the cave whence gushes the perennial spring of Cyre, took a draught of its bright, cool water, and fixed my temporary home beneath the world-famed fountain, amidst the countless ruins of temples and public buildings.

CHAPTER III.

My first day in Grennah was entirely occupied in the
very matter of fact, but not less necessary, employment
of arranging my encampment, whilst Mohammed was
equally busy in receiving the visits of his Arab friends,
in whose society he entirely forgot me; he seemed to
imagine that he was making a tour of pleasure with
the Frank in his suite, not that he was in the service
of the Frank. He took possession of the Grotto of
the Fountain, and established himself on sundry mats
and carpets in a part which is now dry. I also went
there for shelter from the hot sun, while my larger
tent was being prepared; and sat by the bubbling
water, out of reach of the Bedawin and their fleas, but
close enough to hear the Babel-screaming of their

conversation, and to be amused by its monotony. The
Arabs are great talkers, but the range of their ideas is
remarkably limited, so that the day is often passed in
an unceasing repetition of the same words. I noted
down such a conversation, and, as a favourable specimen of *causerie*, I transcribe it here. There arrived
a gray-bearded old Bedawy, with a long gun, and
pistols in his belt, but in all other respects a striking
contrast to the city *brave* whom he had come to see.
As he came up, he pronounced, "Es-selam alaik"
("Peace be with you"); receiving a long, drawling
answer, "Alaik es-selam" ("With you be peace").
He then went up to Mohammed, and touched his right
hand, whereon each kissed the palm of his own hand;
he then literally fell on Mohammed's neck, and kissed
it on the right side, just below the whisker—a salute
which was immediately returned. Now began a rolling
fire of questions and answers, in such quick succession, that it required a practised ear to follow their
meaning; neither party seeming to pay attention to
question or answer—both being already, no doubt,
aware of their import. After repeating the words,
"Es-selam," several times, then came the inquiry,
"How is your state? How are you? How is your
humour?" The answer was, "May your state be
peaceful;" or "Praise be to God;"—an answer, generally, given only to very pointed inquiries after health.

These questions were repeated three or four times. Then again, " Es-selam, How is your state ? how is your humour? how is the state behind you?"—meaning the family left at home. Again, "Es-selam, How is your state ? how is the state of your house (wife) ?" Again, " Es-selam, How is the state of your children ?" and so continually with the same words, varying the final interrogatory by asking after his brother, and his mare, and his cows, and his sheep,—in fine, after all things that are his, down to the most insignificant of his possessions ; each being the object of a particular inquiry. Next came the gist of the conversation— half an hour having been, perhaps, thus passed in preliminaries — which affected the value of the inquirer's own possessions, for the child of Nature has a keen eye to business. " What is the price of corn in Benghazi?"—then a string of salams. Presently he asks what barley is selling at, and then follow renewed inquiries after his friend's state and humour ; as if the fatigue of answering so many questions may have altered them. When reassured on this point, he slips in an inquiry, " How much do oxen fetch ?" and if he be a keen politician he next attacks the local news: "Why has the Pacha come to Benghazi?" " Is the Bey going to be dismissed ?" " Is it true that there is war with the French in Tripoli ?" and so on he questions ; but the great point of interest is the

state of the markets. Such conversations to one who
has nothing to buy or sell, are naturally rather monotonous; and their charm was not sufficient to overcome my dread of the various parasites which constantly lurk under an Arab barracan. Had I not at
once determined upon excluding the Bedawin from my
tent, I should have sacrificed every moment of study
or quiet. A visit of three hours' duration is not a long
one for an Arab, though the greater part is sometimes
passed in silence, after the first torrent of words has
burst forth ; and on seeing a cool, well-carpeted tent,
few of the tribe would make any scruple, if once admitted, of stretching themselves out, and sleeping
through the heat of the day.

Having settled myself comfortably in a delightful
position, I now set about taking a general view of the
ruins ; and I soon found that, to obtain any true notion of the details, I must form a plan for visiting, in
some kind of order, the vast labyrinth which lay before
me.   There are many miles of Necropolis, extending
all round the city; and, in some places, the monuments and sarcophagi rise in terraces of ten, and even
twelve rows, one above the other. The ruins of the
town itself are in such a state of dilapidation, that it
would require no little study to obtain a satisfactory
idea of their nature ; there are few remains of private
dwellings above ground, and extensive excavations

ENTRANCE TO FOUNTAIN OF APOLLO.

would be required to uncover them. The excavator would doubtless reap a rich harvest, particularly of medals and, perhaps, of other small works of art. Temples, public buildings, and tombs, being more exposed to violation, are less likely than private dwellings to reward the excavator; in modern times, however, none of the visitors who have excavated here have applied themselves to clearing the houses, which would require great perseverance and the expenditure of considerable funds. It is almost impossible for an amateur traveller to attempt such excavations; for they demand his continued presence on the spot, to prevent the abstraction of the smaller objects which may be found, and the wanton destruction of others; and the jealousy of the natives, who regard him as a treasure-seeker, can only be effectually repressed by the aid of the Government. I did not, therefore, push my researches beyond the platform on which the ancient agora stood, as, my tents being pitched there, it was easy to watch the excavators.

On arriving at Grennah, the first object which naturally attracts the traveller's attention, is the fountain of Cyre—the cause which led to the choice of this site for building the city, and, in the days of its prosperity, the spot round which most of the public buildings were grouped. Though the volume of water which it pours out has much diminished, even in the

memory of man, it is still the most abundant spring
in this neighbourhood; and flocks of sheep and goats,
and herds of cattle, daily cover the ground where once
the sacred rites of Apollo, or the affairs of their
prosperous commerce, assembled the citizens of
Cyrene. The stream of water issues from a natural
passage, artificially widened; it falls into a shallow,
square reservoir, cut in the ground of the cave; and
hence it was formerly distributed, through a series of
stone channels, of which many fragments still remain.
The external rock is smoothed to receive the addition
of a portico of that beautiful white limestone, closer-
grained than marble, which acquires in time a warm
golden hue. The line of the fronton, deeply cut in
the rock, shows the outline of its architecture, and the
three lower courses of masonry, its material. In the
rock to the right is an inscription, beautifully cut, recording a restoration of the fountain, which, from its
position, as well as its clear, simple characters, may well
be of earlier date than the first century, which is generally assigned to it. In front of the fountain, two
massive walls support narrow platforms, the lower of
which is covered with the foundations of buildings,
whose marble fragments indicate considerable magnificence. Beneath these extends a broad terrace, 700
feet in length, supported by a lofty and very massive
wall, which is still in great part entire. One end of

this terrace is closed by a wall of more recent construction, built apparently to shut out the old Greek
theatre, which lies beyond it; the other opens on the
street of Battus, and, in part, is bounded by a road
running from this, round the base of the eastern hill.
On this platform, which formed the agora, stood many
temples and public buildings ; and it is here that the
monument of Battus, mentioned by Pindar, as standing at the end of the market-place, must be looked
for. As one stands in front of the fountain, looking
to the sea, this platform, covered with ruins, lies at
one's feet ; while beyond, the long lines of the Eastern
Necropolis wind round the curves of the hills, and the
plain beneath is seen dotted with ruins, or intersected
by old roads. To the left, immediately beneath the
fountain, are the remains of a very large building,
whose massive fragments of marble cornices and columns indicate its importance, as well as its more recent date. Among the rubbish lie fluted columns, the
headless statue of a sitting female figure, and some
fragments of inscriptions. No building in the agora
seems to have equalled this in size ; and I believe that
all my predecessors agree in considering it to be the
Temple of Apollo. To the left of this building, behind, and almost touching it at one angle, is a temple
of more ancient construction, the lower parts of four of
whose columns still remain *in situ*. Still further to

the left, is a small building, in front of which some
former excavator has uncovered a finely-draped statue
of a Roman empress, and on a marble near, is an
inscription, nearly defaced, belonging, perhaps, to its
pedestal. The arms and head, originally separate, have
been removed, as well as the, probably, metal girdle of
the waist. I continued the excavation round this monument, with no other result than finding a coarse
white mosaic pavement, and a long subterranean passage, which seems to have been a sewer. Almost in a
line with this building, still to the left, and close to the
boundary-wall, is a monument of great interest. It is
of massive construction, and evidently of ancient date,
and, in plan, bears a strong resemblance to some of the
finest monuments in the Necropolis. Its situation, its
size, its antiquity, leave no doubt on my mind that
this is the Heroon of Battus, whose monument was
erected in the market-place, while the kings, his successors, reposed each in front of his own palace. I
had the greater part of the interior of this monument
dug out, without finding anything but a few fragments
of bronze and ivory, of *terra cotta* of the very oldest
workmanship, and a part of an alabaster vase, of remarkable thinness; but no inscription rewarded me,
either by confirming my conjecture, or by assigning
another origin to the monument. Whilst digging here,
the excavators were interrupted by some Bedawin,

who came to prevent my further researches in the
ruins ; but, as they were armed, and seemed half inclined to violence, and were very impertinent, I refused
to listen to them.   I told them that the land was the
Sultan's—a proposition which they did not controvert ;
and then I asked if they, or their fathers, had either
built or bought " the castle."   My argument might be
bad, but added to a resolute countenance, it was good
enough to prevent any renewal of such obstructions
from the natives.

Turning to the right, we behold a vast mass of
confused substructures, the ground plan of a very large
collection of buildings, though it would be difficult to
assign to them a name.   One very large chamber,
near the edge of the platform, I found, on excavation, paved with a coating of the stucco used for
reservoirs, and beneath this a broken pavement of
Cipollino marble.   The remaining parts of the
building give no indication of its having been a bath,
and its position forbids the idea that it was a reservoir.
Further to the right are two other ruins, with arches
and columns of Cipollino and a coarse white marble.
To the right, the buildings advance to the edge of the
platform, while in front of the fountain, and to the
left, there is a wide space between the large masses of
ruin and the well which supports the terrace.   In this
there are few remains of old buildings, the ground

having been long used by the Bedawin as a corn-field; but the few fragments scattered here and there render it probable that buildings were not wanting in this direction ; at least, such as would be required for the accommodation of the assemblies of the citizens.

Proceeding along the platform, and crossing the wall which closes it to the west, we come to the best preserved monument in Cyrene, the old Greek theatre. Its form, nearly three-fourths of a circle, occupied by seats, is almost perfect, but the proscenium has disappeared. Some attempts which I made to discover the line of the stage were fruitless, as they brought to light only loose stones which had fallen from the wall above. The external wall is still perfect, rising perpendicularly from the ground beneath in a curve, and I am inclined to ascribe the disappearance of the stage and its decorations to a very remote date. It seems, from the wall which completely sequesters it from the agora, that this theatre, notwithstanding its admirable position, must have fallen into disuse, and been dismantled, for not a fragment of marble is to be found in its circuit. Had the present ruin resulted only from the barbarians, or from natural causes, there would have remained, at least, blocks of marble, as in the other monuments of the town, but none such would be found, if, as I conjecture, the ancients them-

selves removed these decorations to use them in some
one of the other theatres, of which we shall find remains. I counted twenty-seven rows of seats, and
conjectured twelve or fourteen more buried under the
ruins fallen from above. I much regretted that the
enormous masses of these ruins made it impossible
for me to attempt clearing the interior, as no building
of Cyrene is of a more interesting epoch, and none
so perfect; its form, also, is uncommon. It is built
in the side of the hill, and the rampart wall which
supported the stage is nearly forty feet high to the
level of the orchestra. A flight of steps from the
top leads down to the orchestra; and there seems also
to have been an entrance on a level with it from the
east. Immediately beneath the theatre, on a lower
terrace of the hill, are the ruins of a large building,
consisting of three very perfect and beautifully pro-
portioned arches, with a fourth at right angles to
them. In front of them is a large quadrangle now
occupied by a Bedawy, as garden ground, and beneath lie many remnants of fluted columns in white
marble, and their capitals, whose execution is more
pure and careful than that of any other fragments to be
found in the ruins. In Beechey's plan this is noted as
a temple, and though, at first, I was inclined to regard
it as a reservoir for the waters of the fountain, which
were in part carried in this direction, I, on further

examination, found nothing to justify a disagreement
with so great an authority.

Leaving the fountain, we proceed in a southerly direction up the ravine, which forms the street of Battus; on either side the hills are steep, presenting surfaces of rock, in some of which tombs had been evidently excavated; while to the right, although the
rock has been in many places smoothed away, or
even hollowed, it is more probable, from the remains
of masonry, that the ground was occupied by public
or private buildings. The facility with which cellars
and magazines can be excavated in the soft limestone,
of which the hills are composed, would naturally be
taken advantage of, for increasing the accommodation of the private dwellings, and in two instances, as
I shall afterwards have occasion to mention, I found
unmistakable evidence of this. Where the ravine
widens, to the right above the road, are remains supposed to mark the site of the temple of Juno, an
inscription relating to the priestesses of the goddess
having been found here by Beechey; but the little
that remains of the temple presents nothing of peculiar interest, a remark which, unfortunately, with few
exceptions, is applicable to almost all the ruins
found within the circuit of the city. Above this, on
the summit of the western hill, is the corner of a
building, which, seen from below, looks like a tower,

and here the substructures are very large, covering a great portion of the plateau. All this part has been extensively excavated in certain directions, by order of the Grand Vizier, who presented the spoil to France. Some small statues in the best style of Greek art, I am told, were found here, but I speak only on hearsay. There still remains a good cubical altar of white marble, which the Arab labourers were obliged to abandon on account of its weight; it having broken down the rude carriage which they had constructed for its removal. On the four sides are bas-reliefs, each representing a figure standing in a quadriga; and when I first saw it there was on one side a votive inscription, which it was difficult to decipher; unfortunately I deferred copying it at the time, and on my return, some days afterwards, I found that it had been defaced by the Arabs. They had probably seen me stopping before and examining the inscription, which was, I fear, with them, reason sufficient for its destruction.

Proceeding up the street we reach the line of a large building, marked by many fallen columns, and then we come to the well-defined outline of a large theatre, once adorned with a colonnade of marble; among the *débris* of which are many fragments of red and gray granite, and some mutilated statues, once the decorations of its proscenium. A flight of steps leads to the orchestra from the rising ground above. Further on is a large building also, with many fallen columns, having in its north-west extremity an apsis of small dimensions. It seems to have been a basilica, as its architecture is too good to suppose that it was a Christian church. On the left nothing but scattered formless heaps of stone are to be seen, until after passing this building, when we reach a lofty tower, of which one corner remains; extensive ruins also attract attention on account of the numerous arches, not of the best construction, which still show their curves above the encumbered ground. An apse, having the same direction as that in the other building, is still standing, and many marble columns strew the ground. This is marked in Beechey's plan as a church, a conjecture which the debased style of architecture, as well as the general plan, fully justifies, and which is, perhaps, confirmed by a stone which I turned up among the ruins, on which a Greek cross is coarsely carved. On either side are smaller heaps of ruins, and thence a grass-covered plain, almost unmarked by any building, but once, perhaps, covered with private dwellings, reaches to the city walls. Just beyond there is a piece of ground covered with what seems to be gravestones, some marked with the cross, and others with the double triangle, commonly called Solomon's Seal. This may be an old Jewish and Christian burial

ground, and the tradition of the Arabs points it out
as the place where the last battle was fought between
the Christian inhabitants and the Moslem invaders.

On riding up the eastern hill from the fountain, one
finds it formed of a series of terraces, partly natural
and partly artificial, with a broad plateau overlooking
the street of Battus on the summit.   On one of these
terraces, the form of the ground and the beautiful
site induced me at first to suppose some ruins I found
to be those of a theatre ; but the ground in these
hills so often takes a semicircular form, and the remains of masonry were so few, that, on further examination of the spot, I was inclined to believe
that the appearance was accidental.   A winding road
led from the plateau to the agora, and steps cut
in the rock afforded a shorter cut for pedestrians.   In
the sides of the terraces are many excavations, which,
judging from the disposition of the interiors, must
have formed parts of private houses, and some of them,
if cleared out, would form commodious enough adjuncts to an encampment.   On the summit are the
remains of several buildings, one with five arches still
appearing above the ground, and there are others of
not inconsiderable size.   Further to the east are several hillocks, two of them covered with the ruins of
temples; one of them, called by the Arabs Kasr' Sharkyeh, is supposed by Barthe to be the temple of Æscu-

lapius, the treasury of the state. It is evidently of
early date, and still shows traces of the colonnade
which surrounded it. On a terrace below, a little
to the north-west, a small stream issues from a
cave, most picturesquely overgrown with maiden-hair
and mosses; into this cave the water filtrates from
narrow rents in the rock. Here, as in all similar
cases, the industrious hand of man is visible; a
second passage is cut in the rock to increase the flow
of water, but this is now dry, and one narrow stream
trickles only from the natural passage. In front there
are remains of a reservoir built to collect the water.
From this point, near which there are remains of a
tower, the city walls are distinctly traceable in a large
circuit to the deep ravine, which forms the boundary
on the west. A group of rocks rising from the soil
near Kasr' Sharkyeh seems to have been in some way
connected with the sanctuary, as they are cut into
niches, small chambers, and seats, and having been
thrown from their original position, probably by some
natural convulsion, they now present a most singular
appearance of elfish disorder. Proceeding southwards,
and passing a small temple, whose longer axis runs
perpendicularly to that of Æsculapius, we see the stadium a little to the right. Long parallel lines closed
at one end by a curve, mark its form most perfectly; in
a few places the seats may be traced, but in the long

grass, which has overgrown its area, I could find no
traces of the spina or goals.   The city wall is, in its
lower courses of masonry, well preserved from a point
immediately east of Kasr' Sharkyeh, where it makes a
right angle, flanked with two square towers.   Others
succeed at short intervals along the line which runs to
the west, but they are not placed at any regular distances ; the rock in general forms the lower course in
the walls, and in one place it has been built into it to
a height of twelve feet, being cut away on both sides
to the thickness of the wall.   This continues to run
in a westerly direction till it reaches a gigantic rectangular reservoir, of the most solid construction, but
apparently never finished.   Three massive arched con-
duits seem destined to distribute the water, and the
vastness of the design and solidity of the execution
render it worthy to be ranked with the greatest of the
Roman aqueducts.   In the arches, where the cement
has fallen away, are to be seen on the stones letters
deeply carved.   They are the builders' marks, and here
are all Greek characters, though the Θ lying on its
side (Ⓓ), and the Ψ (Ⓨ) look strange.   Among the
most frequent are Τ Η Ⓓ Π ٩ Ⓨ Σ.   The stones were
doubtless thus marked in the quarry where they were
cut in the curve of the arch, and the characters appear
in a certain symmetry.

The wall from this point continues to run westwards

for some space, then, turning towards the north, it
follows the edge of the western valley (Wady Bil
Ghadir) up to a point where the perpendicular rocks
render no artificial defence necessary, and here it
terminates in a lofty tower. Beyond it I remarked
two small reservoirs; a building of a large size, of
the Roman epoch, having a central chamber terminated in an apsis; and near this another, evidently a
stronghold of Byzantine, if not Arab, times. Many
other smaller ruins lie beyond the walls on this
side; among them a small temple, with fallen Ionic
columns.

Without riding on to the tall tower which overhangs
the steep rock of the Wady, we turn to the right,
entering the strongly-fortified gate on the old Barca
road. After passing the indications of many small
buildings, fragments of marble and substructions, the
most extensive ruin remaining in Cyrene presents
itself. This is an immense quadrangle, whose north-
west side is broken to inclose a small and very perfect
theatre, which still shows three of the five vaulted
entrances which gave admittance to its interior. The
larger area, whose entrance gate is still entire, is supposed to have been a forum of the Ptolemaic or Roman
time. Excavations have laid bare a number of small
chambers and a reservoir, along the eastern side, besides a large building in the centre. No inscription

is at present visible; but there remains enough of the old decorations to show that the interior and the exterior, at least on the south-east, were decorated with colonnades.   Continuing down-hill, to re-enter the street of Battus, we find, near the temple of Juno, another large monument, having many columns, with marble capitals; this was probably a palace. On the exterior of the north-east side are the remains of a series of vaulted chambers, ingeniously conjectured to have been coach-houses—a necessary convenience in the land of chariots.

There are very many small buildings to be traced on the sites I have endeavoured to describe, but they are in general only quadrangular foundations, in great part overgrown with grass; and in our ignorance of those details of Cyrenean life or history, which lend an interest to every spot in Athens and Rome, it would be tedious and, in truth, impossible to particularise them. The muse of history has not deigned to notice the vicissitudes of her prosperous commerce, and scarcely mentions the bloody factions of her pampered citizens. None of the great scenes which influence the world's destiny were acted within her walls. Her sons were nurtured in wealth and luxury, and though among them were numbered physicians, philosophers, grammarians, and arithmeticians, history records not that other arts than those of the fancy—the charioteers,

and the pugilists—were cultivated with eminent success. The medals often found in its soil are both
rare and beautiful; but the marbles are not of first-rate
merit. Many valuable inscriptions are probably buried
beneath its surface; but it would require both large
funds and much time to attempt, with fair prospect of
success, an investigation of its ruins.

I believe that this account of the present condition
of Cyrene, though vague, conveys a not unfaithful
idea of its state. The destruction is, in fact, so complete, and the masses overthrown so gigantic, that one
can hardly ascribe the present havoc to the hand of
man, or the wasting decay of ages. Though there are
now no appearances of volcanic action, we find mention of earthquakes in Synesius; and the whole of the
sea-coast, as seen at Benghazi and Apollonia, has
subsided—an evidence, at least, of the presence of
volcanic forces; and by this agency alone does it
seem possible that such utter destruction could have
been caused. The greater devourer of the cities of
antiquity, a modern town rising in the vicinity, has
not here aided the destroyer; for the seventh century
is the very latest date that can be ascribed to any
single building in a very wide circuit; and the nature
of the country, cut up by ravines, and for ages destitute of roads, renders the transport of heavy blocks of
stone impossible. If its present destruction be due to

the nomad tribes (of whose attacks Synesius speaks), who feared that Cyrene might again become a flourishing city, and their mistress, we cannot, after admiring the laborious energy of her builders, but wonder at the persevering fury of her destroyers.

The remains of sculpture, as I have indicated, though not few, are all of a late age, and none in the best style of art; I except the three dancing figures, a bas-relief on limestone, near the fountain, now, alas! sadly mutilated. They are even now worthy a place in a museum, as they are of great artistic interest, showing the passage from the archaic style of the Egina marbles to the more graceful execution of the classic school. I think I recognised, near the theatre in the street of Battus, the torso of a statue designed in Pacho's work, and by him called a Cæsar, but it has suffered much from mutilation, and can never have possessed the merit he ascribes to it. Very many headless statues are scattered about, which would be beautiful decorations for a garden, but are all unworthy of a museum.

The rock which forms the hills, and of which the town is built, is a yellowish limestone, filled with fossil shells, for the most part bivalves, and of very unequal compactness. By exposure to the weather it acquires a gray tone, and frequently becomes honey-combed. In some places the marks of the chisel in the stones are as sharp as the day they were cut—in others, the air and rain have rounded off their edges; and one sees walls still standing which look as if built of flattened eggs, showing large interstices between the now rounded stones.

To sum up in a few words, the traveller finds enough to convey the general impression of the past splendour of a luxurious city, but little to satisfy a refined taste, and nothing of which it can be said, if we except the great reservoir, "This is indeed magnificent!" In a commercial community, containing philosophers and physicians, the theatre and the turf may be cultivated as relaxations from the money-getting toils of the desk, but, as far as I remember, excepting aristocratic Venice, history furnishes no example of such a people having attained more than an initiative excellence in the fine arts.

CHAPTER IV.

AUGUST 10.—A few days after arriving in Grennah, having obtained a general idea of the ruins, and made such arrangements as were likely to conduce to a comfortable stay, I went to pay my respects to Bekir Bey, as the Turks call Bu Bekr Hadud, the Governor of the Arabs in this district. I had been introduced to him by the Kaimahan in Benghazi, who, besides a verbal recommendation, had furnished me with letters to him. His residence is a castle, which I found him still engaged in building, at Caicab, a place about four hours distant from Grennah, lying between the two roads to Derna; and from here, with the fifty soldiers who are at his orders, he manages to keep the country in subjection, and his enemies—who are many—say, to rob it into the bargain. His family

has long been one of the most powerful in the country;
and he is sheikh of the Berasa, a tribe counting ten
clans.   The sheikhs of the other clans are subordinate
to him ; and by intrigue or violence, each employed at
the right time, he has made himself really the independent governor of the country, which he rules with
an iron hand, under such protection as his guards
afford him, amidst clans of his own tribe who have
sworn his death.   His life has been one of strange
vicissitudes ; at one time—under the last native sove-
reign, Youssouf Pacha, whom the Porte, with the
help of the English Consul General, so cleverly de-
throned, or rather, I should say, who so stupidly
allowed himself to be smuggled out of his country—
he was fourteen months a prisoner in irons in Tripoli.
His language is now that of the most abject submission, but he carries things his own way notwithstanding.   He pays to the Porte a yearly sum of 48,000
dollars, extracting from the Arabs nearly twice as
much ; the greater part is destined to swell his own
money-bags, the rest being used, according to the
approved receipt in this country, to anoint the eyes
of his superiors in Benghazi and Tripoli.   In person
he is strongly built, but not tall, having the finest
chest and arm I ever beheld ; but his features are
coarse, and his eye twinkles with indescribable cunning.

I arrived about eleven o'clock, and found the Bey seated in his divan, and surrounded by at least forty persons, most of whom were squatted on the floor; he was seated in the corner, on a raised board, not unlike a tailor's, which ran about twelve feet along one side of the room. When I entered, the assembly was dismissed; and I seated myself beside him, having on my other hand three sheikhs of his tribe, one of whom, his brother, Mansour, is a still more ferocious, though less cunning, politician than himself. He it is who can eat an entire sheep at a sitting—a tale which I believe after seeing his performance at an extra meal which was prepared for me, when he excused himself for eating so little, on the score of bad health. In addition to these three, there remained also the Deftudar, or Secretary-Accountant, whose functions also included waiting at table. His place was on a straw sofa, on which were collected all the implements of his calling: a small box, a ream of paper, a pair of scissors for cutting his despatches or orders into proper form, a board for counting money, and a waist-inkstand; open letters with their answers were scattered round him, in what seemed inextricable confusion. After all the usual inquiries after health and temper, and when coffee and lemonade had been served, the Bey resumed his business, while several of the former assembly returned, some to have their complaints discussed, others

to get a nearer view of the stranger. He, knowing
that the Bedawin do not smoke, regarding this habit
as a dirty trick (they only chew tobacco, mixed with
nitre), had taken the precaution of carrying his pipe
with him, to keep himself in countenance during the
long pauses of an Arab visit. This and Mohammed's
exaggerated stories of him—how he ate and drank,
and above all, how he washed in a tub, and slept on a
bed—which were circulated in an undertone, made the
company vote him no better than a Turk, a hateful,
but highly respected character. The Bey from time to
time turned round to bawl out some phrases of exaggerated compliment, in a voice like that of one of his
camels, and then would continue to investigate the
case before him, till, getting animated, he would utter
a dozen "Wallahis" in a breath, throwing his arms
about in a manner that might well alarm his neighbour ; then he would pull his beard two or three times,
and, finally, would finish the discussion by applying
the interior of his thumb-nail to that of his upper
teeth, making a slight cracking noise, which meant
that nothing more was to be got out of him. But it
is not to be supposed that the audience sat listening,
in respectful silence, to this torrent of words : the subjects were as energetic as their ruler, and he who listened to the tones, or beheld the gestures which accompanied them, would think that they must soon come to

blows.   When I first met Bu Bekr in Benghazi, I was
astonished at the loud, rough tone in which he spoke ;
but after seeing a little more of the Bedawin (who all
speak as if from the mountain-tops), and assisting at a
council at Caicab, it was easy to account for it.
Indeed, the good man could not whisper : he tried to
do so, putting his arms round a servant's neck, and
placing his lips close to his ear, when he ordered a
luncheon, dinner, or whatever it must be called, to be
prepared for me. I had arrived too late for their
dinner; and, after much whispering in a loud tone,
and the interchange of one or two notes with his
Secretary (perhaps to show me that there is one Bey
who can write), he ordered another dinner for me.   I
was not supposed to hear or understand anything of
his hospitable intentions; and, after an hour and
a half of fatiguing inaction, in the midst of this Babel-
like hubbub, I rose to take my leave.   This he would
not allow, and seizing a shoulder with one iron hand,
and a leg with the other, he pulled me back to my
place.   I thus had to sit, making what little conversation my confined vocabulary would admit of, for
four hours longer, whilst the banquet was being prepared.   When the carpet was at last spread, and the
tray placed upon it, I confess I was disappointed,
though little inclined to eat, to find that the ladies of
the harem had not profited by this long interval to

furnish some delicate cates. There was soup—a sort
of greenish porridge, filled with rice and onions; then
came two dishes of stewed mutton, with vegetables;
this was followed by two dishes of stewed mutton, with
potatoes; and, finally, a huge wooden bowl of rice,
some thirty inches in diameter, crowned with an entire
roasted lamb. Plates of water-melon, from Benghazi,
completed the feast. I have described the dinner, all
fear of criticism notwithstanding, as it was meant to
be a splendid feed, and the host is the wealthiest man
in the country. The chief fault I found with it was
the long time it detained me in Caicab, thereby occasioning me two hours' ride in the dark. The Bey,
his brother, and Mohammed (whose last wife, by the
way, was a *divorcée* of Bu Bekr's), did honour to the
entertainment; the two former picking out, and
putting beneath my fingers, the delicate morsels;
and I must do them the justice to say, that, with true
politeness, not an effort was made to make me eat
more largely than I was inclined to do. The appetite
which comes in eating aided me to make a most substantial luncheon; but, beside the others, I was like a
canary-bird amongst ostriches. Mohammed, I heard,
could eat no supper; he was ill and useless all the
next day.

This rough, but abundant hospitality, not unbefitting
the traditional idea of an Arab sheikh, is exercised on

a most liberal scale by Bu Bekr; and the enormous drain it must be on his fortune may, possibly, justify him in his own eyes for the unscrupulous means by which he augments it.   At some seasons, the expenses of his court can be little short of 20*l.* a day ; and to meet this, the Turkish Government allows him 11*l.* a month.   An acquaintance, who spent some evenings with him this summer, told me that he had counted 378 rations for horses, given out in one evening for the guests ; while 86 sheep had been slaughtered, to supply their personal wants.   Perhaps he is by nature thus liberal, and only from education succumbs to the Arab fondness for the clinging metal.

CHAPTER V.

AUGUST 23.—I have described, as I can, the ancient city ; but the Necropolis, which yet remains to be visited, is, in fact, still, as in old times, the glory of Cyrene. Among its thousands of monuments, many retain traces of their ancient magnificence, and some still present great beauties of detail. My descriptions, such as they are here given, were written on the spot, after repeated visits ; and this morning, in no unfitting mood, I began my task. The growling camels round my tent, the bleating sheep at the fountain above, roused me earlier than usual ; and I prepared to set out upon my round, while the cool air invited to exertion, and the first rays of the sun gilded the summits

ROCK TOMBS IN THE NECROPOLIS OF CYRENE.

Page 62.

of the hills.   To most men such bright mornings are exhilarating ; and the pursuit of the red-legged partridge, with dog and gun, would seem more suitable to the hour, than a walk among the tombs.   But to me they are associated with recollections too painfully in unison with my present task.   Twice at this season the sun has shone for me on scenes of deepest affliction.   By its morning light, I have received those heart-wounds which never heal—the loss of the well-loved parents, whose affection no love can replace ; of the friend of youthful days, which can never return. Such a morning was it, this day twelve years ago, when thou, O Marcellus, wert snatched from us, in the springtide of youth, in the force of thy strength, and talent, and manly beauty.   After that long, weary night, during which I had sat watching alone, by the dim lamp, each unconscious movement, when all hope was gone, and each long-drawn gasp sent a fresh pang from thy heart to mine, the morning light stole through the ill-closed shutters ; and hoping without hope, I opened the window to admit fresh air to thy labouring chest.   The gay sun-rays burst in upon the chamber of death, the swift waters of the Rhine danced by, refulgent in the morning splendour, and unsympathising nature seemed to awaken to gladness, whilst the tenderest ties that friendship ever formed were immaturely rent asunder.   Long years have

passed since that sad morning; yet have I not learned
to forget, or ceased to mourn thee.   No companion
thou of the debauch; the friendship which survives
the long parting was not formed in the haunts of
dissipation.   If thy wit flashed bright at the festal
board—in the intimacy of the chamber, thy tender
feeling elevated, as thy learning and taste instructed.
Cut off in earliest youth—cruel favour of the gods!—
a few friends alone knew thy worth; one, at least, still
mourns, and never has replaced thee in his heart.   In
the wilderness of the great Babylon each turn recalls
thee; and here, in the city of countless tombs, thy
image rises to my memory, and accompanies my
pilgrimage.

Some feelings of melancholy must be awakened in
every visitor, as he follows those long lines of violated
sepulchres, ranged along the sides of the hills, ob-
truding far into the plain below, and stretching in every
direction across the table-land to the south.   The
simple sarcophagus and proud mausoleum now alike
gape tenantless; perpetuating neither the affection of
the survivors nor the merits of the dead, they are mute
as to their history, their fate, and almost their names.
Barbarian hands have disturbed the relics, and rifled
the treasures which they once contained; the existence
of such treasures must have been the incentive to, and
can alone account for, the universal violation of the

ROCK TOMBS ON THE WESTERN SIDE OF THE NECROPOLIS AT CYRENE.   *Page 65.*

tombs — hatred, if profitless as well as toilsome, is seldom thus unrelenting.

The influence of the vicinity, and, at one time, the domination of Egypt, seems to have inspired the Cyreneans with the same anxious reverence for the dead which distinguished their neighbours ; and they seem early to have abandoned the habit of increma-tion, though it is not evident that they adopted that of embalming. Few of the monuments are fitted for the reception of urns, and the very few bones which are sometimes met with, bear no marks of burning.

The northern face of the eastern hill seems to have been the first place used for sepulture; and, judging from the style, I should think that some monuments, about half a mile from the fountain, on the road to Apollonia, are among the earliest.   They are large sepulchres, with façades cut in the solid rock, with porticoes, in a very early Greek, almost Egyptian, style.   I am inclined to think that the sepulchres, which are entirely excavated, without any adjuncts of masonry, are of two epochs, the earliest and latest : the former, though generally rude, impressive in their monolithic vastness ; the latter, in their meretriciously minute though graceful decorations, reminding me forcibly of Pompeii.   Some of these one finds, in which the smoothed rock is scored with lines, to imi-tate masonry, like the stuccoed houses of Belgravia.

To an intermediate period—that of the greatest prosperity—I ascribe the cave-tombs, faced with masonry,
and the circular and temple-shaped monuments which
are so frequent; while the plain sarcophagus, rising
from the rock on which it was hewn, may belong to
any epoch. The road to Apollonia ran along the side
of the hill, at about half its elevation; and, above and
below, the tombs are built in long lines, tier above tier,
forming, in some places, as many as twelve terraces,
connected together by flights of steps.

The disposition in each form of tomb varies but
little. The sarcophagus contained, in general, room
for one occupant; though I found an instance where
two bodies had been deposited in the same excavation,
one above the other, with a stone to separate them.
The cave-sepulchres have, in general, a forecourt, excavated in the hill, presenting internally a low chamber, containing four or six plain sarcophagi, cut in the
sides, and as many, or even a greater number, of
similar cavities sunk in the floor. There are some
which form a long, narrow gallery, on which open
lateral chambers, each capable of containing two sarcophagi in length, and two or three tiers, one above
the other. The interiors are, in general, left quite
rough, without remaining marks of decoration : a few
have been plastered and painted, and others present
beautiful finishing of the stone-work inside. Those

hewn in the rock, and adorned with a façade of masonry, were, in their original state, undoubtedly the
most magnificent, as shown by the frequent remains of
columns and statues, but they are now the least interesting. The façade has, in general, fallen away,
leaving the sepulchre, with its bare wall and shapeless
entrance, the ghastly spectacle of a fleshless skull. In
only one case did I find such a façade still entire ; it
has separated from the rock, and leans slightly forward,
ready to fall in the first violent rains. It seemed to
me the better worth remarking, as it explains the many
smooth surfaces the rock presents, as well as the
decoration applied to the fountain.

Among the most interesting tombs in the northern
Necropolis are three, standing together, at a place
where the road, following the outline of the hill, makes
a deep bend. They are monolithic, and in one, the
Doric columns, which support the excavated porticoes in
front of the cave, are of abnormal proportions. Beneath
them, descending the abrupt hill, on the third or fourth
tier—it is difficult to say which, the tombs, principally
sarcophagi, being so closely grouped—is a sepulchre
without any external ornament, but exhibiting on its
interior walls the only frescoes of any merit I have
found. On the right hand, and on either side of the
doorway, the paintings are well preserved; those on the
other two sides are, excepting two groups, almost obli-

terated by the peeling off of the plaster in some places, in others by a hard, stalactitic crust which has formed on them.   The inscriptions scribbled over the ground, partly with the brush, partly scratched with a point, have bestowed a certain interest on these paintings, in which Pacho, who has not given quite a correct delineation of the paintings, thought he had discovered indications of Judaism.   The inscriptions, scarcely legible, seem to consist of the names of visitors, and to the unlearned offer no interest.   The whole series evidently refer to the games of the ancients ; chariot-races, gladiators, wrestlers, and pugilists, occupying the two sides which are damaged.   There are two wrestlers, with a third figure, who seems to be taking a flying leap over their heads, but who may be intended to be lying on the ground overcome, while the judge, with the prize-cup, or, perhaps, the oil for anointing, looks on in the corner.   To the right are two figures, one of whom seems to be inviting the first, a youth, to enter a doorway to which he points ; which I conjecture to be the introduction of a youth to the study of rhetoric or poetry.   It is here the inscriptions begin. The action of the next two figures is indistinguishable. We next see a figure in long drapery, crowned with ivy or vine-leaves, his right hand extended, in his left a lyre.   An orator, or poet, with a roll in his hand, follows next ; and, after him, the same draped figure, now

WALL PAINTINGS IN A ROCK TOMB IN THE NECROPOLIS AT CYRENE. No. 1.

Page 68.

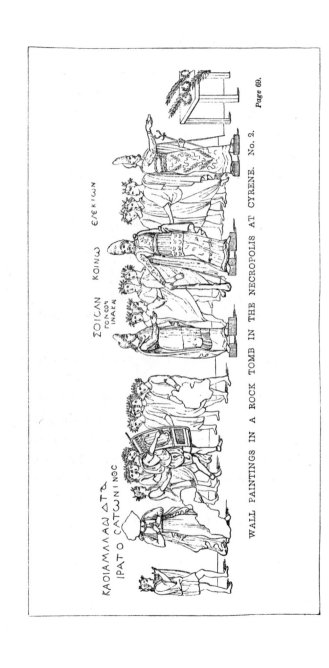

ΚΑΘΙΑΜΛΛΑΩ ΔΤΟ
ΙΡΑΤ Ο CΑΤΩΝΙ ΝΟC

ΣΟΙCΑΝ ΚΟΙΝΩ ΕΛΕΚΙΩΝ
ΤΟΝ ΘΟΝ
ΙΝΑΚΑΙ

WALL PAINTINGS IN A ROCK TOMB IN THE NECROPOLIS AT CYRENE. No. 2.

Page 69.

playing on the lyre. The next group is, unfortunately, much damaged, as its composition is remarkable. It contains eight figures, all crowned with ivy; the fourth blowing the double horn; before them goes a nude figure, bearing a square chest. Here there is a figure now headless, and again the musician playing on the lyre, surrounded by seven persons. A male figure, in a tragic masque, appears to be declaiming to a female also masqued, who is surrounded by seven other females, crowned with garlands. I could discover in these paintings no trace of Jewish origin; two of the figures still remaining, which Pacho has represented wearing mitres, are certainly tragic masques; the lofty hair on the foreheads of which may have deceived him in the obscurity. Though roughly executed, they are drawn with great breadth and freedom; in style they much resemble many of the Pompeian frescoes, to which time, or rather later, they may be assigned. On either side of the door, are an animal-fight and a hunt. On one, a bull attacked by a lion, while a tiger is preparing to spring upon his neck; above are stags, a gazelle, dogs, and a chacal. Spears are flying all about the picture. On the other side is a column supporting a vase, a man launching a greyhound, almost in the position of Gibson's hunter, a stag, two hares, and some more dogs.

Further on in the same range, at a place where the
old road, with the deep-worn ruts of the chariot wheels,
is still visible, is a very large collection of sepulchral
chambers, called by the Arabs Kenissich, or the
Church. There are remains of a large forecourt of
masonry, of which only parts of the sides are still
standing; but though very spacious, exceeding in
extent any other excavation in Cyrene, it contains
neither inscriptions nor emblems. Nothing in it indicates that it was ever used either for the religious rites
or the burial of Christians, as from its name some
travellers have supposed. It must be remembered
that names such as this have no origin in traditions of
the country, as its present inhabitants ascribe all that
they see to the Christians (the Roum); they have
no idea that any race of men occupied the country
before them. To this is to be ascribed their excessive
jealousy of antiquarian travellers, whom they believe
to come furnished with information which will enable
them to remove the treasures left by their ancestors,
according to Arab belief, in secret places. I should
conjecture that this vast series of chambers must have
been appropriated to some civic or religious corpora-
tion, as its extent is far too great to have been intended
for a single family.

This line of sepulchres, with its terrace, connected
by flights of steps, extends in unbroken succession for

about a mile and a half, till it reaches a beautifully-
wooded hill, where the tombs become rarer. Amongst
the immense heaps of stones fallen from the façades
of the larger, are often seen fragments of marble, and
excavations have uncovered many portrait-statues in
every part of the Necropolis.

Turning back to the old theatre, there is found
immediately beneath it the most splendid tomb which
the ruins of Cyrene present, both from its gigantic
dimensions and the excellent style of its architecture.
It is entirely excavated, without any additions of
masonry, presenting a large portico, supported by five
square pillars, which forms a stately entrance to a very
large chamber, succeeded by a smaller one.   The
centre pillars, with the rock which they supported,
have fallen, and lie in one huge mass in front of the
cave.   It is now the habitation of a Bedawy, who one
day very pressingly invited me to enter, to see his
marble boxes, the fragments of two very elegantly-
carved sarcophagi.   Beneath this are the arches
which I have already mentioned as belonging to a
temple ; and in the face of the hill, still further down,
are some very large tombs, now devoid of all appearance of decoration.

In whatever direction one leaves the city, the tombs
extend in long lines along the principal roads, they
are found cut in the rocks of the most secluded valley,

or built in groups on the summit of rising grounds. Of these the most interesting, beside the northern Necropolis, are those which flank the old road leading to Baria, and the long terraces on the western side of the Wady Bil Ghadir. I did not see the former till after I had been some time in Grennah, other objects having engaged all my attention; but, even when accustomed to the variety and vastness of its northern Necropolis, this struck me with astonishment. It was a lovely summer evening when I first came upon this long street of tombs, which is called by the Arabs the Market-place (El-suk), and passed for such with one of the earliest European travellers in this country—Lemaire. The long, deep shadows, with the glowing yellow of the sinking sun, concealed the ravages of time, and gave to the scene an air of solemn mystery which impressed the imagination and the eye. At every step some picturesque group of sarcophagi, or some large mausoleum, arrested the attention, and the sun had long set before I turned homewards. I often revisited this scene, and each time with renewed enjoyment. To reach it, one leaves the city by the gate near to what is supposed to have been the market-place of later times, when the traces of the old road soon show themselves. It is flanked on the left by a rock, artificially smoothed, and covered in a long row with niches square or oblong, and about one-third of

their length in depth. Some have a square hole at
the bottom, about three inches deep, which, though
sometimes in the centre, is more often on one side. Such
niches I have met with in other places, but here they
are more numerous, and in a continuous line for some
distance, interrupted once or twice by the door of a
sepulchre. Their object it is difficult to determine;
they could not have contained urns, for they are too
small, as well as too exposed, being not more than
three feet above the level of the road. They might
have been regarded as receptacles for exvotos, had
they been placed at a greater height. In this line of
tombs are some remarkable structures, peculiar, I believe, to the Cyrenaica—circles of five or six feet high,
surrounding a sarcophagus of the usual form. Most
of them are in a very dilapidated condition, but there
is one still nearly entire. It is formed of three layers
of good masonry, making a square platform, on which
the sarcophagus is placed, with a circle inscribed in
the square of the base, formed by a ring of stones
placed endwise in juxtaposition, no cement remaining
between them; their dimensions are about five feet by
three.

At the end of this street of tombs, turning to the
left, and riding between low hills, where excavations
and remains of buildings are rare, one comes to a
quarter of the Necropolis unique in its *ensemble*, but

not in its individual parts. I have already mentioned
the sarcophagi hewn out from the solid rock, which
are found so frequently mixed with tombs of other
forms; here they occur in large groups, rising one
above the other, on the tops of the low hills out of
which they are cut. The four sides of some of these
sarcophagi stand clear of the rock, which is levelled
all round; in others, only three sides or two are thus
freed; many are in connected groups, three or four in
a line, with no other external separation than a small
space between their lids, and a narrow watercourse,
to drain off the rains falling from their sloping
roofs.

Continuing to make a wide circuit of the city, one
comes upon the ruins of two forts, in one of which is
a large cistern; thence, keeping to the left, the monuments are more scattered, but they assume larger proportions, and date, probably, from the times of the
greatest prosperity. Some are circular towers on a
square base, like the tomb of Cecilia Metella, near
Rome; others have the form of a double cube, with
roofs sloping at the sides, and terminated at the ends
with triangular frontons. A partition, running the
length of the building, generally separates these into
two chambers, having a further division in height, so
as to form two stories. The greater number of tombs
in this direction present vestiges of former enrichment

TOMBS OVER EXCAVATED CAVES.

Page 75.

with statues or marble, and their sides are invariably
decorated with flat pilasters. Most of these monuments are erected over excavated caves, which gives
the idea of their being connected; the monument may
have been added to the original cave-tomb, or the
former destined for the master, and the latter for his
slaves or freedmen. No part of the ruins of Cyrene
offers so good a chance of profitable excavations as the
tombs in this direction, but I am not sanguine in the
hopes of the discovery of any objects in the highest
style of art. Not a trace of an inscription is to be
found on any of these monuments.

In the western valley, Wady Bil Ghadir, some of
the finest tombs are found, on the side of the hill
opposite to that one on which the older part of the
town lay. This part is very attractive by its bold and
picturesque scenery. Here is a deep ravine, forming an
impregnable defence to this side of the town, the rocks
on either hand towering almost perpendicularly above
the narrow bed of the streamlet formed by its three
fountains. Towards the higher point on one side is
a small grove of most venerable cypresses (the remains, perhaps, of that planted by Battus), which
crown the rock, and overshadow the tombs on the
terraces below. The fig-tree, the olive, and the
myrtle (here a tree twenty feet high), surround the
tombs with luxuriant thickets, out of which streamlets

issue, whose course far beneath is marked by thick bushes of oleanders crowned with their rosy flowers, and brambles covered at the same time with their pale blossoms, and with ripening fruit. Some of the tombs in this valley are the most elegant in their proportions, and the most carefully executed of any I have met with in this country; two or three still exhibit the polychromatic decoration of their architecture, and in a few are inscriptions, giving, indeed, only the names of the tenants without either title or date; but even these are interesting, when among them one finds a Jason, an Aristotle, and a Themistocles. The interesting pictures in fresco, representing a black female slave, which decorated the exterior of a tomb high up in one of the branches of this ravine, have been removed by M. Bourville, lately consular agent for France in Benghazi, and I hope that the intrinsic merit of the paintings, of which the engravings certainly make it difficult to judge, is such that their removal may add to our knowledge of ancient art. If not superior to those in the tomb I have described in the Northern Necropolis, their acquisition will add little to the treasures of the Louvre; their absence here is a disappointment to the lover of art. Two of the fountains show the remains of ancient sanctuaries near them, and inscriptions have been found connecting their erection with the name of

a pious matron.   Many statues have been dug up on
the sides of the hill, the best of which have been
removed by their discoverers; those that remain exhibit the worst taste in design, and the clumsiest
execution; their style is that of the statues produced in the masons' yards at Leghorn, and intended,
I believe, by the artists and the purchasers, whoever
they may be, as ornaments for gardens.

CHAPTER VI.

Charming Scenery.—Arab Summer Dwellings.—Ruins of Apollonia. —Ancient Granaries. — Chapels over Saints' Tombs. — Abd-el-Kader's Warriors.—Temple of Bacchus.

THE Wady Bil Ghadir, the Valley of Verdure, was one of the many beautiful ravines in this country which particularly attracted my admiration; it was one of my favourite haunts; and often did I climb its sides—occasionally at the risk of my neck—or saunter more safely in the perpetual shade of its stream-course. In the neighbourhood of Grennah, the hills abound with beautiful scenes, and these I gradually discovered in my rides; some of them exceeded in richness of vegetation, and equalled in grandeur, anything that is to be found in the Appenines. About a mile from the town on the south, one comes upon extensive remains of a fortress situated on the edge of one of these ravines, the Wady Leboaitha, which runs nearly due east; the valley is filled with tombs, and frequented by countless flights of wood-pigeons. Following the ravine, and turning to the left, we enter the Wady Shelaleh, which presents a scene beyond my powers of description. The olive is here contrasted with the fig, the tall cypress and the dark juniper with the arbutus and myrtle, and the pleasant breeze, which always blows through the valley, is laden with balmy perfumes. In the midst of this wonderful richness of nature appear the gray rocks, hollowed into large and inaccessible caverns, or gently receding in wooded slopes, and sometimes rising perpendicularly, and meeting so as to leave but a narrow passage between them.

Between the range of hills on which Cyrene was built, and the rising ground which so abruptly descends to the sea-shore, the broad plain, which from above seems a flat expanse, is found to be deeply indented with many wood-clad hollows. On their borders, ruined buildings or crumbling tombs contrast with the wooden hut of the present occupant of the soil—the monumental industry of fallen civilisation with the slothful hut of victorious barbarism.

August 29.—It was a bright cool morning when I started to visit Marsa Souya, the old Apollonia. The road follows the line of the cemetery until it reaches the hill whose secular cypresses I have so often admired; hence it descends into the plain, taking nearly

a north-east direction. At an hour from Grennah I
came upon excavations which must have formed part
of the dependencies of a country-house. In a good-
sized cave, into which one descends by three steps, is
seen a large circular basin hollowed in the rock, four
feet in diameter, and standing about ten inches above
the floor. In its centre is a square hole, as if for fixing
an upright beam. One side of the cave is occupied
by a long stone bench, in which is hollowed out a
larger mortar, having a slit down the outer side.
There can be no reasonable doubt that this was an oil
press. The country still abounds with fine old olive
trees, but its inhabitants have forgotten their use ;
when the fruit is ripe, they assemble their sheep and
cattle round the trees and shake and beat the branches,
while the animals greedily devour the precious produce
as it falls to the ground. The plain is in this direction
covered with the olive mixed with the caroub, now
loaded with its long dark pods. When left thus to the
hand of nature, the caroub becomes an immense bush,
pushing out suckers all round the parent trunk, which
in size is hardly to be distinguished among them. The
Bedawin have taken possession of many of the largest
of these trees, and make them their summer residence,
clearing out the centre and filling up the lower parts
with walls of dry branches, above which the dark-
green foliage rises with strange effect to the eye, but

affording a most grateful shade from the sun. In such a bower I found four men seated round a rude forge repairing broken muskets ; while in others women were employed in household cares, such as the grinding of flour, or the weaving of the coarse hair-cloth of which the winter tents are made. From here we turned to seek a pass through the hills, and as the old road has now become, if not impracticable, at least most difficult for horses, we took a path a little to the left, passing over ground covered with old junipers ; the twisted and contorted ash-gray trunks of these trees, and their small tufts of hoary green, for they have no other vegetation when very old, give the forest an appearance of decrepitude. The trees look like little old men bent, and bowed, and bald. From this the descent to the coast, even by the better road we had followed, is very precipitous. The supply of water had been forgotten, and a leather bag of milk, offered by a goatherd whom we met, was most welcome. Having at last, after much slipping and stumbling, reached the point where the pass emerges from the hills, we found ourselves in a fertile plain, which it took nearly an hour to traverse before reaching the sea. The water is bad and scarce, and this plain is, therefore, only inhabited in the winter, when it is sown with wheat and barley, and as soon as these crops are cut, the Arabs, with their tents, remove to a station in the hills. The inhabitants were long since in the summer retreat, but we found two men threshing corn by the antique process of treading, which, as all readers of books of travels know, is still practised in parts of Egypt and Syria. I do not remember to have seen the process described as I found it practised here, and there may be others who may think it as curious as it seemed to me. Four oxen abreast are fastened together by the horns, their heads close to each other; a fifth is in like way fastened to the inner one of these four, but the rope which secures his horns is tied round the middle of the belly of a sixth, whose head is in the same way fastened to him. This last pair, when driven, form as it were a revolving pivot, round which the four others move. One man drives them, and another is employed in heaping fresh corn upon the floor, and removing the straw which, by this process, is broken into small lengths, while the grain is, after all, but imperfectly separated from it. Riding on through the plain, we found it, though cultivated, extensively covered with the beautiful evergreen shrub, called in Italy, and here by the Arabs, *Baturne;* it yields a medicinal berry. We now reached a group of low rocks hollowed out into many sepulchral caves. The soil has a reddish tint (whose reflection is heating to the eyes), which with a bright sun made the ride a hot one. On the sea-shore, just without the town, and opposite to a

rocky island covered with excavations and ruins, we
found a well of very brackish water, which is the only
one in this neighbourhood; the town had been formerly supplied by the water of a fountain nearly three
miles off, conveyed to it by an aqueduct, portions of
whose ruins we had passed. This want of water renders a stay here very inconvenient, and prevented me
following my original intention of spending some days
in this place. The city was built on a semicircular
line of rocks close to the shore, and buildings are still
visible beneath the waters which have here encroached
upon the old boundaries, probably by subsidence of
the land. The fortifications on the land side are well
preserved, and remarkable for a large round tower still
almost entire, which rises at the south-west corner;
it is connected with some large buildings in this part
of the city, apparently of a castle; towers flank the
wall at irregular distances, and the position of one
gate is well marked, though now blocked up by fallen
ruins. Clambering over the wall one gains the interior of the city, which is crowded with heaps of ruins,
and presents the same confusion as a child's castle of
wooden bricks when the last story has rendered it
top-heavy and the whole falls upon itself. Some
arches rise above the soil, and in a few places pieces
of wall; the ground is thickly strewed with large
heaps of stone, columns of white marble and cipollino,

whose capitals are in general of indifferent workmanship. The sites of ten large churches, each with
an apse, are easily traced ; and the columns and
cones of the capitals, adorned with the ball and cross,
seem to indicate the fifth century as their date. The
difficulty of excavating would be extreme, on account
of the size of the heaps of stone which cover the
ground, and the weight of the masses ; but this circumstance, rendering it almost impossible for the
Arabs to make any researches among the ruins, may
probably have secured for the first person who is able
to undertake the costly task, a rich harvest of early
Christian antiquities. The theatre, outside the town,
is more perfectly preserved than anything within it ;
nearly one-half of the seats remain, but the proscenium has long since fallen into the sea, whose en-
croaching waters now fill the orchestra.

Returning by the same road I turned to the right,
about an hour and a half from Grennah, to see the
great caves called Maghyenat by the Arabs, and which
are, in fact, supposed to have served as magazines for
the merchandise coming from Apollonia to Cyrene.
They are situated at the foot of a hill, which is covered
with ruins, including those of a temple ; everything
seems to indicate that in this spot a considerable town
must have once existed, though the imperfect notices
of the ancient geography of this country which have

reached us, do not mention a town or village in this place. The caves are very extensive, supported by rude columns, irregularly disposed. One has a square fore-court cut in the rock, and seems to have been adorned with a façade; another has a broad flight of steps leading down to the interior, which is covered with an archway in masonry. There are three of these caves, from 100 to 120 feet square, and they show nothing that could lead to the conjecture that they were ever intended for sepulture; while their situation, as well as the name they have preserved to the present day, render the supposition that they served as magazines highly probable. I found one filled with hay and grain, and another was occupied as the habitation of several families. Turning homewards from this place, and crossing a deep ravine, we reached a very large natural circus at the foot of the hills, from above which flowed an abundant stream. The elliptical form was so perfectly defined that it was long before I could persuade myself that it had not been used as a circus in ancient times; but, though there are remains of building about the fountain, the remainder showed no appreciable marks of cutting away of the rock to form seats, or of the addition of masonry to complete the circuit. Another hour brought us, with the setting sun, back to the tents.

Tuesday, September 7.—This morning I rode to

the sea-shore, taking a north-west direction, to visit
some ruins, which an Arab had assured me existed
there. I was in hope of finding some remains of
Phycus, which must have existed in this direction, or
of the Garden of the Hesperides, which Scylax and
other old authorities place in its neighbourhood. The
country as far as the hills differed in no respect from
that I had already seen—exhibiting a plain partly of
rich soil, partly of rock, and cut up with deep ravines.
We rode down the Wady El Agâra, and reaching the
hills, found, at a distance of two hours from Cyrene,
ruins, apparently of a stronghold, on which is now
built a marābut, called Sidi Kelileh. It is remarkable
that so many of these chapels, raised over the graves
of reputed saints, should be met with in all Moslem countries, and that even the tomb of the Prophet
should be a mosque ; for this mode of honouring the
dead is the object of a special prohibition, uttered, one
would think, in too solemn a moment to be lightly
transgressed. In El Tabaray's account of the Prophet's death, he relates, on the authority of a tradition
derived from Aïsha, his favourite wife, that on the day
when he died, as he lay covered with a black cloak,
his face to the wall, almost his last words were, "May
God be unpropitious to those who make the tombs of
his prophets places of prayer." I know not how the
difficulty is got over ; perhaps, such tombs (being inside

the chapels, or inclosed in railings, so that prayers are not said *upon* them) are not supposed to come within the meaning of the prohibition; in all Moslem countries many such chapels are found, and in no country more frequently than in this, where ignorant fanaticism still exists in a degree unequalled in the other Turkish provinces I have visited.

From Sidi Kelileh we reached the summit of the range in an hour, and saw the sea at a gun-shot from the base of the thickly-wooded hill.   Far to the right, the promontory of Nanstathmus, and about half-way between, on the shore, the ruins of Apollonia; to the left, the mountain gradually closing upon the sea, which, a little further on, washes its base; but there is no promontory here visible, nor had any of the natives ever heard of Ras-sem or Razat.   The only indication which I could find of a promontory was at a point called El Bilanîch, where the shore makes a very slight bend outwards, and above it the hills rise lofty, and very thickly wooded.   A little to the right of the place where I descended we found a spring of sweet water, the only one on this coast—perhaps therefore the same at which the companions of Ulysses landed, when driven by stress of weather from off Cape Malia to the country of the Lotophagi.   On the sea-shore, to the left, are the ruins of a strong tower, built of squared stones without cement, called by the Arabs Arbîah, which seems to have served only as a fortalice, for there are no remains to indicate here the site of a town. Further on to the west is a curious shallow quarry cut in steps, from which the stones for the tower seem to have been extracted; and a little further on, a modern Arab khan, called Furtâs, in the walls of which ancient materials are built. Thence I rode on to Bilanîeh, where I found some excavations and levelled places on the rock, which may mark the site of Phycus. The sea-line from here turning slightly west by south-west, there seems no other place which will answer to the description of Phycus. I now climbed the hill above El Bilanîeh, and not finding the Garden of the Hesperides, whose golden fruit would have been most grateful, I rested for a couple of hours under a stunted ilex. The face of the hill was very steep, and the horses had hard work among the smooth rocks in some places, but it only took half an hour to reach the summit, from which the table-land at once extends. Two hours and a quarter west by north-west of Grennah, we came upon considerable ruins, consisting of a large open reservoir; a small building with a well-preserved apse; and a larger one, probably of Arab construction, as it contained several pointed arches as well as one round arch. My guide called this place Shuni. Eastward we met with nume-rous remains of building and tombs, presenting no-

thing remarkable ; their frequency, however indicates
the populous condition of the country in former times,
of which another proof presented itself on our road
homewards in a large and deep cistern, excavated in
the rock, to receive the rain-waters.   After my Arabs
had drunk of its very muddy water, we rode onwards,
crossing the Wady Mala'ab, pursued on our very
horses by the fierce barking of the dogs of an Algerian donâr, which had been for many months pitched
in the plain below Grennah.   Its inhabitants were as
fine specimens of uncivil fanatics as one need wish to
meet; they did not even deign to call off their dogs
when the Christian stranger passed their circular
encampment.   Their chief is somewhat more politic;
he frequently visited my tents, said that the English
were good men, who beat the French, and then begged
a supply of shot or writing-paper.   He and his companions had long fought under Abd-el-Kader, and
quitted their country rather than submit to infidel
domination.

    To conclude my account of the more remarkable
excursions around Grennah, I shall here in a few
words speak of the vast conduit which exists at a
place now called Saf-saf.   It lies to the south-east of
Grennah, at a distance of an hour and three-quarters,
and is remarkable not only for its magnificent structure, which resembles in size the Cloaca Maxima of

Rome (though of a much later date), but also for the
inscriptions, or rather quarry-marks, which are found
on the stones of which the noble arch is built.   These
are very curious, containing not only Greek characters,
like those in the reservoir at Cyrene (which this conduit seems to have been destined to supply), but also
other characters, resembling those of the Tawaricks,
or the Thugga inscription.   The following I copied,
and I believe it is a tolerably complete list of all that
exist in this place: A, Ⴑ, △▽, TPO, Ⴉ, Π, ⅃P, ⊻T,
K + Ⴝ, Ω, Ⴣ, Ⴗ, +, ×, W, ⌒, the last six being
apparently Libyan characters—a circumstance not to
be wondered at, if we consider that the aboriginal
population of the country would probably furnish a
large contingent to the labouring classes.   At one end
the walls are covered with Arabic inscriptions, recording the visits of various Beys of Benghazi and other
personages—a mark of interest rarely met with in the
East.   The winter rains were still collected in this
reservoir; and when I was there at the end of summer,
notwithstanding the drought of the last years, there
was still a small supply of water remaining in one
part of the vast archway.

The walls of the town are still to be traced, and the
ground-plans of several buildings; but none are of
any importance, excepting a small temple, with fluted
pilasters, only wanting the roof and fronton, which,

with the entablature, lie on the ground before it.   It
is mentioned by Della Cella as a temple of Bacchus,
with a frieze of vine-leaves and grapes, but of these I
could distinguish no trace, and I am inclined to think
that the lichens with which it is overgrown may have,
at a distance, deceived him.   The line of tombs extends
the whole way from Cyrene to Jafsuf, and a large
conduit covered with heavy stones runs along the side
of the road.

CHAPTER VII.

Grennah, a Charming Retreat—Pleasant Camping-ground.—Ren-
contre with an Arab Saint—The Son of a Rich Prince.—Striking
Cures.

AFTER spending six weeks in Grennah, I struck my
tent most unwillingly, and made preparations to continue my journey eastwards. It was too late in the
autumn longer to sojourn here, as I wished to see the
other remains of antiquity which exist in this country.
The rains set in usually about the middle of November,
and then come down with a violence which no tent
can resist. But I cannot quit my pleasant quarters
near the fountain without a few words in praise of a
country where I have found both recreation and health.
I have already told what abundant materials of interest it offers to the antiquarian. The sportsman will
find ample employment among the red-legged partridges, quails, and kata'ah, a sort of yellow grouse, and
a little further south, he will meet with the gazelle and
the houbāra, or bustard; while the lover of a luxurious

climate, decked with all the beauties of nature, will
sympathise in the story of the Odyssey, and easily
picture to himself the difficulty with which the Ithacan
tore away his companions from the land of the
Lotophagi. A more delightful residence for the summer months cannot be imagined. The nights and
mornings are always cool. In the daytime the thermometer ranges from 75° to 98°, the highest I have
seen it; but there blows all day a cool breeze from the
sea, which renders the heat insensible in the tent, and
quite endurable on horseback. The means of comfortable existence are by no means wanting. A sheep
costs from 4s. 6d. to 6s., and will keep good for four
days; vegetables and fruit can be obtained from
Derna, where the grape, the banana, the pear, and the
water-melon, are abundant; potatoes, bamias, tomatoes,
cucumbers, and many other vegetables, may also be
had there. Vegetables are likewise cultivated in this
neighbourhood, in the little gardens of the Bedawin ;
and the milk of their cows affords the richest cream
I ever tasted, though the pale butter which is made
from it is not very good. A man must, therefore, be
very hard to please, as far as the substantial necessaries
of life are concerned, if he be not satisfied with such
fare as this country affords; of course, wine, beer,
biscuits, cheese, and such other superfluities, must
be obtained from Malta. There is also to be had

here a substitute for the Swiss " *cure de raisins,*" in the camel's-milk, which, from experience, I can recommend as singularly efficacious. When drunk fresh, it is hardly to be distinguished from the milk of the cow, though richer ; but in cooling it acquires a most disagreeable salt-taste. Warm or cold, it is equally efficacious, and might fairly take its place among the remedies prescribed by the faculty. If nowhere else in Europe, it might probably be obtained in Pisa, from the farm of the Grand Duke.

To the traveller who has tarried in Egypt till the spring—who is tired of Syria, and unwilling to go to Europe, a more delightful retreat for summer cannot be suggested. The air is far purer than in any part of Italy, the scenery more beautiful and more varied, and fever and dysentery are unknown. From early spring to the middle of October, no rain ever falls, though the sky after the middle of August is almost always cloudy ; a heavy night-dew supplies the moisture which, at this season, covers the hills with a fresh coat of verdure. The distance from Alexandria to Derna is not great, and there is constant communication by sea between the two places. I should recommend for encampment one of the terraces in the eastern part of the Wady Bil Ghadir, a little beyond the first fountain, in descending the Wady from the south, rather than the fountain by which I pitched my tents. There

is here a triangular patch of ground, beneath a lofty
rock, which shelters it from the mid-day and evening
sun ; trees rise on every side, and there is a break in
the hills, giving a lovely peep of the sea. The ground is
dry gravel; along the edge of the terrace runs a streamlet of water from the fountain ; and, near at hand, are
some caves, which, if cleaned out, would make commodious store-rooms, or would serve other useful purposes.
It is not, like the fountain, a place of resort for the
camels, oxen, goats, sheep, and Bedawin, in the neighbourhood ; and is free, therefore, from the dirt and insects they leave behind them. Where I was, the wind
is sometimes disagreeable, raising clouds of dust which
filled the tent ; the other spot is more sheltered, and
even in high wind, is secure from dust. If the tra-
véller is accompanied by such a guide as Mohammed,
who spent all his time in buying beeves, let him be
prepared to have a hundred objections raised to the
situation, as this place is not convenient for such pur-
chases —" *experto crede.*"

From the disagreeable experience I have had of the
servants of this country, I should advise travellers to
bring with them all the servants they may require,
even to a groom, either Maltese, or what is better still,
Egyptians. Their ignorance of the roads is of little
consequence, as few of the Benghazi people are acquainted with them ; for guides it is better to trust the

camel-drivers : by doing so the travellers will have servants who know their duty, and who, having no private
interests to serve in the country, fear not to dis-
please the people; Mohammed, serving his own, utterly
neglected my interests. Egyptian servants would not
be more expensive than Benghazini, and they have
none of that overweening Moslem pride, which
makes the latter regard a Christian as something
infinitely beneath them.

There is one nuisance in Cyrene, too characteristic
of the country not to be mentioned. A small community of Derwishes, or Marābuts, as they are called
here, has established itself lately in one of the largest
tombs not far from the fountain. They belong to an
order recently founded by a reputed saint, called the
Sheikh Es-Senousy, and their president in Grennah is
a fanatic of the first water, who will not defile his eyes
by even looking at a Christian. He busily employed
himself after my arrival here, in impressing upon my
servants the degradation of serving me. The consequence was, that they all grew so uncivil—I must
except the cook — that I was at last obliged to
change them. The groom—an eater of pork and
drinker of wine in the town—here missed none of the
five prayers ; and, between the devotion of my servants and their visitors, the encampment resounded all
day long with " Allah akbar !" I was glad to see so

much religion among my people; but I could have wished it productive of a little more civility.

Not content with giving such good lessons to the servants, his saintship was, it seems, seriously annoyed by my presence here; and particularly at my having once or twice passed before the cave which he inhabits. He sent some of his people here, to say that, if I or my Christian servant again passed before his door, he would fire upon us; but Mohammed, who received the message, knew me too well to deliver it. By chance, that same afternoon, whilst I was engaged below, among some of the other tombs, my servant took this path, little suspecting that he should thereby incur the holy man's displeasure. Two Arabs, armed with large stones, came to oblige him to turn back; but he, luckily, had his gun in his hand, and they consequently retreated. Next morning, I sent to Abou Bekr, to complain of the insult offered to me, assuring him that not a day should pass thenceforward without my taking the tabooed road. It was too delicate a matter, it seems, for him to deal with directly, the church assuming here, as elsewhere, a separate jurisdiction; he, there-fore, sent one of his sons to the superior of the chief convent, with letters to request the punishment of the offenders. Meantime, I kept my word, and, in going out in the evening, I took this road; when I found an assemblage of some thirty Arabs, of all ages, prepared

to bar my passage.   As I advanced quietly, they drew
on one side, but as I passed them, one small stone was
thrown at, but missed me; on which I turned, and,
going straight among them, desired to know the name
of the fellow who had thrown the stone. This information, naturally enough, I could not obtain from them;
but I had seen the man who threw the stone, remarking that he was more than ordinarily ugly ; I, therefore, threatened that I would have both him and them
punished.

The next day the offenders were brought before the
great Sheikh's secretary—a man, I discovered, of good
sense and manners—who condemned them, with their
superior, to fifty strokes a-piece of his three-tailed
courbaj— a punishment which was immediately administered, and will not, I hope, be soon forgotten.
It was really necessary to enforce such punishment,
however painful to one's own feelings ; for lenity to
these people, whose chief intelligence lies in the
soles of their feet, would only have emboldened them
to more serious attacks.   The next day, Hamed, son
of Abou Bekr, arrived to enforce their superior's
orders on the Derwishes; and he then came to pay
me a visit, to make his father's excuses for not
having returned mine ; his soldiers, he said, were busy
collecting the miri, so that he could not assemble a
sufficient escort to enable him to come with safety.

This excuse, though strange, was perfectly true, for, in fact, this Arab Sheikh and Bey could not venture beyond the walls of his castle, even to his hareem, at the distance of a bow-shot, without a guard. His visit, including the dinner, did not occupy more than four hours, a very reasonable visitation from an Arab. He seemed not wanting in intelligence ; and yet he could not, or would not, tell me the number of men under his father's jurisdiction, nor even the number of tribes. Indeed, he appeared to have doubts as to the exact number of his ten brothers : first, he said they were nine ; then, on counting them all over on his fingers, eleven, but he included himself. This son of a prince of great comparative wealth—Abou Bekr being worth at least some 5000*l.* a year—the possessor of wives, and herds, and flocks, wore a shirt as filthy as the Catholic Isabella's, a cotton skull-cap to match, a burneau far from clean, and a pair of slippers as shabby and worn as the meanest Bedawy's. At the end of the visit, he told me he was badly off for soap, as his appearance too plainly testified, and asked for a square, which, with not a little grumbling, my servant gave him. Poor fellow ! he has an abscess in the side, which threatens him with consumption, unless the favourite remedy for all inward complaints in this country— burning with a hot iron—should effect a cure. He promised to consult a medical man who is at Derna at present; but I know that he will not do so, for fear of having to pay for a consultation or the medicines. The Arabs are fond enough of taking medicine when they can procure it gratis, but to pay for it seems against their creed. When the purse-strings are to be drawn, then they say, as he did, " Allah houa es-shafry"— " God is the curer," to which I answered him, by completing the sentence, as it is inscribed over the pharmacy of the Benfratelli in Rome, " *Nos remedium, Deus salutem.*"

The people of the country, when seriously ill, will go long distances to obtain advice from a European doctor; but rather than pay for the medicine he orders, they will hand over more than its price to one of their Fikkehs for an amulet or an incantation. These are the learned men generally employed as tutors, or schoolmasters, or readers of the Koran. They ascribe all illnesses to Satanic influence; and their exorcisms are directed to drive the Devil out of the patient. I am somewhat incredulous as to this origin of disease; but I confess that the cures they sometimes perform are astonishing. When called to a sick person, they generally begin by telling his friends that he has so many devils; then, after a time, they will say only so many remain; and, finally, after further exorcisms, not unaccompanied by an increased honorary (no pay, no pater-noster), they sometimes

really succeed in effecting a perfect cure.   Even Jews
and Christians resort to them; and I heard a well-
authenticated instance from a medical man, who had
himself visited the patient, of a rheumatic fever cured
in this way.   On this occasion the invalid was confined
to bed, unable to move, and his Fikkeh assured him
he was held down by many devils.   He, therefore,
after some prayers, belaboured them soundly with a
courbaj, to make them depart.   The strokes intended
for the devils, naturally enough, made the patient also
smart; and the pain of the flogging exceeding, I suppose, that of the rheumatism, the sick man at last
started up to escape it, and the devils were declared to
be expelled; but next day they returned, when the
Fikkeh was again summoned, his remedy was again
applied with undiminished energy, and the man was
really cured.   Poor old Keate would have been as
great a Fikkeh in the East as he was in the West.
Whilst I was in Benghazi, a Jewish girl who had been
mad for a long time, was restored to her senses by one
of these men; but on this occasion only prayers and
fumigations were used.   I have not seen any of these
cures performed; but relying fully on the sources from
which I obtained my information, have no doubt of
their truth; admitting certain of the strange mental
phenomena produced by so-called animal magnetism,
I do not see, indeed, why I need disbelieve them.

Whilst on the subject of wonders, I may mention, that discoverers of stolen property are not less frequently met with here than in Egypt; and that they often succeed in indicating either the thief, or the place where the missing goods are concealed, but never both, though more frequently the latter than the former, which indicates pretty clearly that their knowledge is to be attributed to the fears of the culprit.

CHAPTER VIII.

An Arab "Vendetta."—Coquetry at the Wells.—A Bridal Procession.—The Okbah Pass.

September 12*th.*—It was late in the day before the camels which I had engaged to take my luggage to Derna were ready, and much time was lost, even after a start was made, before they were fairly in march. This is almost always the case the first day of a journey with new camels, as their owners are never content with the distribution of the luggage, each seeking to lighten his own load at the expense of his fellows.

The road for an hour and a half follows the direction of Safsaf, and then turning to the right proceeds over an undulating country, from which, occasionally, ravines run down to the lower ground, and in these the cedar or cypress trees afford a welcome shade. I have already spoken of these trees, the universal ornament of this country; but I must not omit to mention that they are of a peculiar species. The wood is of a pale yellowish colour, like that of the cypress, and has the same perfume; but the tree itself assumes an infinity of shapes, and in this respect is certainly the most beautiful that I have ever seen. It rarely grows in the straight spiral form of the common cypress; more frequently its branches stretch out at right angles to the trunk, like the cedar of Lebanon, and sometimes it assumes a parasol form, like the stone pine; but whatever its form, it always throws a deep broad shade. At two hours and three-quarters from Grennah are the ruins of a square fortalice; these, and large heaps of squared stones in the neighbourhood, marking the site of other buildings, seem to show that it was a place of some size. Beneath the ruin is a well, called Labrak, in a wide grassy plain, where some twenty years ago a bloody battle was fought, which resulted in the establishment of my friend Abou Bekr's power, and in the total overthrow of the tribe of Beni Hadhra, seven hundred of whom are said to be buried in this spot. The remainder, with their chief, a cousin-german of the conqueror, fled to Egypt, where they obtained a settlement in the Fazoum; but they are ready to return the instant a chance of obtaining revenge presents itself. This may not be distant, as the Bey has a feud with another branch of his family, which feud the government of Benghazi is endeavouring to put an

end to, but with small hopes of success, his enemies
having sworn, "by the divorce," to destroy Abou Bekr
or leave the country. The continuance of his rule
hardly seems desirable, as both he and his son are
accused of the wildest excesses and basest meannesses
of which Arabs can be guilty, in addition to systematic
oppression of the people.   Our excellent Vice-Consul
in Derna told me that, a few days before my arrival,
one of the sons of my host of Cariab came to beg a
little sugar of him. He was then living in the Bazaar,
and came to the Consul's residence outside the town,
hoping thus to save himself the few piastres, with
which he could have bought what he wanted.   These
men will ask for or take, according to circumstances,
whatever they see, were it only a scrap of cotton
enough to make a skull-cap.

An hour and a quarter from Labrak lies Gabiout
Younes, marked by large ruins, among which are many
arches; a large building which, from its style, I thought
Byzantine; and another, certainly Saracenic, approached
by a lofty arched gateway. This building is composed
of vaulted chambers, and was the first specimen of Saracenic architecture I had met with, but it is entirely
destitute of other decoration than the beautiful light
arch of the gateway. Here, as in every spot where
ancient buildings are found, are large reservoirs. Only
three-quarters of an hour further on are the more

extensive ruins called by the Arabs Tirt (like dirt), in the maps Tereth, containing four castle-like buildings and many tombs. Two old reservoirs serve as a Zavia, or habitation of Derwishes, of the same order as my friends of Grennah, and I found here the largest encampment of Bedawy (of the 'Ailet Ghaith) which I have yet seen. They suffered me to wander about the ruins without molestation, but showed no signs of friendliness—thanks, doubtless, to the instructions of the Derwishes, who have been of late years very active in these countries in spreading a feeling of hostility to Christians. Northwards from the ruins extends a plain called Haou el Zouz. From here, continuing nearly eastwards, in two hours and a quarter we passed the ruins of Lamloudeh, formerly Limnis, covering a large space of ground, but, as usual in this country, without a trace of inscriptions. There is a tolerably preserved castle, which seems to have received at a period long subsequent to its erection an additional fortification in a sloping embankment, some eight feet high, of small unsquared stones piled against the walls. Here, and at Tirt, I remarked large numbers of round and oval flat stones hollowed on one side to a depth of about six inches, with a square hole in the centre. Excepting one which lies flat and, I think, in its original position, all the others are sticking upright in the ground. They are more like mill-stones than anything

else; but, besides some of them being oval, their
size is so large, varying from forty-five to sixty
inches in diameter, and their number is so great, that
I can hardly think this their original .destination.
There is to be seen in Rome a stone called the "Bocca
della verità" which has nearly the same form as these;
it was the mouth of a sewer, according to the general
account, and perhaps these stones may have served as
the covers of cisterns ; but I found none connected with
any existing excavation.   The ruins are built on the
side of a hill and contain many arches, all bearing
the impress of the Roman period.   Beneath the town
lay four very large reservoirs connected with each
other, partly cut in the rock, partly built.   A little to
the east is a subterraneous passage, now very much
choked up, which the Arabs pretend communicates with
the citadel, and near it are many broken sarcophagi
and cave tombs, as far as I was able to see, all devoid
of ornament.

From Lamloudeh the road passes through a beautiful wood of arbutus, over long low hills, which, leaving Zimah to the right, gradually descend into a
plain, watered by two fountains, which is called the
Kubbeh.   The stream issues in considerable volume
from the rock, in front of which still stands a portico
(El Kubbeh) supported by five (formerly eight)
square pillars.   In front the ground is covered with

remains of buildings apparently connected with the
fountain, and the rocks behind contain a great many
large tombs, as well as a flight of steps leading to the
ground above. Round the fountain I found large
flocks of sheep and goats, with their shepherds, who were
busy drawing water, with which they filled troughs
formed of stones taken from the old buildings;
women also, who, with their donkeys, had come for the
supply of water required for their households. Here
I seated myself on the top of the portico, in the shade
of the rock, against which it is built, waiting for my
camels to come up, and found amusement enough in
watching the coquetries of the ladies and the awkward gallantries of the men. The well is still, as in
the days of Rebecca, the place for flirtations. The
filling two skins and tying them on the donkey were
so adroitly managed, that, with many words and much
laughter, the men seeming to aid, but really impeding
the operation, at least two hours were consumed at the
well. The Bedawin, as I have already said, are very
sparing in their use of water, their bread even being
generally made with milk, so that the visits to the
wells, often at a great distance, are only made once in
three or four days. Whilst I sat on the Kubbeh, a
wedding party conducting a bride to her husband came
in sight, and for two hours I had the amusement of
watching them, as it is a point of honour to consume

the whole day on the road from the bride's house to
her husband's tent; and as this was at no great distance, and the Kubbeh a sort of public place, it took
the party two hours to go over a space which I rode
along in five minutes. The bride was invisible, shut
up in an arched box called a carmout, placed on a
camel, the centre part or arch covered with black hair-
cloth, the ends with white cotton, the housings of the
camel being also of a dark colour. The cortège consisted of six horsemen (among whom were neither her
father nor her husband), several men, and eight or ten
women on foot. At every hundred paces the procession stopped, the women raised the wild cry of re-
joicing called Zaghazhit, and some of the men performed a sort of awkward dance in front of the camel,
which ended with a discharge of guns. Whilst in
sight they once varied the entertainment with a mimic
fight, when there was much waste of powder, and once,
on a level piece of ground, the horsemen gave chase to
each other, the only graceful feature in their sports.
Then, with a fresh burst of the Zaghazhit from the
ladies, the procession moved on. From what I hear of
the fair sex in this country, they do not seem to have
much degenerated from the reputation which Herodotus has given to their predecessors the Gindanes.
Of course I am unwilling to believe all the scandalous

tales which were told me, but the existence of such
stories seems to prove that irregularities, unknown or
carefully concealed in other Mussulman countries, here
excite little attention.   Divorces are frequent, but they
arise most frequently from the caprice of the men, and,
far from being considered disgraceful to the lady,
many persons prefer those who have already made
the happiness of second husbands to inexperienced
maidens, as their successive dowers, paid in full at
each divorce, frequently make them, for the country,
wealthy.   The usual *corbeil* given to a bride consists
of four rotoli of silver, half a rotolus of gold, and some
pieces of stuff for dresses.   Only a part of the metal
is in general paid down, the remainder a debt due,
in case of divorce, to the lady, or, in case of her death,
to her heirs, that is, her children, or, if she have left
none, to her family.

To the north of El-Kubbeh, not in the direct road
to Derna, lies Messakit, where are some curious caves,
one of them containing rudely-carved emblems, of
Christian origin.   A gently-undulating plain leads
eastward to Beit Thamr, near which are many excavations, one of them evidently part of a country house,
where the apparatus for pressing oil is still to be seen,
hewn in the living rock.   This is one of the places
where bees are reared in great numbers, for the sake

principally of their wax. Our English bees would, perhaps, rebel, if one attempted to house them in the long wooden boxes, which here supply the place of the elegant and commodious habitations they are accustomed to ; but their fellows of the Cyrenaica, though less pampered, produce larger supplies of wax, and the honey almost vies in flavour with that of Hymettus. After passing Beit Thamr, the road enters a valley, called Brouk, filled with small streams, the last which are met with till close upon Derna. Above, on the heights, are ruins of a castle, and along the valley many excavations, one of which, containing a fountain, has a number of niches, as if for votive offerings or statues. Here the road begins to ascend through a beautiful wooded country, affording cover to numbers of the red-legged partridge, of which we started whole coveys at every turn. The grave of a Marābut, called Sidi Yadem, on the top of this ridge, was our sleeping place. From this point to the summit of the steep descent which leads to the coast, is a journey of four hours and a half, over rising grounds, affording, in the breaks of the hills, occasional glimpses of the sea ; and on the heights are many remains of ruined fortalices. The descent, called the Okbah, though certainly steep, is not the fearful pass which it has been described ; and in all this journey I never had occasion, from the badness of the road, to dismount from horseback. In the last years, I believe something has been done to improve this piece of road, which may be considered good by any one who is acquainted with the passes of the Lebanon.

CHAPTER IX.

Improvidence of the Arabs.—Derna, its lively appearance.—
Ruined Battery.—Curious Bargain.

FROM the summit of the Okbah one looks down upon
a long line of coast, the view extending to the promontory Ras el Hilal (Nausthasmus) on the left, and
eastward to the Ras el Tin. The hills which run along
the sea-line to the right are barren sandstone; the
coast, a line of low rocks; and from this point Derna
is only just visible, as a dark spot on the sea-shore in
the midst of glaring sands. It took an hour to descend
from this height to the more level ground; and the
intense heat reflected from the sandy soil, where not a
shrub affords the slightest shade, made this the least
pleasant three hours' ride I had yet had in this
country. Neither well nor fountain is met with in
this day's march till about an hour from Derna, where
a brackish spring issues from the rock, and flows
directly into the sea, in a situation where it is difficult

to find it. At length, after ascending a low hill of sand, which had hitherto bounded the view ahead, the green gardens of Derna relieve the eye, lying between the foot of bare rocky hills and the sea. Here I was most kindly received by the English Vice-Consul, Mr. Aquilina, whose ready hospitality I with difficulty declined, being unwilling to inflict the presence of strange servants on his establishment. Through his kindness I was soon put in possession of a garden, where I pitched my tent under the shade of its palms and fig-trees. Though we had not before met, I was already indebted to this gentleman for many of the attentions shown me while at Grennah; and during my stay here I derived from him much valuable information—the result of his thirteen years' residence among them—regarding the people of the country and their governors.

Leo Africanus, in the sixth book of his "Description of Africa," gives an account of the poverty of the inhabitants of Barca, and tells how they were in the habit of bartering their children for corn with the merchants of Sicily. The spontaneous fertility and pastoral wealth of the country, as I saw it, seemed to contradict this account, though the general fidelity of the author inclined me to place almost implicit belief in him. In Derna I afterwards learned, that his description, instead of exceeding, falls far short of

the truth during the seasons when the country is
desolated by one of those blights which occur at uncertain periods. The Arabs of Gebel-el-Achdar are
among the least provident people in the world; and
when a reverse befalls them, are one and all, the
poor and the wealthy, reduced to the greatest straits.
When the crops are abundant, everything becomes
dear, labour can be obtained on no terms, the Arab
refuses to sell either his cattle or flocks, he buys slaves
and horses at any price, and setting his cap on one
side, spends all his time in riding and gormandising.
But sometimes a flight of locusts descends upon the
country, and in a few hours every blade of corn or
grass, and every leaf, have disappeared; or successive
years of drought wither up the crops, and then, no
provender remaining for the cattle, the wells are exhausted, and pestilence, which spares neither man nor
beast, follows hard upon the scarcity and the drought.
Then, though too late, the Arab is as anxious to sell
all he has at any price he can obtain, as he was before
hard in his dealings and careless of reasonable gain.
He eats the corn reserved for seed, and when the rains
at length descend to fecundate the country, the fields
remain unsown. Such a visitation came upon them
some eight years ago. Their cattle, the great wealth
of the country, died for want of food; the next year
there was no grain for sowing, and then the misery

was so terrible that it would require the pen of a Defoe
to describe it. The strongest guard was insufficient to
insure the safety of the traveller in such a season;
misery rendered the people desperate, so that it seemed
easier to them to die in combat than by the slow
agony of want. Parents sold their children literally
for a few measures of barley : a very pretty girl was
offered to one of my acquaintance for two dollars; and
I know some persons who, through pure compassion,
bought children at this price. The dying were devoured
even before life was extinct; and in the ravings of
hunger, as eye-witnesses have related to me, the poor
wretches would gnaw the thighs and arms of those
who, more reduced than themselves, were too weak
to defend themselves. Thousands emigrated into
Egypt, and hundreds of them died of exhaustion
on the road thither.

We read in antiquity, even in the flourishing days
of the empire, of terrible famines in this country;
but these, doubtless, were alleviated by the resources
of the other provinces. Though again subject to an
extensive empire, the country can now look for no
such assistance when these disasters fall upon it. The
duty of the provinces is, to send yearly subsidies to
the capital; that of the Government is, to send rapa-
cious satraps to enrich themselves by the spoils of the
people, and to stifle their complaints.

The town of Derna is composed of four villages—
Upper and Lower Derna, and Upper and Lower Bou
Mansour, the former separated from the two latter
villages by a broad, stony wady, which in winter forms
the bed of one of the two streams whose abundant
waters, diverted by a former governor into many
channels, flow through all the streets, and are at
regular periods distributed to the different gardens in
which the houses of the town are situated.   These
many streams of water, and the gardens from which
rise thousands of splendid palms, rich in the bright
green of the banana and the reddening leaf of the
vine, give this place a strong resemblance to some of
the villages on the outskirts of Damascus, a resemblance which is still further increased by the arid
barrenness of the hills above and of the surrounding
country.   Unfortunately this luxuriant vegetation, as
too often happens in these lands, is accompanied by
periodical fevers, dysentery, and ophthalmia, which the
sea-breezes seem to have no effect in preventing.   An
old castle, now in ruins, which once commanded the
town from the hill above, and the lanes which lead to
to it, overarched, as they are, with verdure, through
which the rays of the sun pierce in chequered patches,
form a most picturesque scene.   The whole town has
an air of prosperity far surpassing that of Benghazi,
though its population, about 4500 souls, is smaller, and

its trade is comparatively insignificant. It consists
principally in exports of wax, great quantities of which
are produced in the neighbouring country, occasional
cargoes of cattle for Malta, and sheep, which are
yearly sent in vast flocks by land a journey of thirty-
five days to Alexandria.   Antiquarian remains are
few, Darnis having been a place of not the slightest
importance until about the fourth century : they consist of some traces of the ancient port at the western
extremity of the town, a Roman gateway, and some
excavations in the hills.

Derna has no harbour. From September to January
its roadstead is sufficiently secure, but after this month
no ship can anchor there in safety, as it is entirely
exposed to the north and east winds, which then blow
with great fury. There is, to the east of the town, a
point where the shore makes a bend, on which may be
seen a ruined battery, with half a dozen dismounted
guns ; it serves as a monument to record the fact that
this place was held by the Americans, for a short
period, about thirty years ago.*   Probably the diffi-

* When at Derna I was unable to obtain information concerning the origin of the American battery which seemed here so
strangely out of place. I am indebted to Edwin De Leon, Esq.,
Consul-General for the U.S. in Egypt, for the following account of
it. Achmed, Pasha of Tripoli, having been deposed by his brother
Yusuf in 1801, took refuge in Tunis. Before long the new pasha
found himself embroiled with the U.S., through capturing some
vessels bearing their flag. Determined to punish him, they offered

culty of making a harbour (they had planned an excavated basin in the wady which separates Derna from Bou Mansour), as well as the traditional policy of their country, always opposed to distant settlements, decided them to abandon the place.

I spent a very pleasant fortnight in Derna, en-

the ex-pasha the means of recovering his throne, but after long negotiations he left Malta without effecting anything, and retired to Egypt. His American allies had not, however, lost sight of him, and they induced him, by a grant of supplies and the nomination of an officer in their service, General Eaton, who took the command of his forces, to march upon Derna. Of this place he easily got possession, and it was then that this battery was erected. After a few months, being deserted by his allies, who made a treaty with Yusuf Pasha, in which his interests seem to have been little cared for, he retired to Malta, and thence to Syracuse, where he lived, partly supported by occasional sums granted by the Government of the U. S., partly by a small pension which their representative obtained for him from his brother. After various vicissitudes, he returned to Egypt, where, as the guest of Mohammed Ali, he enjoyed a liberal income. On his death a part of this was transferred to his only son, but was suppressed by Abbas Pasha. I found the son, now an old man, bedridden with palsy, in a state of frightful destitution, dependent for his support on the charity of servants. Mr. De Leon applied to the present Viceroy to obtain a restoration of the pension the son had so long enjoyed, and by his recommendation induced the Minister of the U. S. at Constantinople to ask the Porte to restore a small property in Tripoli, once belonging to his father, and of which he had enjoyed the revenue during the late Pasha's reign, but which the Ottoman Government seized for its own benefit after his deposition. Hussein Bey Caramanly, the surviving son of Achmed Pasha, is, as his father was before him, an American protégé, up to the present time a very useless title, but from which he is now, thanks to Mr. De Leon's energy, likely to obtain some advantage. His father's story, in all its details, is told in the Acts of Congress, 1807–8.

camped within reach of the sea-spray when the winds blew strong; but before I left I began to experience that feeling of discomfort which malaria is apt to give when it does not produce fever; and, notwithstanding the beauty of the place, and the attentions of Mr. Aquilina and his family, I was glad to find myself once more on the heights of the Okbah.

October 1.—I returned to Ain-esh-Shehad nearly by the same route which I had followed in coming to Derna, and there I spent ten days in revisiting some of the most beautiful spots in its neighbourhood, and in the enjoyment of the pure light air of its hills. I had left a part of my baggage in the charge of one of the Arabs of the place; and though the eatables must have been tempting, I had not to complain of any great indiscretion in his visits to my sacks. Though my neighbours were fanatical, I had, on the whole, no reason to be dissatisfied with them; with the exception of the Marābut and his pupils, they gave me very little trouble, and their thefts were confined to articles of trifling value. I had got rid of my friend Mohammed at Derna, with the servants, children, and horses which he had quartered upon me, so that there was no longer a daily fair held round my tents; and thus the last days I spent at Grennah were among the most agreeable of my residence there.

The advancing autumn, the threatening clouds

which now overshadowed the sky, and the increasing cold of the nights, warned me not to prolong my stay; and with regret I tore myself from a place where I had spent two quiet months so pleasantly, and, as far as health at least was concerned, so profitably. I find among my notes of these last days mention made of a curious bargain, which was struck in my presence; it was the sale of half a mare. The price of the entire animal was fixed at a certain sum, half of which was paid down by the purchaser, who took possession of the mare, which he was bound to keep in good condition. The foals were to be joint property, and the original proprietor could at any time have the use of the mare, or, by repaying the purchase-money, again become her sole proprietor. This is a common transaction; and as a fourth, or even a smaller fraction of a mare may be thus sold, some have many masters, and serious quarrels often arise from such joint possession.

It was not without many a long look that I rode away from the fountain towards the western gate of the town and the street of Tombs, which I have described as the old road to Barca. I was now on my return to Benghazi, not by the road I had taken in July, but with the intention, after visiting Nurdj, of following the coast by Dolmeita and Tokra.

CHAPTER X.

October 10*th*.—The old road, with its deep-worn
ruts, from time to time reappears among the underwood, and its course is marked for a great distance
from the city by groups of broken sarcophagi and
excavated tombs. In four hours and a half, pursuing
a W.S.W. direction, we reached a beautiful hilly
country, with fine old caroub trees and numerous
ruins. Here is the chief Zavia, or convent of the
Senoosy Marābuts, called Sidi Rafa'a ; it is still in
course of erection, and is a stately building for the
country. The neighbouring ruins supply the materials for the building ; and, by good luck, I arrived
while the extensive foundations of a very large temple,
which they were digging up to employ in building the
convent chapel, were still traceable. The masonry of
the substructures, consisting of passages or under-

ground chambers, was formed of very large stones,
squared and cemented with remarkably white lime.
The lintel of a doorway, of very good chiselling, and a
part of a fluted pilaster, were all I could discover of
the architecture. Its situation, in respect of its distance from Cyrene, and the extent of its ruins, leave
no doubt in my mind that here was the site of
Balaerai and its great Temple of Æsculapius. Its
position on the summit of a slight elevation is lovely ;
the remains of many other buildings, some of them
not insignificant, cover the ground all around. I
should have expected to find a fountain of medicinal
waters near a Temple of Æsculapius (no trace of
which is to be found here), yet none such is mentioned by old writers, nor could I hear of any place in
this direction, or elsewhere at a similar distance from
Cyrene, where such waters exist.

On either side, the country here exhibited signs of
more laborious agriculture than I had yet seen in any
other part; the underwood had been in great part
cleared away, and the fields were black with ashes of
burned weeds and brushwood, spread over the ground
as manure, preparatory to sowing. The secret of this
unwonted industry is the possession of the country by
a religious order who, here as elsewhere, spare no
effort to turn the property which they have acquired
(partly by purchase, but more largely by donations)

to good account. In this way they may exercise here the same beneficial influence over husbandry which, during the middle ages, the religious orders exerted in Europe ; they are also active in giving a sort of Bible-Society education (instruction in reading the Koran) to the children in the neighbourhood of their dwellings. Unfortunately, however, it is only in these points that they emulate the Christian institution to which I have compared them ; for with the elements of learning they instil into the youthful minds of their pupils feelings of hatred and contempt for the professors of every creed which differs from their own—a creed very alien from the practice of Christian charity.

Two hours further on is a fountain with ruins around it, and on a hill opposite many tombs. The place is called Belandsh, and its waters fertilise some gardens which are cultivated by Arabs, who live in the numerous excavations of the neighbourhood. When I left Derna the grape season was long over ; in Grennah, on my return, not a cluster remained on the few vines grown by the Bedawin : here, I bought white grapes, with which the trellises were loaded, and which were not yet ripe. Herodotus speaks of the three climates of the Cyrenaica, in consequence of which the harvest is carried on during eight months of the year ; and it was interesting to meet with this practical confirmation of his remark.

From Belandsh the road runs for many hours
through a country thickly strewed with shapeless ruins
and sarcophagi, the hill-sides being almost everywhere
burrowed by excavations.   Just before reaching a
spring called Maten Ma'as, two hours from the last, is
a ruined castle, to which the people of the neighbourhood have given the name of Kasr Djemal.   It seems
to have been originally a Roman stronghold, added to
or repaired in Saracenic times.   Riding in a N.W.
direction from this place, along an ancient road, I
reached in an hour and ten minutes (horse-pace), a fine
old castle on a hill to the left.   On a square base of
rock, formed by an excavated ditch fourteen feet wide,
rises a square tower, which, with the exception of one
vaulted chamber, still entire, is filled with fallen
rubbish.   In addition to the ditch, very extensive out-
works, which are still to be traced on all sides, formed
its defences : it is now called Sirt Nawara.   That it
must have been a place of some importance may be
conjectured, not only from its position, but also from
the many tombs in its neighbourhood, and the care-
fully-chiselled decorations of many of their façades.   I
here found that I had missed the road, which takes a
turn more to the south, and, consequently, had to ride
back to Maten Ma'as, and thence over a range of low
hills, which afforded little shade, and were very hot,
being screened, by a higher range to the north, from

the sea-breezes. This road, however, led, after two hours' travelling, to a succession of the most beautiful scenes I ever beheld, even in this beautiful country. A steep ravine forms the descent from the high ground which we had now reached, surrounded on either side by lofty rocks, in some places perpendicular, while in others they slant sufficiently to allow an accumulation of mould on their slope. Down this the path winds over fallen rocks, among venerable olive trees and gigantic cypresses, which grow up among the *débris* in the bottom of the valleys, while the receding hills are thickly covered with junipers and olives. This valley, if cultivated, might produce annually an almost unlimited quantity of oil: it took me nearly three hours to ride through it. The trees are probably self-planted, and, doubtless, the descendants of those which supplied the old Cyrenian commerce with the oil for which it was so famous: they were covered with an abundance of fruit. No care is bestowed upon them; many are rather immense bushes than trees, and their valuable produce serves only as food for the goats, which eat the fruit greedily as it falls. In the hands of a speculator possessing capital, an enormous profit might no doubt be obtained in the course of three or four years, by the cultivation of these trees; all they require is pruning, and to have the earth collected round their roots, in order to give a splendid harvest.

The trees are not the wild olive species, though their fruit is small. Not even in Italy have I seen a country apparently so well adapted to the cultivation of the olive ; but the uncertainty of tenure of property, the deplorable weakness of the Government, and the un-tamed savageness of the Arabs of the neighbourhood, would certainly render the speculation a hazardous one.

The name of this lovely scene is Aggher bi Harou-beh. On a hill to the left, on emerging from the ravine, is seen the Castle of Benigdem, the best pre-served of the old forts which are met with everywhere in the Cyrenaica. It is a rectangular oblong building, with two square towers slightly advancing from the line of the wall, in the centres of the longer sides. One of these towers is still in great part perfect, having three stories of windows. The second story is vaulted, and has on each side two windows looking outwards. The walls are built double, of stones carefully squared both within and without, leaving a space filled in with rubble, thus increasing the thickness and strength at little expense. I have remarked that the same method of building is employed in many of the old forts in this neighbourhood, and also further south. On the north side, a low arched gateway, commanded from the tower, seems to have been the only entrance to the fort, which was further defended by a low outwork, built of squared stones,

still easily traced. The interior is now so filled with
the ruins of fallen walls, that it is impossible to distinguish its arrangement. Hence, I rode on through
the hills to another old fortalice of very small dimensions, where I slept. The distance from Maten Ma'as
to this place, for which I could learn no name, is eight
hours of camel travelling. The tents were pitched
among hills of great beauty, covered with wood, overlooking a rich plain, through which runs the lower
road from Grennah to Merdj. This we followed the
next day; and during ten hours of travelling, the
country presented a succession of richly - wooded
scenery, frequented by innumerable covies of partridges. This day, five hours after starting, I made a
détour to the right through a long winding valley,
which leads towards the coast, through the country of
the Dirsah Arabs, but did not meet with any ruins of
importance. The camel-drivers took advantage of my
absence to journey on to a later hour than I usually
travelled; the process of pitching the tents and preparing dinner being very much impeded after sunset.
They were, however, disappointed in their hopes of
reaching water; and we had now travelled two days
without finding any. The skins had all been filled;
but, during the first day, with the ordinary recklessness
of Arabs, they had drunk a large part of our provision,
and there would have been none left for the evening,

had not my servant taken possession of the last remaining skin, so as to secure it for the evening meal.
In consequence of this, there was great suffering from
thirst among my followers. The Arabs here are not
abstemious, for they drink water in enormous quantities
whenever they can get it, and when they cannot thus
indulge their thirst, they seem to suffer very much.
My own rule in drinking is to take a cup of coffee in
the middle of the day, rarely adding a small cup of
water, flavoured with raki, to destroy any insects it
may contain. I make a practice of not drinking at
other times during the journey; and I do this both
from finding the advantage of such abstinence, and for
the sake of example to the servants, in a country where
water is sometimes so precious. The day following
there was of course great haste to reach the wells,
which the evening before, when I stopped them, the
camel-drivers represented as close at hand. I rode on
through an open country, anxious to obtain water for
the horses, which had not drunk for two days; but it
took three hours and a half to reach the Wady el
Gharib, at the upper end of which are many wells.
When at last I reached them, we had no means of
drawing the water; and some Arabs, who were watering their sheep there, absolutely refused, for love or
money, according to their own expression, to supply
us. They were only five in number; and I had great

difficulty in persuading my servant (though he had
only the previous evening wounded his right hand so
as to make it useless), not to take possession of the
well by force.   This would have been easy enough,
but after my complaints against the marābut at Grennah, I was anxious to preserve a good character for
peaceable conduct.   It took the camels nearly an hour
and a half longer to reach the wells ; and not doubting
that, on seeing the number of the party, the Arabs
would yield us a supply, at least enough for the horses,
I possessed my soul in patience in the interval.   When
at last they came up, I acknowledge that, in my heart,
I was not well pleased to see my people quietly submit
to be refused accommodation by the Arabs, without
taking forcible possession of their cord and bucket ;
but, true to my system, I kept the Sultan's peace, and
contented myself, when the caravan had moved on, with
riding down to them, and assuring them that I should
have them punished, having in the meantime found
out their names.   The Governor of Merdj, on my
complaint, promised they should be sent for and
punished ; and to make sure of his having kept his
word, I renewed my complaint, through the English
Consul, to the Bey of Benghazi.   These Arabs belonged to the tribe of Abid, whom I have already mentioned as notorious for their predatory habits and
discourtesy to strangers.   From the well we rode on

for five hours, in hopes of reaching Merdj that evening; but an hour after sunset, when we had climbed a steep wooded hill, we found that we were still only on the edge of the vast plain thus named. It was already dark ; on all sides a hundred fires marked the dwellings of the Bedawin, who encamp here in great numbers for the convenience of the wells, of which there are in all upwards of forty around the castle. I sent a camel for water, but it was midnight before it returned ; so that we were in some discomfort, no cooking having been possible, though I found an unhoped for consolation in my nargila, in filling which a servant had stupidly used the last drop of our water. The next morning, starting early, it took the camels four hours to reach the Medina, as the part of the plain on which the newly-erected castle is built, is called. In the maps, two large lakes are marked as existing in this locality, and before us, immediately in front of the castle, lay an immense expanse of clear water, unruffled by a breath of air, and every object on its banks reflected in it, as if in a mirror. It receded as we approached, and at length disappeared altogether; but on turning round, I saw my camels, which followed at a considerable distance, wading up to their knees in the magic fluid. I had often seen the mirage in the Desert, where it is of frequent occurrence, but the deception was much less real. Here, for some time, I

had no suspicion that the lake, round which I contem-
plated a long *détour* in the hot sun with no pleasant
feelings, would vanish on coming nearer. These lakes,
which make a formidable appearance on the map,
really exist sometimes for years together; they owe
their origin entirely to the autumnal or winter rains,
and dry up after two or three seasons of drought, such
as of the preceding years. On approaching the castle,
in front of which lie the greater number of the wells,
the scene presented to us was the most primitively
pastoral I had ever witnessed. Immense herds and
flocks, collected in groups, covered a very large space,
while boys and women were busily engaged in drawing
water, which they poured into skins stretched on hoops,
for the cattle to drink from. Many short trunks of
columns are placed near each other triangularly, so as
to support the edges of the hoops, while the skins
form a basin. The sun was very hot, and the earth here
is of a red colour; and, though not yet midday, the
air, from these causes, seemed to have that warm tone
which we admire in some of Both's evening landscapes.

I rode at once to the castle, after procuring water
for my horses from one of the fair Rebeccas at the
wells, and was very kindly received by the Kehia or
Governor. The ill-lighted, cool council-room to
which he conducted me, empty of everything but the
divan at one end, was most refreshing after expo-

sure to the fiery heat of the plain. Dinner was almost
immediately afterwards served, and I sat down with
him, the commandant of the few soldiers stationed
here, and half-a-dozen Arabs, whom he summoned by
name from the door. When dinner had been dispatched, the only term applicable to Arab eating, I
remarked a custom which had on other occasions
struck me. Of those who had dipped their hands in
the same dishes with us, all went out after washing
except my host, the commandant, and one of the
Arabs, who was specially invited to stay: after their
departure coffee was served.   I remember having
heard a story from one of the most spiritual of my
friends, which is applicable to the case in point. Several years ago he spent some time at one of the
smaller German courts, where the number of the rules
of etiquette is in the inverse ratio to the numbers of
the population. For many days one of his neighbours
at dinner—a most agreeable and well-informed man—
regularly left the room when the *rôti* was served,
making a low bow in rising from his place. His
departure did not at first attract my friend's attention,
but as the same scene occurred daily, he at length
turned to his other neighbour and asked him the
meaning of it ; expecting to hear that the man had
an aversion to roast meat, such as some people have

to cats. The answer was simply, " Herr N. ist nicht
bratenfähig ;" that is, Herr N. may sup his soup, and
enjoy the entrées and relevés, but he is not well born
enough to partake of roast beef in this company.
Thus any Arab may with propriety enjoy the Bey's
good dinner, but he must not hope to drink his coffee
after it. A similar custom seems once to have existed
in England. In Shadwell's " Lancashire Witches," Sir
Timothy says to his uncle, " What a murrain do we
keep you for, but to sit at the lower end of the board
at meals, rise, make a leg, and take away your plate at
second course."

The site of the castle, surrounded by many fragments of ancient buildings, is that of Barca, daughter
and rival of Cyrene, and even under the Arab domination (long after the parent city was a heap of ruins),
a flourishing town. The ground is literally strewn
with fragments of small columns, the ruins of the
Saracenic city, and the line of its walls is still distinctly traceable. The castle, which was only begun
a year ago, on the site of the ancient citadel, is built
of ancient materials dug up on the spot. Many capitals of columns, of debased Greek workmanship, and
many entire columns, have been found in digging out
materials for its construction, but nothing dating even
as far back as the time of the Ptolemies. I found the

base of a column, of white marble, lying among the
rubbish, which had formerly been a cube, having on
four of its sides Greek inscriptions. Judging from the
form of the letters which remain, I should suppose
them to be of about the first century of our era; but it
was not possible to decipher the meaning of the inscription, as each line was more than half effaced on
the side which has been turned downwards, and only
single letters of each line remained on two other sides.
In its present condition it may be of the fourth or
fifth century.   Cufic inscriptions are not unfrequently
discovered here; one, lately found, had been placed
above the door of the council-room, but was so thickly
whitewashed as to be quite illegible.   Two capitals of
columns, in white marble, with the Moslem profession
of faith beautifully inscribed round each in raised
flowered letters, had just been built into the sides of
the minbar of a mosque which the Kehia is building,
one of the capitals being turned upside down.   He
begged me to go to see the progress of the work, to
assure him, by means of the compass, if the Kibleh
was rightly placed, and this gave me an opportunity of
seeing the simple, or rather rude, fashion in which the
light arches are thrown from pillar to pillar.   There
was no scaffolding used beyond two planks for the
mason to stand on, neither was there any wooden

centering, but the stones, cut to the proper shape,
were, one after another, handed up to the mason, who
secured them in their places with cement ; a few loose
stones were made to support them : the arch being
thus gradually built up from each side, the keystone
was at last added, and then the planks were immediately removed, the arch being considered solid
enough to require no further care. The arches were
pointed, and each composed of eleven or thirteen
stones. In another building, intended for an oil-
press, I found a large circular arch, twenty feet in
width, in process of erection. Here a long board had
been run across the breadth of the building ; in its
centre a nail served as a pivot for a long strip of
pointed wood, by which the mason decided the position of each stone as he placed it. There were several
small houses in progress, destined to form the nucleus
of a town, which the Kehia hopes to see rebuilt. This
was the only place in the whole country where I had
seen anything like enterprise. The Kehia is a clever
man, and, in conjunction with the Bey of Benghazi,
whose dependant he is, he had undertaken these works
in hopes of making a profitable speculation out of the
oil of the uncultivated olive trees in the neighbourhood.
It was with a sincere wish for his success, which cannot
fail to be followed by increased industry and gradual

civilisation of the district, that I took leave of him, having spent two days in the Medina, during both of which the hot south wind had blown with great force, raising clouds of red dust. It was the first time I had experienced this wind in the Cyrenaica.

CHAPTER XI.

October 16*th.*—Right glad to escape the furnace-like
blasts which swept, stifling, over the plain of Merdj, I
started, though late in the afternoon, on the way to
Tolmeta. The camel drivers, who had been furnished
to me at Grennah by Abou Bekr, in addition to their
ignorance of the road, proved themselves the most
unmanageable beings I had yet met with; having
complained of them to the Kehia, he gave them an
admonition, and also provided me with an Arab of
the country, a soi-disant relation, to conduct me on
my way.

It took three hours in a north-east direction to reach
the edge of the plain, when, night coming on, I encamped, and continued the journey the following
morning. There are two ravines which lead towards
Tolmeta, of which we took the one to the west, called

Wady Shebbah ; this route is rather the longer of the
two, but affords an easy descent, which, to travellers
with heavily-laden camels, is a consideration of no
little moment.   The other descent was called by my
conductor Wady Hambes, or Hambesh.   It is described by Beechey as very beautiful, and, being more
difficult, its scenery is probably grander than that of
the route followed by me, which is rather a pass than a
ravine, running over long low hills until it gradually
reaches the level of the sea.   On the shore, nearly
opposite its *débouché*, is a group of rocks, and among
them a well with brackish water, where we found many
goats, with their attendants.   From this, riding eastward, we came to another well, and then to a third in
the ruins of a fortalice, which contains the only sweet
water in the neighbourhood.   Having filled our water-
bottles, we went on to a large square monument, supposed to be the tomb of one of the Ptolemies who
reigned in this country ; the monument is visible to a
great distance out at sea.   Built on a square base of
rock, it presents a noble mass, and has kindled the
enthusiasm of former visitors ; but, to my eye, excepting for its greater dimensions, it seemed in architectural beauty inferior to many I have seen elsewhere in
this country.   The triangular entrance, on the side
opposite to the hills, is remarkable from its resemblance to that of the Great Pyramid.   Near this are

many large excavated tombs, one of which is remarkable, from the fact that the rock out of which it is
fashioned has been cut away all round, and thus a
monolithic monument, in the truest sense, produced.
It took seven and a half hours in all from Merdj to
this point, where I stayed for upwards of an hour, in
the useful, or at least necessary, employment of bargaining for sheep, a flock of which was drinking at a
pool in front of the large tower. All bargains are
difficult negotiations in this country, the Arabs often
refusing to sell at a price less than double the market
value of their merchandise : they are well acquainted
with the laudable custom of making strangers pay
their way. The price of sheep appeared to have gradually risen since I came into the country ; the first I
bought cost me about five shillings, and those I
bought here more than double that sum. For a party
of six people I found that, with economy, a sheep
would last three days, if eked out with a not inconsiderable supply of rice and biscuits for the Arabs, who
eat voraciously.

With my new friend, Abd-el-Kader Waled Ali, I
had much curious conversation, as I found him more
communicative than the greater part of his countrymen. He is of the wealthier class, and lives in the
country beyond Labiar. He complained, and I believe
with justice (for every one I have spoken with on the

subject confirmed what he said), of the unequal manner in which the taxes are levied, the miri for each
naga varying in different tribes from five to six hundred piastres.   The naga, like the pound sterling, is
an imaginary unit, consisting of ten camels, or twenty
oxen, or a hundred sheep or goats.   Each tribe pays
tribute for a certain number of nagas, according to
a census made some 150 years ago; the Sheikh
being responsible for its partition among the members of his tribe, and its collection.   It is easy to
understand that with such a system the tax falls very
heavily on those tribes which from war or other causes
have sunk in importance in this lapse of time; whilst,
on the other hand, those which have grown wealthy
pay an insignificant sum: thus a tribe rated at a hundred nagas, and which has now only twenty, pays for
each naga five times the sum it was originally taxed
at; while those whose wealth has increased from a
hundred to a thousand, pay for each only a fiftieth
part of what their less fortunate neighbours are
charged.   Ignorant in book learning, the Arabs, aided
by their rosaries, are no mean proficients in arithmetic;
and their applications for redress are as incessant as
fruitless.   From what I have seen of the country a
spirit of discontent is universal—the Arabs regret
their old independent pasha; and I think the arrival
of any Government, Moslem or even Christian—so

only not the Sultan's—would be hailed with general satisfaction.

Abd-el-Kader is married, and I took down his account of the price he paid for his wife. To her father he gave thirteen sheep, valued at two dollars and a half each, with a hundred dollars in cash; and to the lady herself, a pair of silver bracelets (souar or debalg), weighing thirty-five dollars, dress-stuffs to the same amount, furniture, carpets, &c., to the value of fifty dollars; these, with some other expenses, made the cost of his wedding amount in all to three hundred dollars. He confirmed to me the truth of an Arab custom, which I had before heard of from others, that of giving to the mother of the bride a sum varying from a hundred to five hundred piastres, as the price of the milk with which she had suckled her daughter. The sheep and the money are not returned in any shape, as, on her father's death, his wife's brother succeeds to them, and on his death the next male heir. " Well," I said, " you will acknowledge that here you literally buy your wife ? "— to which he retorted, " Of course we do; while in Europe it is the wife who buys her husband; we are up to that;" and he chuckled, and seemed to think he had paid me off with interest.

After passing the pools, where I had stayed so long, we came in sight of the line of the fortifications, which

are now almost buried in sand, and of one of the city
gates, still an imposing mass.   The plain where Tolmeta stood did not become visible until we had
crossed the low ridge formed by the fallen walls.
Great was the disappointment I experienced on my
first view of the city, and greater became my disappointment the more I saw of it.   Three columns
standing over large covered cisterns, and two smaller
ones not far distant, the ruined apse of a Christian
church (probably of the fourth century), catch the
eye; but the general impression of the entire surface
is that of a huge piece of new macadamisation, so
thickly is the ground strewed with small fragments.
The celebrated barracks have been lately despoiled,
by truly Vandalic hands, of the curious inscription
which rendered the building so interesting, and to
obtain which the greater part of the front facing the
sea has been overthrown.   The destruction of it seems
to have been as wanton as the labour of it must have
been great, the architecture being of the most solid
description.   I was told that in attempting their
removal one of the slabs was so broken that the
author of this devastation left it lying on the ground;
and that after an interval of two or three years, when
he had learnt in Paris that an inscription, of which a
third part is wanting, is worthless, he sent for the
remaining fragments, which were already illegible.

If those employed were incapable of taking an accurate copy of the inscription, one would suppose that they might at least have made a cast of it, and at less expense, and thus have left the only monument worth visiting in Ptolemais still retaining its external form, and the disposition of its interior still traceable, and unchoked by newly-made ruins.   The three Ionic columns, which have been described as dating from the earliest times and of remarkable purity, seemed to me of a late epoch, when not a tradition of true beauty remained ; they are clumsy, and badly chiselled, nor did I see in the whole space any fragments of sculpture or architecture in a good style of art. There are ten vaulted buildings, and a very large rectangle rising only a few feet above the soil, whose purpose cannot even be guessed at; scanty remains of a theatre, the outlines of an amphitheatre, formed in a quarry, having no feature of interest, complete the catalogue of the ruins within the town.   The fortifications towards the sea, consisting of a series of forts, are well preserved, though nearly buried in sand ; but the most conspicuous object is the gateway I have already mentioned, whose two flank towers are still nearly perfect.   On the stones of which these are built are many inscriptions, whose irregularity would lead one to the idea that they are of very recent date, or even to fancy them the work of industrious idlers,

REMAINS OF IONIC BUILDING AT PTOLEMAIS.

O. JEWITT SC.

Page 144.

bent upon thus immortalising their names.   Fox's and many other names, carved with a knife on the old walls at Eton, are far better specimens of caligraphy.   More interesting than these are the quarry-marks, many of them in Barbary characters, which are found here, as well as on one of the forts on the sea-wall.

On the second day of my stay here the clouds gathered thick towards sunset, whereupon soon followed a storm of lightning and rain, such as I have seldom witnessed.   The autumnal rains had commenced, and it was evident that my proper course was a speedy return to Benghazi, as when it does rain here it continues, almost without intermission, for many days, and with a frantic violence which no tents can withstand.   I had been too much disappointed with the remains of Tolmeta to regret having to shorten my stay here; and when the rain ceased the next morning, or only continued in fitful showers, I had the wet tents and baggage placed on the camels, and took my departure for Tancra, the ancient Tenchira.   It was, however, so late before a start could be made, that at sunset we were still at no great distance from the ruins, and finding a good place for encamping near some wells, and fields sown with *izra*, I stopped there.   The route is along the sea-shore, through a wide plain covered with briars and baturne

bushes, showing only in very few places slight marks
of cultivation. A soft warm wind, like that of a spring
morning, made the ride through the clean-washed
underwood delightful, and I fancied I could already
see signs of fresh vegetation in the briars. It took, in
all, nine hours and a half to reach Tancra from Dolmeita.   Near the old town are many patches of cultivated ground, producing vegetables and fruit, the
property of Arab families, who inhabit many of the
excavated tombs in the quarries on either side of the
town.

The first view of Tancra rather disappointed me.
So much has been written about the perfect state of the
walls, that I arrived there with the expectation of
finding them more perfect than the walls of either
Rome or Constantinople; and what, indeed, have these
cities, amidst all their remains of bygone days, to offer
of more interest than their venerable walls, which, after
withstanding unnumbered hostile attacks, still retain
so much of their historical significance ?   The circuit
of the walls of Tenchira is on three sides entire; the
disposition of the towers is well marked, and the places
of the gates may be conjectured: in many parts the
wall is not more than two or three feet high, in some it
is reduced to a mere heap of stones, and in none does
it exceed fourteen or fifteen feet.   At the eastern extremity, a quarry has been taken advantage of, to add

strength to the wall by being made to serve as a ditch;
on the ground above there are remains of a strong
fortalice. Within these is another quarry, which serves
to isolate the fortress—a narrow ledge of rock, along
which the wall ran, alone affording access to it; this,
with a third parallel to the sea, seems to have completed this curious defensive structure, for such I
suppose it may be considered. The walls are, doubtless, interesting to the military antiquarian, exhibiting,
as they do very perfectly, the system of fortification
used at the time of their reconstruction or repair by
order of Justinian; but they disappoint the traveller in
search of the artistic or the picturesque, who had
hoped to find in Greek or Roman style what Alatri
presents in the Cyclopean. The ill-carved inscriptions
with which they are covered—mere records of names
which have evidently belonged to other buildings, and
many of them now turned upside down—possess no
kind of interest; and I am inclined to think that the
walls of Apollonia, if cleared of their rubbish, would be
found more perfect, as well as more picturesque. But
if disappointed with the exterior of the town, I was
equally surprised by finding the contents of the interior more interesting than anything I had met with
in the Cyrenaica; and then I had to regret that I
had allowed myself to be so long enchained by the
delightful climate of the hills, as to render a long stay

in Tancra impossible on account of the rains, which
this year set in nearly a month earlier than usual.
The town, indeed, contains no monuments of any great
elevation, which accounts for the little attention which
seems to have been bestowed on Tancra by previous travellers; at the season when they visited it
everything must have been hidden by the long grass;
but when the ground is bare of vegetation, as at my
visit, many lines of streets become as distinctly traceable as those of Pompeii, and even the ground plans of
the houses which bordered them. Among the larger
buildings, are to be remarked the ruins of a church in
the west of the city, and those of a large quadrangle,
with a well-preserved reservoir within its precincts,
which, from its similarity to the hapless barracks at
Dolmeita, must have had a similar purpose. Further
eastward, is a striking edifice bearing inscriptions,
which may have been a temple or a basilica, but its
interior is so completely filled with rubbish, that its
plan cannot be distinguished. No trace of a theatre,
amphitheatre, or stadium is visible; so that the inhabitants of Tenchira must, in all probability, have had
the misfortune to be destitute of any place of public
amusement. I have remarked with surprise in other
parts of the Pentapolis, as well as here, the absence of
any well-defined ruins of public baths; though I cannot suppose that any town, even of small size, was in

Roman times destitute of so necessary and favourite a
luxury.   The only hypothesis which presents itself to
me as explanatory of this, is the fact, that these towns,
as we see them at the present day, belong to the later
empire, during whose existence the opposition shown
by the bishops and clergy to the delicacy of the bath
(*balneorum deliciæ*) may, in some places, have succeeded in suppressing its use.   No place in this
country promises a more abundant harvest to the
excavator than this : medals must be buried in great
quantities, and perhaps other articles of value, among
its ruins ; and the tombs sunk in the rocks all around
are, with those of Benghazi, the only ones in the
country that seem to have escaped desecration.   All
those which were excavated in the quarries have been
long since rifled ; and even those have not escaped
which are now sanded up, as was recently proved, to
his great disappointment, by an Arab antiquarian, who,
no doubt, having read, adopted Beechey's suggestion,
and employed money, men, and much time, in clearing
one of those nearest to the town, on the west side.
Beechey, judging from their situation, had conjectured
that these tombs were the most ancient; and that, as
they had probably been early sanded up, they would
offer a good chance of rewarding researches.   The
event proved that his opinion was incorrect, as the
tomb, a large square cavern, was empty of everything

but sand; above the door of it is a cross in a circle, with the letters I C . X C. There are tombs cut like troughs on the summits of the rocks on which the quarries are sunk, which yield great numbers of vases, but all that were found, whilst I was there, were of very coarse manufacture. I saw in the hands of an Arab a small fragment of a large and very finely-painted urn of the latest style, and although such are not, of course, common, I believe they are occasionally found. I had intended to spend some days here, and to open a large number of tombs, whose position I had conjectured from the hollow sound the ground above gave out when struck; but the rains had now set in, descending every night in torrents, and frequently lasting all day; so that no working was possible, and in the small tents a dry spot could not be preserved. The discomfort produced by the rain, however, was even exceeded by the destruction it brought to books and instruments; I therefore left Tancra, and firmly resolved that my first purchase in Benghazi should be one of the hair tents of the Arabs, which, though not quite impervious to rain, are yet the best protection one can have against it. As used in this country, they are generally about eighteen feet long, by fifteen broad, the roof formed of long stripes of coarse hair-cloth woven by the women. The roof is sometimes made in white for winter use; but more generally it is of a brown, earthy colour, with stripes of black and white. No cutting out or other fashioning is necessary, for the cloth, being sufficiently elastic, accommodates itself to the slope of the roof. Two poles, three feet apart, support the tent, giving in the centre a height of about seven feet, while the corners and edges are stretched by cords, and supported by slender spars, at about half this height from the ground. Three sides are closed by stripes of the same stuff, rudely attached to the roof by wooden pins, the fourth—that turned to leeward—being left open. In summer, the sides are removed, and branches are used to replace them, while, in general, an older roof is substituted for the better one used in winter. With a little management, they might be made comfortable enough, and, with the exception of the great weight of the hair-cloth of which they are formed, they would be very convenient for travelling, as they are easily set up, are exposed to no accidents which could not be remedied on the spot, and are less liable than cotton tents to rot when packed up wet. Against this evil I have found M'Gregor's anti-dry-rot preparation of no use. I have one tent of prepared, and one of unprepared canvas, and have yet found no difference in the condition of their materials.

On the third day after my arrival in Tancra, I reluctantly pursued my journey to Benghazi. In an hour and a quarter we reached Bon Jera'a, which has many gardens and wells. An hour and a half further on lies Birsis, with its few insignificant ruins and its many wells; it afforded one of the pleasantest autumnal scenes I had beheld for a long time : whole villages of tents in quick succession, fields everywhere separated by well-made inclosures, and the whole landscape animated by a busy industry, in which all ages and sexes seemed equally to join. This is the only part of the Pentapolis which has the appearance of being inhabited. The damp, warm air of the morning communicated a sensation of enjoyment to the frame; and the unwonted life of the scene recalled more civilised lands to my mind.

The appearance of the country soon, however, changed; and we entered upon a tract most dreary and desolate. The path winds further inland, being separated from the sea by an extensive marsh, along the edge of which it runs at the foot of low rocks; the dark, stunted vegetation interspersed among the stony wastes gave an air of indescribable melancholy to the landscape. A journey of six hours and a half through this dull flat brought us to Sidi Suaiken, a marābut on an eminence ; beyond this the country becomes more wooded, and green meadows appear, in one of which I encamped. There is a place of the name of Handouleh, consisting of a few gardens and rich pastures, which lies about an hour and a half from the marábut; further on to the right is the large salt lake of Ez-zajana, a favourite resort of the Benghazini in their excursions.   Near here are extensive ruins, showing only the ground plan of many buildings, which, from the name, are supposed to mark the site of Adrianopolis.   Soon after this the road enters the dried sandy bed of the salt lake, which, filled by the winter gales from the sea, gradually evaporates in the course of the summer.   At length, we again reached Benghazi, after an absence of rather more than three months.

CHAPTER XII.

On arriving in Benghazi I found a house prepared for me, by the kindness of one of my friends, who gave up to me the only waterproof rooms which, I believe, exist in the town. The sensation of sleeping within walls, after three months spent under canvas, was not the less agreeable from the circumstance that the rain poured down in torrents, and only ceased for short intervals during my ten days' stay. The second day after my arrival there fell a deluge of rain, the effect of which was to wash down some thirty houses, while there was not perhaps one in the place which had not suffered more or less. This is owing to the houses being built with mud instead of lime, which might be had at a very small cost. In the Frank quarter some new houses were in process of building, and not being roofed in, were more liable to suffer than finished

buildings. As I passed them the next day their interior literally presented mere heaps of ruins.   Year
after year the same devastation is produced by the
same cause ; the flat roofs, formed, as they are, of
mats laid over beams, with a heavy superstructure of
sea-weeds and mud, are never waterproof; yet such is
the apathy, even of the European residents, that they
make no attempt to secure dry quarters for the winter.
One would think from their conduct that it had never
rained here before, and that the visitation, instead of
being as regular as the almanack, had taken all the
world by surprise. In one house I found workmen
repairing fallen walls; in another, I heard that the
whole family had to sleep on the bales in the ware-
house, which admitted the water in fewer places than
the other rooms.   The streets were in many places
impassable from the ruins ; and many houses were
literally melted away, the beams and stones remaining
imbedded in huge puddles of mud.   It sometimes
occurs, when the rains are more than usually heavy,
that the houses are in so menacing a state that the
whole town takes refuge in tents, where, though the
ground be damp, there are certainly no walls which
threaten to overwhelm them.

I had the pleasure of finding the newly-appointed
English Vice-Consul, Mr. Werry, a gentleman well

known to our officers who served in the Syrian expedition. I was glad to offer him personally my thanks for the ready politeness with which he had taken measures to insure my safety while in the interior. Though he had only been two months in Benghazi, he had already secured the good-will and confidence of the British subjects for whose interest he is placed there, as well as the respect of the Turkish authorities. During the ten days I stayed in Benghazi he gave me frequent opportunities of increasing my debt of gratitude to him. I regretted to leave behind me, in so dreary an exile, one whose official experience, whose activity, and familiar knowledge of all the Oriental languages, would enable him to render essential services to his Government in places of more importance. I do not by this mean to insinuate that the presence of a British Consul in Benghazi is of little utility, although the number of Europeans (they are nearly all British subjects) be very small. Unconnected with trade, our Vice-Consul holds an independent position, which those of other nations, fettered by their personal interests, cannot attain, and he is thus frequently able, in cases of gross injustice affecting the natives, to exercise a salutary influence with the governor. His house is the ready refuge of the ill-used slave and the oppressed Arab, and his exertions in their behalf,

rarely unavailing for them, give a prestige to the name
of Englishman, of which I more than once experienced
the value.

This portion of the pachalic of Tripoli, in which I
passed nearly six months, is, like so many countries
belonging to the Turkish Empire, most bountifully
endowed by nature with every source of wealth.
Under former rulers it was flourishing and populous,
but it has now become a waste; its scanty inhabitants are sunk in hopeless barbarism, and even their
poverty is no defence against the grasping avarice of
their governor— " Inter continuas rapinas, perpetuò
inops." I do not accuse the present Sultan or
ministers in Constantinople, individually, of the tyranny and ignorance which render his rule a curse
wherever it is acknowledged ; but— after seeing the
fields of Roumelia lying waste to the very gates of
his residence, the cities of Asia Minor depopulated,
its mineral wealth a sealed treasure, even the Arab
glories of Syria faded, the palaces of Damascus crumbling, and its marts deserted—the traveller cannot but
long to see a government changed whose oppression
is less mischievous than its neglects, and which tacitly
permits wrongs greater than those which it sanctions.*
Well has it been said, that where the hoof of a Turkish

* Johan. von Müller.

horse has touched the ground, there the grass grows
not.

During the last twenty-five years, since the fall of
the Janissaries (which seemed to strengthen the central government while it weakened the empire), there
has been much law-making, and many abuses have been
abolished, as far as edicts can abolish deeply-rooted
customs; but the old spirit still breathes in the new
régime, and injustice and oppression are as frequent
under the present Sultan as under his predecessors.
It is, indeed, no longer a matter of indifference to the
Grand Vizier, "whether the dog devours the swine or
the swine the dog." A wholesome fear of European
opinion has succeeded to undisguised contempt; but
the Turk of the people is still in his' own eyes the
first of human beings; his Sultan is still the suzerain
before whom all kings bow, and at whose orders the
French and English krals send their fleets and troops
to chastise the rebellious Egyptian or Muscovite; and
in the remoter provinces, which are beyond the immediate eye of the Elehi Beys, as they call the foreign
ambassadors, the old system of peculation and robbery
exists in full force.

Much has been written in praise of the new organi-
sation of the Turkish Government, and the Tanzimat,
as the regulations for the service are called; but the
good which this contains is for the most part evaded

or neglected.   The most real result of the reform has been to introduce a number of new functionaries, or, in other words, to increase the points of contact between the governors and the governed, whereby more frequent opportunities of peculation are given to the former.   The sanitary regulations, so ridiculous in the way they are enforced and the way they are neglected, are one instance of this; another is the prohibition of presents from inferiors to superiors, which all employés take an oath to observe; yet it would not be easy to find ten per cent. of the higher officers who are insensible to, or unwilling to accept such an argument.   In trifling things they are, of course, careful to wear the mask of austere virtue, as Izzet Pacha, the Governor of Tripoli, lately recalled on the complaints of the French Government, showed, when he was here in summer.   A merchant of the place sent him a basket of grapes, when they were still scarce, and he returned them, saying, that, according to his oath, he must either pay for or refuse them.   Yet this is the man who, after keeping an Arab sheikh in prison for many months, released him on receiving 150,000 piastres, about £1500 ; and whose sons, youths of eighteen and twenty years, established in their father's pachalic a trade in all the produce of the country, which amounted to a virtual monopoly.   The European merchants sent a remonstrance on this subject to Constantinople, and

they received an answer, in the advancement of the
elder of these enterprising young tradesmen to the
dignity of Mirabi, or pacha of one tail.

After the last harvest the cultivators of the soil
complained that the tithe in kind due to Government
was taken in such a way as to amount to nearly one-
half of the entire produce. This had been contrived
by Izzet Pacha's son and some of the local authorities; the tenth only being carried to the public account,
and the remainder divided among themselves. Many
representations to this effect were made to the French
consular agent, who, after obtaining satisfactory
evidence of their truth, reported the case to his superior in Tripoli. Not long afterwards, on some dispute
with the Pacha, the Consul brought this up as a proof
of the malversation of the subordinates, on which the
other pretended great indignation, and insisted that he
and the Consul should send to Benghazi for information. The books were, of course, in good order; the
witnesses, on whose testimony the Consul had relied,
were by threats reduced to silence; the charge could
not be substantiated (the Bey who was judge being
himself the chief delinquent) ; and the upshot of the
inquiry was, that the Vice-Consul had to make apolo-
gies for the slander, while he and every Frank in the
place knew the truth of the accusation, and could point
out the magazines where the grain thus extorted was

deposited. Many weeks had not passed after this when ships belonging to the Pacha's son arrived in the port, and openly loaded with this very corn on his account

When a pacha acts thus, we cannot wonder if his subordinates imitate so good an example; and the director of the customs may be praised for the honesty which consigns about three-fourths of their produce to the treasury. An Arab said to me one day, on this subject, " The Pacha eats, the Bey eats, and the Gumruckdjy (director of customs) eats," each buying his superior's silence with a share of his own peculations; the friends who protect his interests at Constantinople coming in for their share of the pacha's profits. A Turk is, in fact, capable of learning many things; he may be *civilisé*—a Frank word, now adopted in Turkish; he may cease to be what *La Jeune Turquie* calls a fanatic; he will indulge in deep potations, or abstain from fasting in Ramadhan; but he will never learn not to eat (Italicè *magnare*) when he can. His appetite and digestion, in this sense, are truly ostrich-like. On inquiring into the truth of the Bey's statement that there are 1200 houses in Benghazi, I learned that there are, in fact, 1400; the two hundred which are suppressed in the official account being " eaten" by the Bey and the Sheikh-el-belid.

An amusing instance of the ruses to which a scrupulous man, who has the fear of his oath before his eyes, will resort, was related to me by one who was in the town at the time it occurred. An Armenian addressed himself to a Pacha in Anadoly, for the decision of a lawsuit in his favour; and, after stating his case, produced a bag well filled with the usual arguments, which he offered to his Excellency. On this the great man, who had listened to his statement with the blandest smiles, drew himself up, frowning in anger, and only answered, "Infidel, be off!" The poor Armenian, astonished at the reception of his well-meant offering, begged and prayed, and seemed to weigh the bag in his hands, that the Pacha might see how heavy it was—all Spanish dollars; but the only answer he obtained was a fresh order to be off, with the surly addition, "He is an infidel who gives, and an infidel who takes"—disobedience to the Sultan's laws being rebellion, and rebellion, according to Turkish doctrine, infidelity. Disappointed and crest-fallen, the poor Armenian withdrew from the presence, and was not a little surprised to find himself the object of the congratulations of the attendants and cavasses in the anteroom. "It is useless," he said, "to ask me for backshish; for the Pacha has rejected my suit, and that, too, with hard words." "What answer is this?" said they; "did you not hear his words—'the infidel gives and the infidel takes?' Go to the steward; is not he also an Armenian?"

One of the greatest blots on the Turkish constitution has not been touched by the Tanzimat: it is that provision of the Moslem law which excludes the reception of evidence given by persons of other religions against a Moslem. Twenty witnesses may depose to the murder of a Christian or Jew by a Turk; but, as was too clearly shown in the case of Sir Lawrence Jones, if there be not among them at least two Moslemin, their testimony is unavailing; while to obtain Moslem witnesses to prove an outrage on a Christian is impossible.* An Arab was wantonly beating a Maltese boy, a few days ago, in the bazaar, when a respectable Moslem came to his assistance; a third then came up, and apostrophised the boy's defender, saying, "Are you a Moslem? and do you take the part of a Christian against a believer?" He spoke what all the spectators felt. Until this odious distinction be abolished, there can be no security either for the life or property of Christian rayahs or foreigners, excepting in the energy and privileges of the consuls; and the representatives of the great powers seem at present disposed to yield the greater part of their own rights and the

---

* Since writing this I have learned that a recent decree gives to the evidence of Christians the same force as that of a Moslem.

immunities of their fellow-subjects. These were wisely considered essential to the welfare or consideration of foreigners among a people who, though little less than barbarians, look with the most profound contempt upon a Frank ; and those who renounce their enjoyment are, I fear, too precipitate in their favourable judgment of the real state of the Turkish Empire.

I cannot close my notes of the Cyrenaica without adding that I spent there (occasional annoyances excepted) some most pleasant months ; I came to the country an invalid, and was exceedingly unwell when I started for Grennah ; but its pure air and lovely scenery restored me to perfect health. For those who seek summer quarters in the Mediterranean, I again repeat to them my former advice, to choose the pleasant solitudes of Cyrene in preference to the Syrian hills, where so much sickness and mortality prevail. I have been many times in the Lebanon, and the rich beauty of Damascus has greater charms for me than that of any city I have seen ; but, still, I have never been there without witnessing or feeling the effects of the pestilential air, which, every autumn, produces fatal fevers and dysenteries. Even in quitting its shores the evil spirit seems to pursue its victims ; and I have seen more than one friend seized with the deadly Syrian fever weeks after he had reached a healthier climate.

CHAPTER XIII.

November 4th.—After many *pour parlers* with a
caravan of Majabra (inhabitants of Jalo), who had
come to Benghazi to sell their dates, and after making
one or two false starts, I at length got under weigh
for Angila. I was desirous of taking with me some
hawks, as the country I was to pass through for the
first days of the journey was represented to be full of
game ; and the trained hawks of this place are said to
be the best in Africa; but I was unable to purchase
any. Some of my friends assured me that I should
find no difficulty in obtaining the birds from the Arabs ;
but I eventually found that my informants were mistaken. Both in Benghazi and in its neighbourhood,
I often met horsemen with a hawk, either perched on
the right hand or seated on the crupper of the horse ;
but I never found any one willing to part with this
favourite companion. Yet there are seasons of the

year when they are to be had at a small price; in
spring, many young hawks are brought to the market,
and the proprietors of trained birds will then willingly
dispose of theirs, at a price for which they can buy a
dozen young ones, whose education they find both
amusing and profitable.

Stopping to rearrange the luggage half a dozen
times while the town was still in sight, our progress
the first day was very slow, and we pitched the tents
for the night at a distance of about eight miles from
Benghazi, having traversed a country unmarked by
any feature but the shapeless ruins of what may once
have been an extensive villa, or a very small village.
The next day, we reached, in three hours, extensive
ruins, called by the Arabs Idirsa, which cover much
ground, but nowhere offer extensive *débris*, nor even
a plan of any large building. The sea, though
still in sight, lay considerably to the right. Avoiding
the promontory of Bozium, and the site of the old
Jewish colony (which presents nothing remarkable), I
followed the road which runs through the middle of
the wide plain lying between the hills which I crossed
in going to Cyrene, and the sea, which here trends
gradually to the west. Two hours further on, we came
to a place, Ourm Sofah, marked by very deep wells
hewn in the rock, beside which was a pool formed by
the recent rains. At this moment, the country is

dotted far and near with such sheets of water, formed
wherever a clay bottom, or a depression in the rocks,
presents a surface favourable for the collection of the
rain.   Herds of cattle render these pools muddy and
uninviting to the eye ; but when they have just been
formed, there is probably no risk in drinking their
water.   For greater precaution, however, as well as to
accustom my servants to the trouble, I had the water
boiled before we drank it ; this process, of course, gave
it an unpalatable flatness, but it is thought necessary,
in order to avoid the risk of fevers, so often caused by
drinking stagnant water.   During this day's journey
and the two succeeding ones, we saw in every direction
groups of Arab tents, inhabited by people from Benghazi, who had come to sow the extensive plain we were
passing through.   The soil is a rich loam, yielding,
without any sort of tilling, abundant harvests of wheat
and barley.   It seems probable that, if a moderate
amount of labour were expended in the husbandry of
this country, its ample crops would vie with those of
Egypt or Sicily.   As it is, nature is left to herself;
when the winter is rainy, the crops are very large, but
if the rains are scanty, the harvest fails.   In autumn,
after the first rains, the seed is scattered broadcast on
the ground, and over this a light plough of wood, shod
with iron, is drawn, turning up, or rather scratching,
the ground, to a depth of about two inches.   By this

process the seed is covered. The husbandman returns
to Benghazi, and no other care is bestowed upon the
crop until the sower returns in spring to reap it. The
land is open to the first comer, the Government receiving a tenth of the produce as rent; but this rent
is very arbitrarily fixed, and thereby ample room is
given to the ingenuity of the Turkish *employés*. The
result is that the taxation is often most exorbitant, as
I have mentioned in a former page. This year the
early rains gave an impulse to speculation. About
one-third of the Benghazini were now squatting on the
plain; every animal—horse, ass, ox, cow, or camel
—that could be made to drag the light ploughshare
having been laid under contribution. The prices of
these animals had, consequently, increased greatly in
the market. If the winter proved as rainy as it
threatened, sundry little fortunes would no doubt be
made. Many of the Europeans and wealthier Arabs,
who do not themselves go to the country, employ a
man to sow seed for them, they providing the seed
and cattle; the man receives half the profit, besides
160 piastres—about thirty shillings—for sowing and
reaping.

Eight hours from Ourm Sofah are the ruins of a
large castle of the same character and epoch as those
of Benigdun, called Tell-i-mout. The walls are, in
the lower part, formed by four courses of large ma-

sonry; and above, to an equal, or rather greater
height (probably a later construction), they are built
of small stones. There remain two sides of an oblong
rectangle, with a square tower at the north-east corner,
whose entrance is by a well-turned arch from the interior. The large stones of the lower courses are
literally covered with Tawarick characters—most probably merely indicating the passage by them of the
Arab tribes, which use one or other of these signs as
their distinctive marks; but the number, size, and
regularity of these characters in this place are truly
astonishing. During the remainder of this day's journey the character of the country remained unchanged,
and nothing marked our course except a solitary
marābut, Sidi Keilani, on the right, three hours and
a half from Tell-i-mout; from hence proceeding as far
again, we reached the first Bedawin tents we had seen
since we left Benghazi, pitched in a place called Keif-
i-djil. Here there are large stores of grain, formed on
the same principle as the *cachettes* or *silos* of the
Algerian tribes, which resemble the grain stores at
Leghorn. A conical hole, dug in the ground, is
lined with straw, and after being filled with grain,
is thatched over with straw and mud. The people
assured me that neither ants nor vermin ever attack
these stores, and at Leghorn I have heard it asserted
that in the similar receptacles there, built of stone and

plastered, the grain can be preserved good for fifty years. Two hours further on are ponds and a well, in a place called Sa'aity. Here the ground is covered with large fragments of stone, and seemed a favourite resort of scorpions, which the Arabs, who were with me, amused themselves in hunting. They brought me one of a greenish yellow colour, fully five inches long. The gerboas also abound in this place; they are about the size of a rat, and one sees them towards evening in great numbers, jumping along like the kangaroo, their long, elegant tail, tipped with white, trailing on the ground; the plain is riddled with their holes, which makes quick riding very unsafe.

At Sa'aity I remained half a day, while the camel-drivers bought food for their beasts from some grain stores on a slight hill above the well. These Majabra were in many respects the worst people I had yet had to deal with; the only good quality I discovered in them was the rapidity with which they loaded in the morning. The time gained in this way, however, was lost in another; their object in such quick loading being merely to get off, and to leave as much of their load as they could behind them. The consequence of this was, that as much as two camels could conveniently carry, fell to the share of the last-loaded camels, over and above their fair allowance. On such occasions I had to make the whole caravan return, which

cost quick riding and loud words ; and then at length
each received his fair proportion of the articles that had
been left.   Day after day the same scene was renewed,
until I at last resorted to the expedient of having
my carpet spread for breakfast on the road they were
to take—a scheme which, united with constant watch-
fulness, I found tolerably successful.   They have another accomplishment, hardly less agreeable to the
traveller who is at their mercy.   They must have
learned, that if eloquence be silver, silence is gold ;
and therefore they show themselves most unwilling
to afford the smallest particle of information, silencing
questions with a prolonged nasal grunt, which seems
to play the same part in their conversation as the
" So-o-o !" of the Germans.   On the journey they sing
their unmelodious chaunts nearly all day long, one
relieving the other ; their song being at rare intervals
interrupted by an occasional admonition to a camel
to make a little more way.   They never swear at their
beasts, however, as European, and especially Italian,
postilions are in the habit of doing ; the ear is not,
therefore, shocked with the obscene blasphemies which
are so offensive on a journey in the Roman or Neapo-
litan States.   Here the driver apostrophises his camel
with one invariable expression of abuse, which seems
quite as efficacious as a volley of oaths—" Oh, you
Jew !" and the camel mends its pace.   It is true that

this is usually accompanied with an admonition from a full-grown stick, which may perhaps have some effect in quickening its step; but I am persuaded, nevertheless, that the insult to its feelings has more to do in rousing it to exertion, than the application of the bâton to its hide. The food of the Majabra is *basina*, like that of the Barca Arabs, a mess prepared with flour, water, and salt, kneaded into a tough paste, then boiled, and eaten with a little oil or butter; it is a tough, and must be a most indigestible composition. They eat enormous quantities of it, re-kneading it with the fingers of the right hand into large balls, and dipping in oil, so as to enable them to bolt it; to see them devour it is one among the most wonderful things in this country.

There are wells, for which I could obtain no name, ten hours from Sa'aity. After this, the country becomes somewhat less level than it has hitherto been, swelling in slight hills, the soil more stony and sandy, less capable of producing grain, and covered with low, thorny, and fleshy-leaved shrubs. Five and a half hours further on, are wells, called El Farsy. These, like the preceding ones, are pierced in the rock, and to obtain the water from them, it is necessary for some one to be lowered into the well, as the water does not lie immediately under the upper orifice. There is a large chamber hollowed in the rock, in one corner of which the well is sunk; I did not descend into it, and it was not till I was far past it, that one of the men told me there were inscriptions on its sides. This is as likely to be false as true, as I have twenty times gone, on the strength of Arab information, to look for inscriptions in places where nothing of the sort was to be seen; but this would have been no reason for neglecting to examine this well-chamber, had I known of it in time. It was now too late in the evening to return that day, and the next I was not inclined for an expedition whose result was so uncertain, while I had before me the more promising ruins of El-Ajdabiah.

These old Saracenic ruins are four hours and a half from El Farsy; they present groups of buildings situated on two low hills, about a quarter of a mile apart. The centre of the intervening space is a flat bare rock, in which several wells are pierced. The first group which the traveller, coming from Benghazi, meets, contains the remains of a castle of excellent architecture, which cannot be later than the third century of the Hejirah. It is a rectangular structure, terminating in three vaulted chambers, the extremity of the centre one of which has an octagonal niche, on which the plaster still remains. This end is flanked by round, dome-covered towers, whose sides are perforated with loopholes for arrows; but neither within nor without, neither above nor below, could I discover ornament or inscription.   Failing here, I now turned to the opposite group of ruins, the *débris* of a very large mosque, in which I had no doubt that I should find something to reward me for having chosen this route rather than the shorter one, which, from Sa'aity, takes more to the eastward.   The mosque is in even a more ruinous condition than the castle, but is of equally good construction; in one corner are still standing about fifteen feet of the light-sided minaret; towards the other, three light and lofty arches, and beyond them the Kibleh niche, or minbar.   Round its arch may be traced remains of a zigzag ornament, and on the capital of one of the two pillars which support it, I persuaded myself that I could trace the first three letters of the profession of faith.   Believing implicitly the accounts I had somewhere read of the ornamental inscriptions of Ajdabiah, I had bargained with my camel-men to stay here two or three days if I required it, in order to examine them ; but no exertion of eyesight or imagination could enable me to discover more than these three letters, if they were really such ; for, after all, they might have been mere accidental scratches in the stone. Whatever may have been the case when the buildings were less ruinous, I can safely affirm that there is in no part of them now a trace of an inscription in any character, excepting those Arab marks to which I have already several times alluded. I was greatly disappointed ; and as soon as the water-skins were filled (an operation which was protracted during four hours), I saw the caravan depart. I took myself a S.S.W. direction, though with little hope of any satisfactory result ; and rode to Henayah, a distance of about seven miles.

Henayah is a strong fortress of very early architecture, and by far the most curious construction I had met with in these countries. The squared mass of rock, on which the keep is built, is not higher than the surrounding ground ; but it is isolated by a dry moat, fourteen feet wide, and nine deep, cut in the living rock. On the square mass, eighty feet on every side, left in the centre, rose the walls of the keep, of which only a few feet in height now remain. It is approached by means of a wall, hardly fifteen inches broad, which is built across the moat on one side. This wall was, perhaps, once the support of a moveable bridge. The interior of the rock's base is entirely excavated, forming a centre chamber, now open to the sky, and entered by a flight of steps; round this chamber are cut a number of vaults, communicating with it, and having small openings, to admit light and air, pierced in the sides. This is, however, only the smallest part of the old stronghold, its size being greatly increased by extensive caves, to the number of twenty-eight, cut in the rock, beyond the moat, into which they all open. In no part of these laborious excavations could I discover any inscription, or any evidence of their origin; but, judging from the beautiful execution of the whole—from the form of the lamp niches which are cut in several of the vaults, as well as from the general style, resembling what is found in some of the Greek isles—I have no hesitation in ascribing it to a date coeval with the best monuments in Cyrene.

The water of its wells, being the last sweet water to be met with before reaching Angila, pointed it out as a natural resting-place for the caravans which brought gold, gems, slaves, and ivory, from the interior to Cyrene. I cannot, therefore, doubt, that it must have served as a fortress, and, not improbably, also as a magazine for the caravans trading with the interior and with Carthage. El Ajdabiah replaced it in the Saracenic epoch; and so little have things changed in the long lapse of years, that the wells of the latter place, though its castles and mosques have fallen, are still the favourite halt of the caravans passing between Benghazi and Angila.

The commerce is now insignificant; Angila and Jalo have only dates to send in exchange for corn and the few manufactured articles which the rude life of these people requires. At uncertain and long intervals, however, when the great caravan from Waday arrives,

life is given to the commerce of Benghazi. Then the
old picture of Cyrenean commerce is for a short time
renewed. The desert, for weeks, is alive with long files
of camels, which arrive, laden with ivory and gum ;
and with them, alas ! as in old times, hundreds of un-
happy creatures—the spoil of war—condemned to
slavery, who come halting in, at the end of this first
hundred days' stage of their misery. How many, hap-
pier than their fellows, have dropped exhausted on the
dreary road ! Twenty-one degrees they traverse on
foot, exposed to the rays of a tropical sun, when, for
twelve days at a time, no water is found ; without
clothing, and having a handful of meal for their daily
food. Fatigue and thirst in vain lessen the numbers of the melancholy caravan ; the number of
"heads" brought to the market diminish, but the
profit of the traffic is still enormous, being more lucra-
tive than that of ivory, which, from Waday, yields at
least 500 per cent. I have heard natives describe the
appearance of one of these caravans on its arrival, and
the sufferings of the slaves, with a simplicity of language, and a reckless thoughtlessness, most heart-
rending. And to think that a single word from
England could arrest these horrors ! In treaties and
conventions we have spurned all the old established
laws of international right, in our desire to put down

the slave trade in the colonies of independent sove-
reigns; but it would seem as though we dared not
put a veto upon a branch of it ten times more cruel
than was the slave trade on the Atlantic before we
declared it piracy.   It may be answered, that we may
indeed force Turkey to abolish the slave trade in words,
but that we cannot ensure the performance of her promises; that we can send no men-of-war into the
deserts to enforce our humane decrees; that slavery is
bound up with Islam; and that society in the East is,
in fact, founded upon the godless institution.   Many
will also say (and this I do not deny), that when at
length the slaves are brought into the Turkish dominions, they become comparatively happy, are well
clothed, well fed, and well cared for; and that, if torn
from their country, they are removed from its idolatries
and ignorance; and that the first care of a Moslem (in
this respect infinitely superior to the more polished
savages of the slave-holding States in America) is, to
teach his slave a religion which assures him that all
men, of all colours, are alike the children of one God,
and equal in His eyes.   All this is true; but it in no
degree lessens the horror of the traffic in human flesh,
or the privations to which its victims are exposed.

Whoever knows Turkey, knows that its many provinces are only held together by the shadow of a name,

and that a stroke of the diplomatic pen will suffice to sever any part from the remainder.   Syria, Egypt, even fanatic Tripoli, would hail with joy a Christian — that is, a European — master.   Wherever they rule the Turks are hated, and their subjects are kept in subjection by a superstitious veneration for the old power, which has long departed—as the genii waited in awe round the throne of Solomon, not perceiving that the master spirit had forsaken its tenement of clay. You have paid twenty millions to liberate your slaves in the colonies; and God knows what vast treasures— how many lives of Englishmen—have been sacrificed to stop this trade on the western coasts of Africa !   Be consistent still ; and if you will not take possession of the lands of Egypt and Tripoli (by whose frontiers the slaves for the whole empire are imported), let your commands go forth to him who is now but the shadow of the shadow of God upon earth.   He dare not dis- obey them if he would.   You will be following, in favour of humanity, an example proposed to you in every page of Turkish history—the strong extorting submission from the weak.   Increase, if necessary, the number of your functionaries, create an *imperium in imperio*, to watch the execution of your orders ; trample, in the cause of freedom, upon every diplo- matic form—forms, alas ! are all that remain of diplomacy—and extend to the Mediterranean the treaties which you have applied to the Atlantic.*

This evening, six of my camels, which had been turned out to feed on the scanty herbage which dotted the plain, wandered away. They were not to be found at their supper-time; so their owners went off in quest of them. The next morning, they had not yet returned; and it seemed a fortunate chance alone which enabled us to start at last about twelve o'clock. They had gone on their way to Angila, probably not a little pleased to have left all their packages behind them; and were met by a caravan of Arabs, coming in the opposite direction, who, understanding the case—no unfrequent one in places where the herbage is scanty— turned their heads backwards. The soil had now become sandy and stony, unfit for cultivation, but covered with dwarf shrubs of three or four varieties, though all having one general character—woody, gnarled stems, and fleshy leaves. The first rains are in the desert immediately succeeded by spring; hence these plants were all green and in full flower; some of them were very beautiful on close inspection; but the

---

* Since these lines were written (in 1853), a decree is said to have been published, abolishing the trade in slaves throughout the Ottoman Empire. In Cairo, in Alexandria, it is at this moment as active as ever.—Cairo, 15th July, 1855.

pale yellow and pink colours of their blossoms, notwithstanding their abundance, had little effect in
tinging the general landscape.

During the two days, after passing El Ajdabiah, we
saw immense herds of gazelles; but they were too shy
to give one a chance of getting within shot of them;
and there was too little cover to stalk them. The
greyhound which I had with me was young, and far
too frightened to do more than run after them for a
short distance; when she thought she was getting
dangerously near, she would stop, and look round.
There is a race of greyhounds peculiar to this country,
generally of a pale fawn colour, with very short hair,
and limbs almost as fine as those of the Italian pet
greyhound. They are very swift, and, when well
trained, will run down a gazelle. They are, however,
not often to be met with for sale, the best being in
the hands of the Zowaya Arabs, who inhabit El Ijherri,
a small oasis to the north-east of Jalo. In winter and
spring, they pitch their tents round El Ajdabiah (it
was, indeed, a party of them who had so opportunely
met our camels), and, in summer, turn southwards to
gather the dates in El Kofrah, a range of uninhabited
oases, of which the last is marked in our maps as
Kebabo. The plain, south of Benghazi, up to the
desert which we were approaching, affords excellent
sport; abounding in hares, the red-legged partridge,

the kattah, or sand grouse with yellowish plumage, quails, and, occasionally, the bustard. There is, besides these, a ground lark, existing in great numbers, which is as large as a quail, and forms no unwelcome addition to a traveller's fare, in the absence of larger game. I should be ungrateful, were I to omit adding to this list of good things the juicy mushroom, which seemed, for several days, to spring up under our feet, begging to be gathered for supper.

Fourteen hours from El Ajdabiah, we came to the boundary of vegetation; a very long range of low sand hills, rising one above another in almost imperceptible gradations. The sand is of a pale yellow colour, and in some places forms almost an impalpable powder, but in others it is mixed with gravel of finely-rounded, variegated pebbles, such as would be invaluable for the walks of a garden. The Arab name for these hills is El-Towaleh, and they are well called so, for they seem long without end, the gradual rise of the range never affording a view of a mile in any direction. It took nearly thirteen hours to cross this range—the thirteen longest hours I remember; for, until the last two were reached, there was no interruption to the constant up and down, through featureless sand; nor was it possible to tell whether one had reached the summit or not. At length, large masses of petrified wood, scattered over the surface, afforded something to look at. In many places, the surface of the sand is blistered with an incrustation of salt, looking as if frozen. Low, flat ledges of white limestone rise above the general line ; and semi-transparent crystals of gypsum are scattered over the sand. A few trees appeared in a hollow, and we had at last reached رسم Rĕsam.

The waters of Rĕsam, mentioned by Bruce, are of a milky colour, and salt, though hardly more so than those of most of the wells which I met with afterwards in the desert; I thought them pleasant enough to drink when cold; but they acquire a peculiarly bitter taste when boiled. Bruce, from forgetfulness, has confounded Rĕsam with the promontory marked as Ros Sam * in our maps—a name, by the way, unknown

---

* On referring to Beechey's Narrative, since these pages were written, I find that he speaks of Ras Sem as a name unknown to the Arabs to designate the promontory marked thus in our maps. The coast, from a few miles west of Apollonia, has a very gradual inclination southwards, but so slight that it is impossible to designate even the place from which it begins to turn as a headland. Shaw and Bruce's account of the well five or six days south of Benghazi agrees perfectly with the place called by the Arabs R'sam; and although the very bitter well is eight hours further on, there can be no doubt it is to this place that they allude. The petrified city, with its inhabitants, does not exist; its magnificent castle is only the Saracenic building, now called Sheikh Es-saby; but the ground is to some distance strewed with petrified wood. The dream of the city where "men are conspicuous in different attitudes, some of them exercising their trades and occupations, and women giving suck to their children," is due, of course, to Arab imagination, and not to those truthful travellers.

to the natives of the country—and the aluminous
water, which he places here, is, in fact, that of a well
rather further on ; which well I reached the next day
in six hours, at Marag, or Marak.   The water at
Rĕsam rises in great abundance to within a few feet
from the surface ; and the slight hollow in which it
lies, partaking entirely of the nature of an oasis, is
diversified by palms and large tamarisks.   As a desert
scene, it is at once highly characteristic.   The slight
mounds which collect round the tamarisks, and out of
which they grow, break the uniformity of the surface,
while their pale, feathery foliage affords a pleasant
shade, and the few stately palm trees rise gracefully
against the clear blue sky.

Two miles S.S.W. of Rĕsam is a Saracenic ruin, of
the same date as El Ajdabiah, called Sheikh Es-saby,
evidently a stronghold.   A square court, surrounded
by four arches, which may once have supported a
cupola (though I could see no remains of this), is
supposed by the Arabs to contain the tomb of the
Sheikh ; and, when I was there, a *carmut,* the cradle
sort of conveyance in which ladies and children are
housed on the camel's back, was in the saint's keeping.
This custom of leaving furniture, and even provisions,
in the keeping of a reputed saint—that is to say, of de-
positing them on his tomb—to be taken again at the
return of the owners with the caravan, is very common ;

and travellers in several parts of Africa have mentioned
it. I have never heard of such deposits being stolen.

We did not stop at Marag; but I tasted the water,
which was quite clear and cool, and had a strong smell
of sulphuretted hydrogen. I did not drink of it sufficiently to test the assertion of the Arabs, who boast
of its purgative qualities; but, from its taste and smell,
I should suspect that it contains sulphate of magnesia.
The bottle, in which I had brought away a specimen
of it for analysis, was broken on the journey. At
several points near the well, the stratified rock rises in
isolated masses from the sand; their weather-beaten
sides, with the slabs which have fallen, and lie scattered round their base, have, at a slight distance,
the appearance of ruins. A few stunted trees in the
midst rendered the whole a melancholy scene.

The next morning the sun rose in a thick mist, like
a November fog in England. Its pale white orb could
be gazed at without wincing; below it was a luminous
spot, like a second sun, and again below this a long
line of bright light rested on the horizon. At eight
the mist began to disperse, and then in the opposite
side of the heaven a distinct bow of white was visible,
faintly fringed at the lower extremities with the pris-
matic colours. Twenty hours of travelling during two
days, over unmitigated sand, brought us to the skirts
of the oasis of Angila. It was near sunset when I

rode into the palm-tree plantations to seek a place for
the camp.   The first appearance presented to the eye
by the large plantation rising in the midst of the
loose sand, was most singular.   The rosy light which
coloured the ground when the sun's rays penetrated
the tall stems, gave the part which was in shade a
white appearance like snow, which, contrasted with the
bright green of the bushy young palms, lent to the
whole the appearance of a winter scene, while the air
was balmy as summer, and the bright evening sky
glowed with orange and purple tints, such as Italy or
Greece cannot show.   The scene one might liken to
a Flemish snow-piece seen in Naples on a summer's
day.

CHAPTER XIV.

November 17. — The palm groves extend for more
than three miles in a curved hollow to the town of
Angila, and nearly as much beyond it, forming almost
a half circle of verdure. The fertile part of the oasis
is considerably beneath the level of the surrounding
country, so that the water being nearer the surface,
the roots of the palm trees, which pierce downwards to
a great depth, reach it, and thus obtain their nourishment. The town is built on a slight elevation, nearly
equidistant from the two furthest points of the oasis.
It is surrounded by a thin mud wall, some twelve feet
high, but not more than nine or ten inches thick; this
wall is in a most delapidated condition, in several
places entirely destroyed, and in others worn into innumerable holes. Six gate towers of equally substantial architecture give entrance to the long and tortuous
lanes of the capital.

Sheikh Othman-el-Fadil, the hereditary Sheikh of
Angila, and the Kehia who happened to be in the
town, came to my tent as soon as I arrived. The
former I had seen in Benghazi, and he showed me
every attention, convenient and inconvenient, in his
power, by way, probably, of asserting his right to the
family name, which means " the complaisant." I returned the Governor's visit, and thus had an opportunity of seeing " the castle," which is situated near
the great mosque—a not less ruinous structure than
the external walls. It is composed of several very
small courts with recesses, which serve as sleeping or
store rooms ; the open court, in which are mastabahs—
mud divans covered with carpets—is the place of reception. The Governor either could not or would not
tell me the number of inhabitants, or even of the
houses, saying they were written in the Deftar, the
domesday-book of Benghazi ; and, in fact, he seemed
quite determined that it should not be in my power to
quote him as giving any information dangerous to the
State.

I looked into the principal mosque in passing; like
all the other buildings it is of mud and small stones,
with many low columns and arches of the same material; the roof being formed of small conical cupolas
like sugar loaves, some of which are four feet in diameter, and eight or ten in height. This is the conse-

crated style of building for the mosques, of which
there are fourteen. From the best information I could
obtain, it seemed that the number of inhabited houses
was under 500. The Kehia, an Arab of Benghazi,
only comes here once a year, and then to collect the
tribute; his visit ended, the Wagily, as the inhabitants
of Angila are called, are left to follow their own de-
vices. The Sheikh has a traditionary, but no legal
authority; if crimes occur, his duty is to report them
to the Bey of Benghazi, and wait for orders before
sending the offenders with the witnesses to the Bey for
judgment. Of course, with such a system, the only
check upon crime and violence is in the natural disposition of the people, or in the fear of blood feuds; re-
course is, indeed, rarely or never had to the distant
and doubtful justice thus to be sought in Benghazi.

The inhabitants of these oases indulge greatly in a
slightly-intoxicating drink, derived from the palm tree.
Sheikh Othman, who himself professes not to indulge
in this forbidden luxury, was so obliging as to take
me to one of his gardens to see the method by which
it is obtained. The tree is stripped of its branches,
and the crown cut off, so as to lay bare the heart; a
small drain is then cut in the edge, to which the mouth
of a jar is applied, and for months the tree yields its
daily tribute of *lagby*. From time to time the crust
is cut from the wound to facilitate the flow of the

juice; for this purpose an instrument is used, in shape like a horse fleam, tied at right angles to a handle of wood. After three or four months, the wound is generally closed; the tree does not yield fruit for some years after this exhausting process, and will die if the wound be left too long open. It seemed to me, however, that the tree never recovers its stately appearance, but ever in after life has a debauched, drunken look about its branches, indicative of its former intemperate habits. The drink itself is of a milky white colour; on the first day it is drawn, it is sweet, like the milk of the cocoa-nut; on the second, acid and slightly vinous; and, on the third, it is already vinegar. Though drinkable in large draughts in the second stage, when it has only a slightly acid taste, it is still a poor substitute for the smallest small beer. The Wagily are rich in about 16,000 date trees, and their gardens produce gourds, melons, tomatos, and onions, with a small quantity of kesab and barley.

I next day continued my journey to Jalo, where I hoped to make arrangements for my further progress. On the same day that I left Benghazi, a Turk, dependant on the Kaimahan, set off for Jalo, to take the census of the date trees, on which the taxes are levied; the result of the last one having been unsatisfactory to a large party of the inhabitants. He was accompanied by Yunes, one of the sheikhs, who had given

me every promise of assistance, though not disguising
the difficulty I should probably find in pursuing my
original plan, which was to go to the Koffra, and
thence eastwards towards the Nile.   Such a route was
quite new to the Majabra, and no one would venture
to join me in exploring it; I could not even find any
one willing to accompany me to Gebabo, كبابو.   The
Zowayah had already returned; after whom parties of
Tibbus often visit these oases to glean the fruit which
remains on the date trees.

Jalo, 28 miles, or eight hours E.S.E. from Angila,
is by far the most important in this group of oases;
the name, now restricted to the first, was probably in
ancient times applied to the whole group.   The oases,
according to the earliest accounts we have of them,
contained no fixed inhabitants; the Libyan nomads
paid them a summer visit to gather dates, in the same
way that the Zowayah now go to the Koffra.   In the
time of the Roman domination of Africa, they contained a small settlement, which, probably, had been
formed to meet the necessities of the caravans.   Jalo
is approached by a hollow, bordered on each side by
rows of tamarisks, which gradually opens into a plain,
bounded by low sand hills.   On two of them, facing
each other, Leb لب and El'Erg العرق, two villages
of much humbler pretensions than Angila, are built.
Each contains a few mud houses, but the dwellings are

mostly huts (zeribah), constructed of palm branches,
generally of a conical form, eight or nine feet in diameter, and rarely more than seven high at the apex.
The mosques are mere square mud structures, without
any attempt at ornament; and, instead of walls and
gate-towers, a simple palisading of palm branches
surrounds each village.   Jalo is, however, more populous than Angila, and a far greater degree, not of com-
fort—this is unknown in such places—but of *bien être*,
is found here.   This arises not only from the great
extent of its palm groves, but principally from the
occupation of its inhabitants, who are all merchants.
They are of different origin from the Wagily, some
speaking Arabic, whilst others, both in appearance
and language, preserve the Berber type.   El'Erg contains 4000 inhabitants, allowing five to a family, which
is rather above than below the average; it contains
seven mosques, distinguished only by little white flags,
and is governed by twelve sheikhs.   Leb, which is but
half this size, rejoices in only three sheikhs and as
many mosques.

I encamped in the plain between the two villages,
where I found Hafiz Effendi's tent already pitched;
he had chosen this central position by way of proving
his impartiality, for there is, of course, great rivalry
between the two places.   I took my ground between
two large clumps of tamarisks (ef-teleh), the only vege-

tation which the plain presented; their graceful foliage affords a relief to the eye, the small crystals of salt with which it is covered giving it an ashy gray colour; here, then, was an imperfect representation of the three Turkish elements of happiness—a bright eye, a green shade, and a running stream. The tamarisk clumps were the only variety in the monotonous yellow which surrounded me on every side, for the date groves are only visible at a distance in one direction. It would be possible to render the whole of this plain productive, but the Majabra have too little taste for agriculture to take the necessary trouble. About three feet beneath the sand is found a layer of whitish clay, which, when uncovered and watered, yields crops of barley, wheat, and a few vegetables; but the labour required for this is great. The people are addicted to an idle roving life, and as the date-trees produce abundant harvests, almost without care, other cultivation is very much neglected. The dates are of an inferior quality to those of Angila, but they afford the principal article of food, not only to man, but also for all his dependent quadrupeds. Horses, dogs, camel, sheep, are all put on this same regimen, which Sheikh Yunes pretended was a very wholesome one, but the blackened jagged teeth, universal here, seemed to contradict him.

The palm groves which surround Jalo contain up-

wards of 100,000 trees, the tax upon each of which is
four Turkish piastres. The former census only counted
45,000, but the new one, which is now going on, will
raise this number to 65,000, an increase of taxation
produced by the complaints of the people themselves,
who are now, as may be supposed, furious at their own
stupidity. For several evenings after the census began,
when the people saw the turn it was likely to take, the
women of the two villages assembled after dark and
filled the air, in alternate chorus, with yelling curses
upon Hafiz Effendi. He allowed them the uninter-
rupted enjoyment of this female form of respectful
remonstrance, and after a few nights, either from
hoarseness or disgust at finding their eloquence dis-
regarded, this expression of public opinion was abandoned. I went two or three times to see the method
adopted for taking the census; nothing could be sim-
pler or more tedious. The commissioners, surrounded
by all the fifteen sheikhs, and the greater part of the
proprietors, male and female, of the plantation they
were visiting, went from place to place, counting and
recounting the trees. Every artifice was put in practice to distract their attention, or to puzzle the commissioners as to ownership; indeed, this latter was no
difficult matter, for many trees have three or four
owners, or one man's property is dispersed here and
there, through the whole oasis. A good date-tree will

yield three hundredweight of fruit on alternate years;
the produce being generally smaller in the intervening
year. As dates are worth about 20 piastres a hundredweight, the tax is about a tithe of the produce.

The wells of Jalo are all brackish, and the nearest
sweet water is at a distance of six hours; hither, at
rare intervals, the ladies of the place resort to wash
the cotton shirts and woollen plaids, which are the
costume of their lords. The scanty fauna is confined
to the fox, wolf, or jackal, fovina and gerboa. There
are snakes, which are said to be venomous and of
large size, but though I offered backshish I could obtain no specimens of them, either here or at Angila.
Some exuviæ, which I found in a quarry near my
tent, at the latter place, proved the fact of their existence and their size. Of antiquities I could learn nothing; the subterranean temple, with a cubical idol,
mentioned by some writer, the oldest inhabitants had
never heard of, and the only curiosity which they
could point out to me, was a single large hewn stone,
about four miles south-west of El 'Erg, under which
they suppose a treasure to be concealed.

The Majabra are, almost without exception, addicted to excessive drinking, owing, no doubt, to the
facility of procuring *lagby*. At an early age they
commence their apprenticeship in trade by journeys
to Benghazi, soon followed by longer courses to

Egypt and Fezzan. They are the great slave-dealers of these countries, purchasing their human merchandise in Fezzan, from wholesale dealers, many of whom are Majabra settled there. The latter make every year an incursion into Bornou, and return with troops of five or six hundred slaves, which they afterwards sell in retail to the men of Jalo. The most valuable black slaves are called Fellatah ; they have nearly straight hair, and their features bear little of the negro type. Their distinctive mark is three slashes on the cheeks and two on the temples. The gains in this trade are very large, and many of the Jalese have amassed in it large sums ; which sums, however, they have no means of spending. The women are generally unveiled, wearing a long blue shirt and a milayah on the head, like the fellah women in Egypt; they enjoy a good reputation for purity of morals.

Finding myself obliged to renounce all hopes of going to the Koffra, I contented myself with gathering such information as I could from those who had been there. The nearest oasis is distant six days' journey, over a flat sandy desert, unbroken by rock or shrub, and having no wells. The remaining ones are respectively at a good day's journey from each other ; the furthest and largest, Gebabo, قبابوا, being considered twelve days distant. These oases are totally uninhabited, except in autumn, when the Zowayah

proceed from their summer station, Ijherri, in a body
to gather the dates and figs, which grow there in wild
luxuriance. They are represented as abounding in
sweet water, which is obtained in large quantities
by merely scratching a hole in the sand. I was
assured that the Koffra contained no monument of
antiquity, and were mere fertile spots, like some I
should see on my journey to the east, inhabited only
by the jackal and wild cow. The Tibbus, as far as I
could learn, are a timid and inoffensive people, not
possessing fire-arms, and, except for the pilgrimage
(they are Moslemin), never visiting Jalo or Siwah.
With Fezzan they carry on an insignificant trade,
chiefly in dromedaries (of which they have an excellent breed) and sulphur, which they exchange on the
frontier for cotton, cloths, and beads.

The caravans arriving from Waday reach Gebabo
in about forty-two days from Warah, and having come
twelve without water, their camels are so exhausted
that they stop here, and send to Jalo to hire camels
to continue the journey to Benghazi ; there they generally spend six months, buying cottons, coral, paper,
and, I think, arms. The Sultan of Waday is himself
the proprietor of the greater part of the caravan, and
in the long intervals between its visits, the Frank merchants lay in stores of such curiosities or elegancies
as his Wadayan majesty is likely to be pleased with.

I heard of a plated dinner service, which had been
ordered by one of them, in hopes the caravan might
arrive this year; at its last departure it conveyed a
carriage to him.   The Sultan is said to have began
to coin dollars from a die sent to him from Europe ;
up to a very recent time the entire circulation was in
Spanish dollars, and writing paper served in lieu of
smaller coins.   A fowl is bought with a sheet of
writing paper, six or eight are paid for a sheep—the
most original paper currency.   The country is said to
be rich in pasturage and arable land, and two mountains yield copper and iron.   No European having
ever visited Waday, its other mineral and vegetable
riches are unknown, though a small quantity of gold
dust is collected either within its frontiers or from
the countries to the south.   The Sultan claims to be
a sheikh of the family of the Abassides, and was for
many years a refugee in Cairo, where he learned to
appreciate the arts of civilisation.   If he still reign,
it is not improbable that a European would be warmly
welcomed at his court, but no one could venture there
without having previously obtained his consent.   While
in Jalo I heard rumours from Fezzan, to the effect,
that he had grown blind, and had been deposed by
his son, a blood-thirsty tyrant, who soon made himself so hateful to his vizirs and influential men, that
they reinstated the father, who is now only a puppet in

the hands of one of the rival factions warring for the sovereignty. Should these news be confirmed, or in the doubts which they suggest, no one could prudently venture into Waday.*

The Turkish Government levies at Jalo heavy duties upon the produce of Waday, 25 dollars on the cantar of ivory (98 lbs.)—a sum more than its original value, and one dollar a head upon the slaves, upon whom a further duty of seven dollars and a half is charged at Benghazi. Those shipped for Constantinople, however, go duty free, the supply of so necessary a commodity for the capital being encouraged in every possible way. The Wadayan slaves are amongst the least intelligent negroes in Africa, and have the reputation of being thievishly inclined; they are, therefore, the cheapest, but the profit on their sale is very great, their value at Warah hardly exceeding a dollar and a half.

Jalo was decidedly not an amusing residence, and my impatience to continue my journey, when I found that I could only reach Egypt by way of Siwah, was not diminished by the delays which I half suspected my friend Yunes of occasioning. In this I did him

* A description of Waday has been published in French, translated from a MS. of the Shiekh Mohammed El Tounsy, who was there about 1814, and who still lives in Cairo attached to one of the mosques.

injustice, for, even if he intentionally sought means
to put off my departure, after-occurrences lead me to
think that he did this in my interest; of his good-will
I had no idea at the time, and I only felt annoyed at
being detained, and certain that some intrigue was at
the bottom of it. He, every day, expected the arrival
of his son, who was on his way from Fezzan with a
few slaves for the Egyptian market, and he wished
me to accompany him. For this I had little inclination, having no wish to join a slave caravan, and,
above all, desiring to be master of my own movements—*Hoc amo quod possum quâlibet ire viâ.*

I had long exhausted every topic of information
upon which the Jalese could enlighten me, and my
only amusement now were the rare visits of the Sheikh
and Hafiz Effendi. At whatever hour they came, the
coffee which was given to them was never the only
refreshment they reckoned upon being treated to, and
they never failed to ask for something stronger. I
was provided with a small stock of rum for such a
contingency, being well aware that many of the Turkish *employés* are eager votaries of the bottle; but, before my departure from Jalo, my friends had completely exhausted my stock; when they had done so,
I may add, their visits became less frequent. Besides
drinking in my tent—not in my company, for I never
joined them—they thought nothing of asking for a

bottle with which to indulge in a private kef in their
own quarters—glad to make something out of the
Frank; they could not plead the excuse of the bottle
being a rarity to them, as they were in constant communication with Benghazi, where the forbidden drink
is plentiful. With us it is shameful for a man out of
his teens to be seen drunk; with them it is only a
sin. One day, during my stay at Grennah, the secretary to the Government, said to be a most upright
man, came to see me; he drank, before, during, and
after dinner, Marsala and brandy to such an extent,
that when, at last, wearied with his meaningless loqua-
city, I insisted upon his going to bed in the tent I
had prepared for him, he fell flat in the attempt to
rise from the couch, breaking the bottles he had just
emptied; and then it was with difficulty that he allowed himself to be put to bed by one of my servants.
The next day he alluded, without an appearance of
shame, to his evening's exploit, saying, if any damage
was done, it was not he but the wine that did it. The
great object in getting drunk, (kef they call it,) is to
procure the soundness of sleep which follows, and
hence the pleasantest liquor, in their estimation, is
that which has the speediest effect.

I was, in fact, thoroughly tired of my stay in Jalo;
and what rendered it particularly exasperating was the
persuasion which every day took more strongly hold

of me—that I was the victim of a speculation, on the part of these people, to detain me, until, tired of waiting, I should be ready to subscribe to any terms they chose to offer me. This idea only made me more determined to refuse what I knew to be an exorbitant demand. Hafiz Effendi possessed no authority, and Yunes, if he had any, did not, as I thought, exert it. After concluding a bargain for camels, at nearly a third more than the usual price, my men returned the next morning and tried to extort another dollar; this I refused, and no one, naturally enough, would incur the ill-will of his people in defence of a stranger, by obliging them to stick to their bargain. Consequently, in a fit of unreasonable disgust—unreasonable, for it is always better to put up with such annoyances in travelling than to subject oneself to fresh and perhaps more serious ones, only to give proof of a resolution which people cannot appreciate—I sent off to Angila to ask Shiekh Othman to provide me with camels to return there, and to look out for others for my further journey. I had now been a month in Jalo, and on comparing my expenditure with the state of my purse, I discovered to my dismay that, thanks to the dearness of everything here, I could not start without sending to my good friend Mr. Xerri, in Benghazi, for a fresh supply of the needful. I must do Yunes the justice to say, that when I announced my determination, he did all he could to dissuade me from it, offering me, after the things were already packed for the return to Angila, money, camels, anything.   He felt that I had come there in a sort of way as his guest, and that leaving him as I did was a slur upon his hospitality.   I persisted, however, in my determination, and in the end was punished for it as I deserved.   I never yet opposed myself to an imposition, that I did not end by submitting to at least as great a one, and having all the annoyance without the glory of martyrdom into the bargain.   After each lesson I promise myself to consult, in future, my real convenience, throwing abstract notions of justice to the dogs on the next occasion, but I rarely, when the temptation comes, am able to resist it.

CHAPTER XV.

WITH bitter maledictions against the fathers of all
the Majabra, I saw my luggage loaded to return to
Angila, and then started with a single servant for the
district called Ijherri, اِجْهَّرِي, eighteen miles to the
north-east.   It is a large village of square palm-
branch huts, lying in the midst of date-trees, and is
almost deserted at the present moment, as not a dozen
persons remain in it during the winter; its situation
among trees renders it more picturesque than either
Jalo or Angila, and the trees themselves are remarkable as the first specimens I had seen of untrimmed,
perfectly wild date-trees.   The Arabs are too lazy to
pay the slight attention to the cultivation of the trees
which the Wagily pay to theirs; and on many of them
the dead boughs of the last twenty years could be
seen drooping in a thick fringe round their stems.   I

found that the very few people who still lingered behind the rest of their tribes, were inveterate *lagby*
drinkers, and had stayed behind to indulge in their
favourite vice.

The next day I turned backwards south-west to
Angila, where I was warmly welcomed by Sheikh Othman, who could not conceal his pleasure at my applying to him, in preference to taking camels from Yunes.
There had been an old feud between them when Othman's father was Sheikh of Jalo as well as Angila ; the
Majabra, however, revolted from his authority, applied
to the Pacha of Tripoli, and obtained an independent
government, but not before Yunes, with some of his
friends, had waylaid and murdered their old sheikh.
How the quarrel was made up I shall afterwards have
occasion to tell.   Othman pretended that I was not
the first victim of the insolence of the Majabra, as the
last Turkish commissioners of the census had been
treated still worse, and had only been enabled to return to Benghazi through his means.   Othman el
Fadil is a perfect specimen of an African Sheikh-el-
bilad, the most despicable combination of cringing
servility and insolent tyranny that barbarism has produced.   These good qualities in him are combined
with extreme cunning and no small amount of natural
talent.   After being despoiled of his hereditary authority, he made shift to repossess himself of it ; he even

managed to resist the authority of the Turkish Pacha
of Tripoli, after the deprivation of the last native
Governor; and he now contrives by art rather than
violence to maintain himself in his position. He is
probably wealthy, for half the cultivated land in the
oasis belongs to him, and he has also possessions in
Jalo and in Fezzan. As a proof of his shrewdness, I
may mention, that since the death of the last Cadi,
which took place fifteen years ago, he has persuaded
the people to do without this functionary, so that all
marriages and other contracts are now made in his
presence. He gains immensely in influence by this
arrangement, and the people probably do not lose by
it; for as the appointment of the Cadi is in the hands
of the Cadi of Tripoli, who buys his office in Constantinople, and as he in turn sells all the posts de-
pending upon him, it is not improbable that the purchaser sells the justice he dispenses.

During my long stay here, his attentions were, after
his fashion, unceasing; he rarely omitted paying at
least one visit a day to my tent, and frequently sent
supplies of vegetables, or fresh baked bread, or new
drawn *lagby*, for all which he took care to exact hand-
some payment, asking for and carrying off everything
he saw which struck his fancy, which was a most mis-
cellaneous one. He pretended that he could speak
four of the languages of the interior, as well as Turk-

ish, but I never could induce him to let me see the vocabulary of them, which he said he had drawn up; more than once I had, in other matters, occasion to admire the liveliness of his imagination, so that he may very possibly be mistaken in his assertions. Whatever the amount of his learning, it is unquestioned by his subjects, who look up to him as a prodigy of wisdom. He was particularly fond of taking a peep through my sextant, and of astonishing any of his people who might be in the tent, by giving them explanations of the use of the " Astrolabe," which would have astonished Hadley, and been new to Sawitsch.

Time wore slowly away at Angila, and the fifteen days, before whose expiration I had been assured my messenger would have returned from Benghazi, had passed without bringing any news of him. A dull Christmas was to be expected in such a heathen place; but what I was not prepared for was the extreme cold of the nights, during which the thermometer sometimes sank to zero; and in the long evening, from dark till bedtime, I occasionally had as much difficulty in keeping out the cold, as in finding occupation. The Wagily, unless there be a *fantasia* on foot, go early to bed, and the Sheikh's conversation was not sufficiently instructive to make me wish for his company; he was shy of speaking about the customs of his people, and they seem to have preserved no tradition of their origin or former history.

I have already described the oasis of Angila as extending in a half circle of about six miles in a hollow, around the foot of a range of compacted sand lying over a white limestone. In this space is comprised a large tract of brown morass, covered with a crust of saline earth, beneath which are bitter waters. Such a morass is described by Beechey on the coast of the Syrtis, and I had reason to respect the propriety of the warning given him by his guide, as only a yard from the path which runs across it the thin crust gave way under my horse, who began to flounder, and was only able by a violent effort to extricate himself. In general, the water of the wells in Angila is very good; the salt which it contains being almost imperceptible to a person accustomed to that of Jalo.

I had encamped on a hill used as a burial-ground, to the east of the town, and water was drawn for me from a well close at hand, which was used to water one of the Sheikh's fields. I was astonished one morning, soon after I arrived, by finding the water of my sponge bath sensibly warm, and, on inquiry, I found that, instead of standing as usual all night ready for use, it had only just been drawn from the well. The thermometer, when immersed in it, showed, two hours after sunrise, a temperature of 74°, while the external air was 52°. Many of the wells have this degree of warmth; others are quite cold, and these are either brackish or very salt. At some distance from the modern town, following the inside of the curve of plantations and to the left of it, there are in a small field some remains of reticulated brickwork, and the ground in the neighbourhood is full of broken pottery. What remains is too little to authorise a conjecture as to its use.

Angila is on the caravan road from Fezzan to Egypt and Benghazi; the intermediate stations between Angila and Murzuk are Maradah, an oasis three days distant, and Zalla as much further on. At an hour and a half, on the road to Maradah, which follows a north-west direction in leaving Angila, I found, at a considerable elevation above the cultivated land, a number of small groups of rock of volcanic origin, forming an irregular oval like the remains of a crater. The rocks are gray and black lava, as heavy and compact as basalt. Ten hours before reaching Maradah, مَرْأَدَه, there is a small oasis, Jabna, حَبْنَه, and two hours further Hairaigah, حَيرَيْقَه, both inhabited by Arabs of the tribes of Hamud and Zowayah. In Maradah there is one of those curious wells whose water contains a salt, doubtless of iron, which imparts to it the property of dyeing cotton and woollen cloths

black.   I think it is Belzoni who mentions the existence of such a spring in the little oasis, without, however, stating that the stuff to be dyed is first boiled in
a decoction of bark.   There is another well of the
same kind in Fezzan, at a place called Agar, which,
like this one at Maradah, is called 'Ain essobagh, or
the Dyer's Well.   At Zalla tame ostriches are kept
in the houses, and it must be in this way that the finer
feathers, imported into Europe, are obtained, for those
of birds killed in the chase and brought to market, are
almost always soiled and broken.   A Fezzan Fikhy,
who came to me while in Siwah, supplied me with one
other fact concerning Fezzan : the place where sulphur is found is called Wady 'ain Ghadga (غدقة),
near a hill called 'Angud (عنقود), ten days east of
Murzuk.

Whilst I was in Angila two marriages took place,
one of them that of the Sheikh (only his thirteenth)
with the daughter of my friend Yunes.   She was old
and a widow; the only attraction I could discover
seemed to be the relation in which their respective
fathers had stood to each other, of which I have
already spoken.   The festivities were commenced,
some evenings before the marriage, with the loud
shrill cries of women, accompanied by occasional mus-
ket shots.   On inquiry, I was told that all the female
friends of the bridegroom were assembled in his house,

each bringing her mill to help in grinding wheat to
make bread for the marriage feast. The usual quantity ground is from six to eight hundredweight, but
sometimes, if the Sheikh might be believed, as much
as eighty hundredweight is consumed on such occasions. This bread is partly sent to the houses of the
principal people, like our old-fashioned wedding-cake,
and partly eaten at the feast, which consists chiefly of
dates and large supplies of *lagby*.

The evening before the wedding, the young men and
boys of the village assembled with all the donkeys which
they could procure, and, loading them with fine sand
from the hill where I was encamped, brought it to the
bridal house, and strewed it in the rooms. In the intervals between the departure and return of the donkeys, the boys who remained danced to the sound of
their own voices and the beating of a drum ; this drum
is made of a circle of wood about the size of a tambou-
rine, on each side of which a gazelle-skin is stretched ;
it is beaten with a knotted rope. The first marriage
was that of a young girl, a relation of Othman's, but
as she belonged to the town, there was nothing remarkable in the bridal procession : it was, as usual, accompanied by the Zaghaghit and firing of guns. The arrival of the Sheikh's bride with a *cortège*, including all
the men in the place, but none of her own relations,

was a much more solemn affair. She was carried in
state in a closely-veiled carmout, covered with white
cotton hangings, round which an old red silk scarf was
tied; a man on horseback preceded her, carrying a white
flag. When the *cortège* arrived in sight of the town,
several halts were made, during which there were rude
dancing, firing of muskets, and evolutions of the three
or four horsemen whom the place furnished. While the
lady was thus being brought in procession to her new
home, the gallant bridegroom was quietly seated in my
tent looking on, and it was not until the *cortège* entered the town that he betook himself to his house.

Here, when the camel knelt at the door, before the
howdah containing its precious burthen was removed
from its back, a sheep's throat was cut over its right
knee, in manner of sacrifice. The Sheikh, after many
ineffectual hints which I would not understand, at last
boldly begged of me a sash woven with gold which he
had one day see me wear; this he wished to form part
of the corbeil, and in letting him have it I took the
opportunity of inspecting the ornaments destined for
the bride. They consisted of two pairs of broad silver
bands to be worn as bracelets, weighing respectively
ten and fourteen ounces, and a pair of very curious
silver earrings of Tunis make. They were in shape
like the young moon, two inches and a half in dia-

meter, two-thirds of the circumference being covered
with filigree bosses, from which five pear-shaped filigree pendents hung, each earring weighing 160
grammes. I felt a great curiosity to see the cartilage
capable of supporting such a weight. The marriage
feast was diversified by dancing to the sound of the
drum, and a curious double clarionet, formed of the
leg bones of the eagle or vulture, which discoursed
sweet music in the tone of a very broken-winded bag-
pipe. The dancing, like that of the Egyptian Alnach
(in whom youth, good looks, and sex hardly excuse
the peculiar style), was here performed by a hideous
man, and was utterly disgusting. When the bride had
entered the house, the festivities were terminated by a
discharge of fire-arms, and the company retired, to
meet again the next evening, and to renew the eating
and dancing.

It is no uncommon thing to find men in these countries who have married twenty or thirty times, the sum
given for a wife rarely exceeding six or eight dollars.
When tired of a spouse, or if she do not prove fruitful, a divorce follows as a matter of course, and the
lady does not suffer in general estimation; having
borne children seems to be no protection against the
caprice of the men. This licence is utterly opposed
to Turkish habits, for divorce is more disreputable to

a man among the Osmanli than with us, but the assertors of the rights of women in Europe would find this régime very congenial to their theories, for a woman can always force her husband to a divorce, even without laying her slipper at the Cadi's feet.

CHAPTER XVI.

JANUARY 13.—My messenger returned several days
ago from Benghazi; and Sheikh Othman had a
fortnight before assured me that the camels were
ready to start with me at a moment's warning; and
then again, after several days' delay, had promised
them for this morning, but I saw nothing of them.
At length, on Saturday morning, Othman, accompanied by several other persons, came to see the baggage
tied up and weighed—a long operation, which I hastened as much as I could, being anxious to get away
from a place of which I was heartily tired. Where
were the camels all this time? They were at the
other end of the town, and would be brought up immediately; but as soon as all seemed in order for
starting, my friend Othman went off, saying, that we
should start with the dawn next morning. I was com-

pletely in his power, and had nothing for it but to take patience, and the more so, since I now found that the camel owners—with whom I had only communicated through my trusty friend, and to whom he, in his anxiety to serve me, had promised an exorbitant hire on my part—were, in fact, himself and one of his friends. I consoled myself with the idea of taking it out of him by suppressing the backshish I had intended to give him; but this was poor consolation for the previous days thus lost.

Sunday, Jan. 16.—The sun had been up for more than three hours before the camels came, and then there were only six instead of nine. These I had loaded and dispatched by a little after midday, having been promised that the others should be sent to me in half an hour. Hour after hour went by, and I sat fretting among the remains of my baggage; at length the day wearing on, I determined to follow the camels which had already started, leaving a servant to come on with the rest as soon as they arrived. I had found out from the people of the place, that the men with whom the original bargain was made had been sent away, as the Sheikh, finding he could make so profitable an investment, had determined to supply the greater number of camels himself; he had not, however, yet purchased them all—and hence the delay.

Half an hour before sunset, no camels appearing, I

mounted my horse and rode off alone, to seek for
my caravan, and—what I was beginning to feel a great
want of—my dinner. The road was over gravelly
sand, and as long as daylight lasted it was easy
enough to follow the tracks of the camels; but as
night closed in, and the sky became overcast with
fleecy clouds, which obscured the moon and stars,
the track gradually grew invisible, and I could only
guess at the right path; so keeping my horse's head
as straight as possible, I rode on. There was no
appearance of fire in any direction, and after four
hours I found myself among palm-trees, which I
recognised as those of Jalo. It would have been
folly to attempt to return to find the road I had de-
viated from, in the darkness, and it was too late to
ask for hospitality in Jalo; I, therefore, tied my horse
to a tree, and lay down supperless and hungry under
a palm-bush near him. I was soon asleep; but, tor-
mented with thirst, I dreamed of the gurgling streams
of Damascus, and the water-sellers in the streets of
Cairo, with their leaf-crowned jars of cool water.
Their cry, " God's fountain for the thirsty," awoke me,
and the first sound I heard was the rumbling of water
in a vase. " Oh, man," I cried, " bring water." There
was no answer, as my voice fell echoless in the still
night, and I turned again to sleep, thinking I had
dreamed; but in another moment I again heard the

sound, and this time I was sure I was awake. I sat
up and listened; presently the noise was repeated, and
then I heard the pawing of my horse, and felt the
branches of the bush I was lying under shaken.   I
rose, and found that my horse, thirsty as his master,
and more sagacious than he, had nosed out a vase of
lagby among the branches ; the booming noise which
had awoke me being caused by his ineffectual attempts
to get his head into a jar which had an orifice of
about an inch. My thirst in the meantime had increased with my dream, and setting aside all sense of
the impropriety of theft. I took a draught of the cool
palm-juice, which, for the first time, seemed to me a
pleasant beverage, and again lay down, after replacing
the jar and tying my horse in a position to prevent his
repeating his vain addresses to the bottle.

In the gray of the morning, I mounted with the intention of retracing my steps and joining my caravan,
but just as I emerged from the palm trees, I saw two
men and a camel coming from Angila. At this sight
my malignant star suggested to me the idea of saving
time, and not returning on my way—a bad omen in
the beginning of a journey; so I rode up to the new
comers, asking if either would accompany me to the
Wadi, the place of rendezvous for caravans starting
to Siwah ; and one of them saying he knew the way,
agreed to guide me. I knew that my servant, when he

saw the camels arrive without me, would at once conclude that I had ridden straight to the Wadi, and
without a misgiving I rode on. I had eaten nothing
since an early breakfast on the previous day, and when
midday came and we were still far from the Wadi, I
turned to see what store of good things my saddle-
bags contained. I found in them only a single sea-
biscuit. Of this I gave half to my conductor, and,
unable to make any impression on what remained, I
reserved it till my arrival in the Wadi. We reached
it at half-past two, but there was no appearance
of the Cafilah, and I now began to contemplate with
some dismay the possibility of the Ottoman having
again broken his word, and having another day to
wait with my not abundant store of provisions. There
was at least water here, and this was all I had to give
my horse and dog; my tarboush served to draw it,
and for them to drink out of. The Wadi was here
and there dotted with tufts of a bright-looking thorny
grass, and to enable him to pick up a few mouthfuls,
and at the same time prevent him from going far off,
I tied my horse's forelegs together, and sent him to
look for his dinner.

Meantime my guide had made me a fire, which he
lighted from the smouldering embers left by a caravan,
which must have started a few hours before we came up;
and I then dismissed him, showing the half biscuit which

remained, as a good reason for his not staying with
me, while I assured him that my people could not be
long in coming up. Evening was fast approaching,
so I ate half the remainder of my biscuit soaked in
water, gathered sticks to feed my fire, and choosing the
sheltered side of a palm-bush, looked to my arms and
arranged my saddle and saddle-cloth, so as to make
something which I persuaded myself was a bed. I
had not even a cloak, as in a fit of carefulness for my
steed I had removed it to save him the weight, never
reckoning on such a contingency as the present; the
only additional covering I had to the white trowsers
and jacket I wore, was one of those light india-rubber
overcoats, bearing a barbarously meaningless name,
such as the classic public of the Strand delights in.
The sky was bright and clear, and the air proportion-
ately cold. I had no provisions, no wine, no brandy,
no covering, not even a cigar, but I had a chronome-
ter, a sextant, a compass, a thermometer, a telescope,
in fact a whole observatory of instruments to console
me for the want of a dinner, and I was thus enabled
to certify, that at dawn the thermometer marked 43°;
and the sharp air, contrasted with the heat of the sun
during the previous day, made this seem still more
piercingly cold.

In one point at least I am a true Englishman, for
I can brook anything better than the want of my

"victuals;" next to this the most painful feeling I know is that of inaction. I had had enough of my two days' fast, and in the morning I thought to avoid further endurance of either evil by mounting my poor horse and going back, somewhere or other; my ambition in fact was to keep moving. The old gray, knowing my temper pretty well, after an eight months' acquaintance, had probably foreseen this; he woke me half a dozen times during the night by rubbing his nose against my legs, by way of asking how I felt, and at last getting some cross words for disturbing me, had made himself scarce. As far as the telescope could command he was not to be seen, and I was in no humour for a tramp in search of him through the loose sand. The morning wore heavily, a quarter of my biscuit still remained, but I reserved it with an idea of keeping rather than eating my cake, while from time to time I took a look to see if " anybody was coming." At last I saw a spot moving in the distance, a single man, but so wrapped in his borneau that I could not distinguish him. He came straight towards me, and then I recognised him as my guide of the previous day, who had brought me a basket of dates, some corn for my horse, and two pieces of stick to kindle a fire. I sat down on the sand with the basket before me, he sitting in true Arab style of hospitality at a little distance to see me eat, and while I picked out a few dates without relish (appetite was gone, and I fancied them dirty), he told me why he had returned. It was midnight when he reached his cottage in Jalo; his mother got up, made him a fire, and gave him something to eat while he told her how he had spent his day. He then lay down to sleep, but his mother said to him, "My son, this is no time for sleep; my heart is troubled for the man in the Wadi; rise and go to him, for he is alone, and I fear robbers; carry him these dates, for he is hungry." Abd-er-rahman started afresh and reached me about ten in the morning, having hardly rested during forty-eight hours. When he had seen me eat, he went to the well and washed, and then employed himself in gathering date-stones in the sand round the fire-places of previous caravans. I was puzzled to see him thus groping in the earth, and visions of truffles, which I had read of in Theophrastus as being found in this desert, rose before me. Were I given to the vice of *gourmandise*, as those whose palates are not gifted with discrimination call the sense of taste, I could not have hastened with more alacrity to join in the search; but my disappointment was great, when I found that he was only gathering old date-stones, which he pounded and then gave, mixed with straw and water, to his cousin's cow.

In about four hours, the caravan and my horse, which

had gone to join it, arrived, and I learned, as I had
anticipated, that this fresh delay was due to my
Sheikh, from whom, however, I thought that I was
now pretty safe. But he had still a trick of villany
in store for me, for when the camels came to load (and
they carried less weight on account of the water I
should require during the first days), his people refused
to carry water unless I paid half a dollar a skin extra.
I had no resource, as I was still too near Jalo to force
them to move on against their will, but to submit,
which I did with secret vows to have them punished
in Siwah for the imposition. I little guessed what
would be my reception there.

It was twelve when I started from the Wadi after
filling a dozen skins at its well, whose water is " sweet
as those of heaven," as Abd-er-rahman poetically
called rain, though the sand from which it springs is
mixed with crystals of common salt, admirably white
and pure. For an hour and a half the ground is
dotted thickly with hillocks of the Tumaran, of which
each camel received a bundle in passing, as during
some days little or no wood is to be found on the road.
This is a low-growing woody plant with spare short
fleshy leaves, whose thick twisted roots creep over the
sand near its surface, forming low mounds. It is
thornless, is easily torn up in large pieces, and though
alive and in leaf, burns with a clear bright flame.

Much of the petrified wood found in parts of the
desert is formed of Tumeran, which even in its living
state seems to be undergoing the process of petri-
faction, as long veins of red brown earth run through
its roots.   Six hours after starting, travelling through
fine loose sand in a N.E. direction, we reached a lofty
sand-hill, the ground at whose base is sprinkled for a
considerable distance with dark gravel and fragments
of black half-vitrified stone.   Many parts of this desert,
seen in a bright sun, seemed perfectly flat, but as day
closed in, and the shadows lengthened, the gentle
undulations of the sand became visible.   For ten
hours we continued our course over a nearly flat
country, gradually trending to the north, when we
came to a long line of low hills, among which we were
soon engaged.   It is here that the two roads to Siwah
separate ; that which I took is the longer, but is easier
for the camels ; the other is the one more usually followed by the slave-dealers, and the same followed by
Hornemann ; it is preferred as being further removed
from the haunts of the Aoulad Ali Arabs.

In gentle swells, these hills ultimately reach a considerable height.   Journeying over such ground is
singularly fatiguing, for the sand offers no variety to
the eye, which is pained by the intense glare which it
reflects, and the horse sinks in it to the fetlocks at
every step.   Nothing marked the road, which is very

rarely used, and a slight wind suffices to obliterate every trace of former travellers. No caravan had passed this way to Mecca for three years, in consequence of disturbances among the Tuarick, to whom this country principally belongs. Thus we continued during fifteen hours and a quarter, constantly ascending between two lines of low hills, which rose on either side like waves driven from opposite directions. By this I mean that they rise on one side in long gentle swells and fall very suddenly on the other, forming an angle of about 70°, while eight or ten feet of their crests are on this, one would say the lee side, perfectly perpendicular. But the action of the wind, to which this appearance is doubtless due, is such, that in this place the lee side of each sand-wave faces that of the other, forming a valley between them, bounded on each side by steep sand. My greyhounds enjoyed themselves famously in running along the crests of these hills, and then rolling and tumbling down their steep sides; but after a couple of days of such gambols, the sand began to distress their feet, and they were glad to mount a camel during the greater part of the remaining journey.

It was on the afternoon of the third day, that, sending on the servant who had waited on me at luncheon, I stayed behind to smoke a chibouque, and having a supply of tobacco beside me I thoughtlessly protracted this amusement beyond a due time. When I at last started I rode straight for the passage, between some distant hills, where I had last seen the caravan, but soon I found that I had lost the track. At the height I had then reached, the wind blew so strongly, that, in exposed places, the footsteps were speedily effaced, and for an hour I wandered sufficiently to convince me how easy it would be to lose oneself in the sand. Evening was not far distant, and I was on the point of returning to my noon-day resting-place, but determined first to try one cast more. With this intent I rode directly at right angles to my course, and happily came upon the tracks of the camels. I soon reached the base of a peak round which they had gone, and, turning it, I beheld the most extraordinary scene of desolation.

I found myself standing on the ledge of an oval basin, some five or six miles long, whose sides were formed of stratified rocks, of a bluish gray colour, in their horizontal layers; across ran low dykes of the same laminar construction, the upper layers being generally of a blackish stone, but all bearing the appearance of vitrifaction. The dykes ran in lines parallel to the minor axis of the ellipse, and one might almost have supposed it the ruins of a construction on a gigantic scale, like that called Solomon's Pool, near Bethlehem. Excepting at points where the rocks crop out, the bottom of the basin was filled with sand; piles of stones, memorials of former caravans, erected on the dykes; many skeletons, both of men and camels, bleached white as the purest ivory, pointed out the path which I must follow. Night closed in while I was still in this lonely valley; and it was with some pleasure that I heard the signal guns, which were fired from time to time, to direct me to the halting place. At sunset, as I had not been seen for six hours, the caravan was halted, although it had only made ten hours and a half journey that day.   The Arabs call this place the Gerdobiah, or Little Gerdebah, قردبه, to distinguish it from the great range of this name, which commences two hours and a half further on. A ridge of round-backed sandhills forms the separation between the Gerdobiah and the immense range of low dark hills and table-lands which here presents itself. A low line of sandstone rocks, with nearly perpendicular sides, bound the line of road, sometimes closing upon it, sometimes leaving a wide plain on either side. In the basins thus formed rocks rise frequently, in the form of low truncated cones, generally in two steps, one rising from the other, so like diminutive craters, that in referring to this day's journey my servant always calls them, " *les Vesuves*." The black appearance of the ground is caused by numberless fragments of flat, dark, flint-like, coarse, broken glass, with which

the sand and rocks are covered; among them are many
pieces of petrified palm-wood; and, in some places, I
found four or five feet of the trunk of the tree still
standing erect as it grew: while, in more than one
instance, large fragments of the tree, like the *débris* of
a broken column, lay scattered round.   In one spot, I
found the trunk of such a tree (judging from its form
at the base) in the position and place where it grew,
and lying alongside of it, fragments of its stem, in all
more than twenty feet long; the fractures of each of
these corresponded to those on either side of it.   It
would seem from this that the trees were petrified as
they grew, and that their general prostration is due to
some convulsion which followed the withdrawal of the
petrifying waters in which they had been immersed.
I believe these trees to be, many of them, date palms,
such as grow in the oases at the present day; they are
similar in appearance; and so were some petrified date-
stones, which I found, to their stones.   It took in all
twenty-six hours to traverse this line, which, judging
from the cold, must be at a very considerable elevation.
The south wind blew so bleakly that even at midday
a cloak was a welcome addition to the borneau.   In
the mornings and evenings the thermometer was rarely
above 43°, and at midday, notwithstanding the bright
sun, I twice found it only 45°.

Towards the last part of the Gerdebah I observed

large masses of beautifully-marked agate, of a coarse
crystalline grain, with colours more vivid than the
Sicilian.   Descending into a plain of sand, the next
landmark is a lofty cone, called Gar Hhot, خوت,
some sixty or seventy feet high, which rising abruptly
from the level, is seen at a great distance.   It was
formerly a stronghold of the Aoulad Ali, who from
it descended to pillage the Majabra caravans.   The
tombs of seven or eight Majabra, who were killed in
one of their raids some forty years ago, are at the base
of the hill; but this was the robbers' last exploit, for
the Majabra are said to have come in overwhelming
numbers, and to have overpowered them.   I will not
answer for the truth of the story which was told me
by my guide, whose grandfather was among the slain;
for in my experience of timid people, I must do the
Majabra of the present generation the justice to say,
that I never met with any who had so strong a regard
for their personal safety.   Along this line they never
light fires during the night, for fear of attracting the
Arabs, and for the same reason they frequently diverge
from the direct line of journey; their cargoes of human
merchandise being, it is said, very attractive to the
Arabs.   However this may be, I have no complaint to
make of the dangers of the road: every night two
large fires were kindled in my encampment, yet I was
never molested, nor during the whole journey saw the

trace of man, excepting in the case of one small slave
caravan, which I came up with the day after passing
Gar Hhot, at the first well we reached, called Maten
Et-Tarfawy, طرفاوي. It is seventy-four hours from
the well of the Wady.

This place was visited by Hornemann, and is the
only spot in which my route (which is the one followed
by the great pilgrim caravans) coincides with the more
southerly one. The slave caravan, which I came up
with here, continued to follow Hornemann's route.
Near the place I found some palm trunks upright,
imbedded in reddish, coarsely crystallised flint. The
sand is in great part composed of *débris* of small
marine shells, and the limestone rocks from here to
Siwah are filled with fossils. A considerable descent
from the high ground we had been traversing, crossing
several hills and valleys, which grow gradually more
sandy as we advanced, leads to a valley clothed with
gum bushes. From it rises a platform of soft, white
limestone rock ; and it is in this that the wells of
brackish water called Et-Tarfawy are pierced. The
white platform is picturesquely crowned with a garland
of the bright-green 'ajrum bushes, which grow somewhat like a broom. Here we watered our camels, and
then went an hour and a half further to a hattych (a
copse) called Bou el Lawah, لوه. The wind, which
had blown for several days constantly from the south,

shifted for a few hours to the north, and was gratefully warm; heavy rains speedily followed, during which it again veered to the south.

From here to Siwah I was six days on the road, but one day I was only able to travel five hours; in fact, I never again got a fair day's work out of my camels, for Sheikh Othman, after making me pay so dearly for them, sent them with so small a supply of food, that they successively dropped off, one after another, exhausted from sheer hunger. I cannot, therefore, state the distance exactly, but as nearly as I can calculate, from Et-Tarfawy to Siwah is forty-eight hours. The road runs through a succession of small oases, of which the first is Faredrah, فغيدرة, twelve hours from Et-Tarfawy. Among sandhills one descends very suddenly into a long basin, which is occupied by a dark brown morass, like that which I met with at Angila; it is bounded on three sides by time-worn rocks, which rise perpendicularly round it, a fringe of palm trees growing about their base. The Arabs pointed out a place in the rocks, on the other side of the morass, in which they said the ruins of a castle were to be seen. Now this, like the other spots of the same nature which I passed through, is uninhabited. The largest and prettiest of these is Caicab, twelve hours further on. Here the rocks of variegated limestone assume a bolder appearance, rising from forty to a hundred feet in fantastic masses, looking in the distance sometimes like noble cities, sometimes like extensive ruins. There is one valley where columns, with their capitals of gigantic proportions, rise from mounds of sand—half buried palaces and temples seemed in the moonlight to make the former the abode of giants. From the uniform abruptness of the sides of the rocks, though weather-worn and varied in colour by the different strata, it would seem that these morasses had been formed by a suddenly falling in of the crust; for the flat tops of all the surrounding rocks have the same level with the desert and with each other, and the wall of rock is only found on the side turned to the morass. In a Wady some twelve hours further on I found wells of a clear water, in very small quantity, but which, after the first draught had been taken from it, filled again by rapid infiltration from the sand, but this second supply had a strong sulphurous smell and taste, which were not perceptible in the first. The morass, the universal feature of these oases, was here a wide lake of a deep blue, inclosed in a ring of brown crust, overgrown with rushes, and a tall, rank grass, of which the camels eagerly plucked the flowering tops. The name of this place is El Ghazalieh, the Gazelle Ground, and though now deserted, it must in ancient times have been inhabited. Sepulchral chambers, entirely devoid of ornament, but well and regularly cut, are

hollowed out in the faces of the rocks. Each open-
ing, of about four feet square, corresponds to a cubical
aperture of seven feet, in two sides of which—in that
facing the door, and in that generally to the left—are
cut receptacles for the dead. I counted twenty-three;
but there may be many more, which, being sanded up,
escaped my observation. Most of them are as empty
as if they had never been occupied; but in some of
these deserted abodes of death the wild bee has stored
her sweets. We made a long halt in this place, for
the camels had to be watered, and I had to dress as
well as to breakfast, for the guide having lost his way,
we had gone supperless to bed, being unprovided with
either wood or water. This had twice occurred to me,
and each time I had promised myself never again to
be without at least one skin of water; but though my
orders were no doubt attended to during the first few
days, it always happened that, when the precaution
would have proved useful, it had been neglected. In
my luggage I had wherewithal to supply every defi-
ciency but this; and the want of this, however little
I care for the pure fluid, is fatal to all hopes of sup-
ping.

This was the last day before reaching Siwah; and,
again, I was sadly delayed through the miserable condition of the camels supplied by my rascally sheikh
of Angila. One after another they dropped, unable

to proceed, and I was obliged to leave them, and the boxes they carried, in the sand. Unable to get further, we slept on a hill, at whose foot I beheld next morning a garden-like expanse—a real island of the blest. A stream, the first running water I had seen since quitting the Rhone, flowed down its centre; the ground on either side was green with young crops, among which rose clumps of date-trees and flowering mimosas. Some cabins dotted the extensive plain, and men and children were busily employed in irrigating the fields; the very water, perfectly sweet, after the thirst-exciting draughts to which we had been for some time condemned, seemed delicious; and, perhaps, by contrast with the barren sand we had so tediously journeyed through, this valley, towards Moragah, مراقة, seemed one of the loveliest spots I had ever visited. I welcomed the exhilarating impression which it made upon me, as a foretaste of the enjoyment reserved for me in Siwah, from which we were now only six hours distant, and I began to believe my Majabra guide might not be wrong in his daily assurances that it was a Belad Mabruk, an abode of blessedness.

After leaving Moragah, the loose sand again reappears for about an hour, leading to the lofty rocks of Kamisah, at whose base are the ruins called 'Amudein, which consist of two lofty masses of brick

work, the façade of a temple, or perhaps of a church,
for the style of building betrays a late date.   One of
the two salt lakes of the oasis lies at the foot of Kamisah, and I stopped for an hour at a well of sweet
water which springs at its edge, to rest the last of
Othman's camels, which here threatened to drop.   The
hill of the mummies, Garah-el-Musabberin, and the
village of Gharmy, where the principal ruins are, were
visible from here, as well as the position, though not
the town, of Siwah.   I sent on the camels, retaining
only one servant with me; soon following them, I
found that one of the camels had again lagged behind
the others.   I therefore stopped, and spreading a carpet in the shade of a tree, I sat down, having first
sent a servant into the town to Sheikh Yusuf, whom
my slave-dealer acquaintance had named to me as the
chief man of the place, to obtain donkeys to transport the luggage of the camel.   Here I sat alone for
two hours, until the sun had set, and began at length
to reflect on the uncertainty of Arab accounts of distances; the town might still be two or three hours off,
and with a strong determination to dine to-night, having been on short commons for the last four days, I
left the camel where it was, and rode towards the
town.   Night closed in before I had come upon any
well-marked path, and I was beginning to feel some

perplexity as to the road, when I luckily came upon the servant I had dispatched to Yusuf's, and one of the men who accompanied him turned to guide me to my tent, while he went back to bring up the remainder of the luggage.

CHAPTER XVII.

IT was soon perfectly night; the ground seemed to be cut up with ditches, and it was only by keeping close to my guide, as he trotted along on his donkey, that I could make out the road. After about half an hour, the guide jumping off his donkey, said to me, " Now you are going up hill," and before I knew what I was doing, unable to see an inch before me in the darkness, I found my horse clambering up what seemed to be the face of a precipice; in about five minutes more, I found myself riding among walls; presently, my guide stopping, began to call out, " Yusuf! Yusuf! " and thus I found that instead of taking me to my tent, he had brought me to the sheikh's. After some delay a door was opened; and a longer time elapsed before a flaring palm-branch was brought to light me;

and then I was conducted, through all sorts of tortuous passages to a small room, where the sheikh and
two young men were seated on mats, before a blazing
fire of olive wood.   He received me very cordially,
told me that my tents were ready, and that whatever I
required I should get through him.   I thanked him
and accepted his offers, giving him at the same time
to understand, that I would take nothing as a present, and that all I required should be paid for.   He
said that the servant I had sent to him had already
told him this.

These preliminaries being settled, there was a pause,
which he broke after looking steadily at my head for
some time, by saying, " Where's your hat ?"   I
thought I had misunderstood, and begged he would
favour me by repeating his remark.   He gravely re-
iterated, " Where's your hat ?"   After the hearty fit
of laughter which so droll a question as this seemed
to me produced, I told him that, for the moment, I
did not keep such an elegant luxury in my establishment; but this seemed to puzzle him sorely, for a hat
was evidently, in his eyes, one of the chief articles of
the Christian faith.   " Have you brandy, wine, ro-
solio, tea ?"   I began to think that he was making a
mental inventory of the good things he meant to ask
for, though I afterwards found it was mere curiosity to
find out whether I was as abundantly supplied with

these good things, as were my last predecessors at Siwah.

This cross-examination began to tire me, so I took leave of him; but before I retired he invited me to return in the morning, promising then to provide me with a guide to see all the curiosities of Siwah. I promised to come early, but explained that by early I did not mean early as he understood it, for, when not travelling, I do not rise till two hours after the sun. "Oh!" he answered, "drunk with araki;" meaning, that I lay in bed to sleep off the effects of the intemperance he gave me credit for; when I assured him that I had never in my life been drunk. "Do you, then, never drink wine or araki?" seemed to be the only solution for the wonder which his experience could suggest. We parted very good friends, and I proceeded to my tent. The night was still too dark for anything but the fires to be visible, and it was only the next morning that I obtained an idea of our position.

I was encamped on a very wide plain to the south of the town; to the right was an extensive palm grove with a few clumps in front of the principal plantation, the nearest about a hundred yards off; behind and to the left rose some limestone rocks, and near them a square building, the castle, in which a garrison was formerly lodged. In front, the town rose like a lofty fortress, built on a conical rock, entirely concealed by the houses, which, joining one another, seem to form a single many-storied edifice. To the west of this, another rock or gara, quarried with numerous caverns, rises to a considerable height; on one side of the rock, and in the space between it and the town proper, houses, in the ordinary style of mud architecture, are built.

It was here that Yusuf's house, the largest in the place, was built, leaning against the hill, and I now proceeded there to obtain the guide he had promised me. I was received in a room open to the street, in which a large crowd was assembled. Yusuf immediately began, in a tone very different to that of the preceding evening, to tell me the old story: that the people did not choose that I should enter their town, or see their wells, which my incantations might dry up, and that they insisted upon my immediate departure. In the room, seated round the walls, were several stupid-looking men, who, he told me, were the sheikhs of the place, over whom he had no authority—his influence being confined to that part of the rock which he inhabited, since his deposition some years before. He tried hard to render the decision of the town council (the Mejlis) palatable to me by frequent assurances, that the Siwyah have no sense. " No sense ! no sense !" he shouted into my ears, as if I had been deaf. "They must learn sense, or buy it," was my answer, "for since I am come here, you cannot treat me in this way; it is contrary to the rights of hospitality and the laws of your country. I am an Englishman. There is my passport, the English sultan's firman, better than 'Abd el Mejid's or any other in the world, more respected by Abbas Pacha and 'Abd el Mejid himself than their own. I ask to enter no man's house. I shall not run away with your wives, nor eat your children; but I have a right to go by every public path; to see all I want to see of the old ruins in your country; and if you, the sheikhs, prevent me, you must be prepared to take the consequences; and if any one insults or molests me, he has only himself to blame for what may happen to him."

I had gone unarmed, but I now sent down to my tent for a pair of revolvers, and after making Yusuf admire their construction, I had them placed in the holsters of my saddle. "You ask me what is my business here? I am a traveller from the west going to Cairo, through the Sultan's and Pacha's dominions; you are their subjects. Your own laws, the laws of Islam, give me full right to travel in your country; the treaties with the Sultan guarantee me protection; you are responsible to the Pacha, and he must answer to my country for anything that befals me here." I now mounted my horse and was riding away, when the

Mufti arrived, and I returned, at Yusuf's earnest request, to explain myself to him. He was an irresolute,
shuffling old man, apparently afraid to speak above a
whisper, but unable to deny the truth of what I said.
Yusuf then returned to the charge with shouts of "No
sense! no sense!" in which he was joined by all the
sheikhs, who pretended to lament the ignorance and
stupidity of their rayahs, while the Mufti seemed very
anxious to get me into a religious discussion, which I
was not foolish enough to engage in. By this time
the room was pretty full, all the great men of the
place, excepting two of the sheikhs and the Cadi, who
had refused to pollute their eyes with the sight of the
Christian, being assembled there. The street also in
front was crowded with the curious, who stared as if
they never could see enough of me; but they did not
interrupt the discussion.

Seeing that the plea of stupidity did not turn me
from my point, they now changed their tone; and one
of them, whose insolent air had from the first been
very offensive, gave me to understand that I could not
be allowed to defile their blessed country with my presence, and that the best thing I could do would be to
return quietly to my tent, shut myself up there, and
get camels as quickly as possible to pursue my journey. "Four hawajahs came here from Alexandria
some years ago, we fired upon them, after forbidding

our people to have any intercourse with them, and
they went away next morning, vowing vengeance indeed, but nothing came of it." " I am not a hawajah,
and I do not mean to run away ;" then, turning to the
Mufti, I added, "nor will there, I am sure, be any
reason for me to do so. I only want to see the old
ruins of your country, and then, without having done
injury to any one, I shall pursue my journey." So we
bandied about the same arguments for at least three
hours, when at last it was agreed that before going to
Omen Beydah I should wait till midday next day to
give them time to persuade their people not to molest
me ; and that my time might not be lost, Yusuf was
to send me in the morning a man to accompany me to
a hot well near the high hill, which lies to the south of
the town. I had now no doubt that I had carried my
point, and returned to dine in great spirits, persuaded
that I had vanquished the opposition, trusting to the
well-known timidity and gentleness of the Egyptian
Fellah, and the activity Mehemet Ali had always displayed in punishing violence offered to travellers. I
found my cook, a black, whom I had brought with me
from Dernah, in a terrible fright, for some of the
people had told him, when he went into the town to
buy some provisions, that they were coming to rob me
during the night. I laughed at his fears, quoting to
him the saying, ' Forewarned, forearmed.'

After dinner, I was smoking my chibouque and marking in my note-book the little I had observed or heard during the day, when three shots were fired, the balls passing with a loud whistling through my tent just over my head. At first I thought little of the incident, believing that it was a rough joke meant to frighten me; so I merely looked at my watch and noted the circumstance in my note-book. It was perfectly dark, and from the door of my tent nothing was visible, nor should I have thought more of it but for the violent barking of my dog, which showed that it heard people, who were invisible to me. I sent a servant, therefore, to Yusuf's to acquaint him with what had passed, and soon after he was gone, the firing recommenced. I now began to think the affair more serious than I had supposed; I heard one gun hang fire close to my tent, and, turning, saw its muzzle pressed against the wall of the tent on the shadow of my head; I therefore had all the lights put out, and went cautiously out to get a view of my assailants. The night was so black that this was impossible, but it also favoured my evasion; after counting eleven volleys, which gave me grounds to suspect that there was a numerous body of men in the date-trees to the right, I, with my servant, went up to the sheikh Yusuf's house, abandoning the tents to their fate. Moving cautiously across the plain, which separated us from

the town, and climbing the steep street which led to
his house, we could still see the fire of the enemy's
guns, and the more frequent flashes in the pan, to
which we probably owed our escape.

The servant whom I had sent there had returned,
saying that he could not make himself heard at
Yusuf's, but when we reached the door a vigorous
application of the butt-end of my rifle roused him;
having admitted me, I told him what had happened,
adding, that I should stay with him till morning.
He immediately sent some of his people to protect
the tents, which they found had not been entered,
though there were seven shots in the one in which I
had passed the day, and one shot had passed immediately over the place where I was reclining when the
attack commenced; had I been sitting up instead of
lounging, it could not have missed me. By one of
those strange chances which one feels to be provi-
dential, I had just after sunset ordered a larger tent
to be pitched, in which to dine and sleep; I had been
all the morning in a small umbrella one, at which the
shots were principally aimed, and to this circumstance
must my escape be ascribed.

I spent the night in Yusuf's house, and the next
day he gave me a small one, containing three rooms,
opposite his own, in which to stay as long as might

be necessary. One of these rooms was built on the roof, with a sort of terrace before it; we were standing upon this, after viewing my intended abode, when our attention was attracted to a large body of, perhaps, four or five hundred men, most of them armed, who were in march with a flag, and several camels against my tents. The rumour had been spread in the town that the Christian was not dead, and the entire male population of the Lifayah had gone against him, with camels to carry off the spoil. They found the tents closed, and no appearance of any one near them, but they thought I and my Frank servant were inside. It was long before they ventured to approach, for the camel men, who had come with me from Angila, had given a wonderful description of the number and power of my arms; at last, some bolder than the rest, went up and tore aside the curtain of the umbrella tent in which I was supposed to be. Meanwhile, Yusuf had sent for some of the sheikhs, and assuring them that anything stolen would have to be replaced ten-fold by the town, he induced them to go to the rescue of my baggage. This they succeeded in effecting, and returned in a few hours to tell me that everything was safe, and to ask for a certificate to that effect. I refused to take their word for it, and at their urgent solicitation, accompanied by them, I

rode down to the plain, which was now quite solitary.
Everything was in strange confusion, but nothing had
been taken away.

Seeing the turn things had taken, I now determined
to continue my journey at once, promising myself to
return to Siwah with an escort from the Viceroy, as
soon as I should arrive in Egypt. But if the Sewiyah
had given me so warm a reception, they had no wish
to lose the advantage of my company; and, therefore, by threats prevented any of the Arabs, of whom
great numbers were now in Siwah, from hiring me
camels. I then proposed to Yusuf to leave my baggage in his charge, if he would procure me a sufficient
number of donkeys to mount my servants, and carry
a few skins of water and provisions; but he declared
that, without camels, it was impossible to cross the
desert, and that if I attempted to get away at the present moment, the people would follow and massacre
my servants and myself on the road. I waited, therefore, a day or two to see what would turn up, nothing
doubting that rather than keep the Christian in their
town, these zealous Moslemin would in a day or two
come to terms. In fact, on the third day of my im-
prisonment, three of the sheikhs came and offered me
camels to go away with, but just before this the Mufti
had sent privately to warn me, that if I accepted the

offer, my caravan would be waylaid a few hours out of the oasis.

I now wrote to Her Majesty's Consul-General in Cairo, acquainting him with the position I was in, and requesting assistance, and Yusuf dispatched my letter by one of his slaves, who was familiar with the country he had to traverse. I had previously endea- voured to persuade a Bedawy to be my messenger, but after bargaining for an exorbitant remuneration, he lost courage and refused to take it. When, how- ever, on the second day afterwards, he missed the slave, he did not doubt I had sent him to Cairo ; and now, regretting the money he might have gained, he revenged himself by telling the people that I had sent to bring soldiers. On this the Mejlis assembled to deliberate ; their first proceeding was to come to Yusuf, to ask if it were true that I had written to his High- ness. He answered that he could tell them nothing about it, and that they had better apply to me. The three who had rescued the baggage, now, therefore, presented themselves, and at Yusuf's request I ad- mitted them. In answer to their questions I said that I was no way bound to satisfy their curiosity, but that being a good-natured fellow, and my messenger by this time a long way on his road, I consented to gra- tify them. I had, indeed, written to tell how I had

been attacked, and how I was imprisoned by them in
Sheikh Yusuf's house, and that I had added, I should
now stay there till an answer was sent to me.

For the first fortnight that I was shut up in the
cabin Yusuf had given me, though unable to stir out,
I found the time passed quickly enough, as, besides
that Yusuf and the people of his clan came often to
see me (so that my house was generally full), there
was every day something exciting, which afforded
amusement.   One evening, for instance, some shots
were fired into my house, probably by way of keeping
me on the *qui vive* rather than with any murderous
intention; another day, the whole of the Lifayah assembled in arms, at the small village called the Man-
shieh, determined at night to march upon my house,
and so end the matter.   They were resolved to get rid
of the Christian; and to encourage themselves in their
warlike resolutions, many of them bound themselves
" by the divorce," to exterminate him, and the big
war-drum was put out into the sun to stretch the skin,
and give it a terror-inspiring tone.   Next, a deputa-
tion of the sheikhs came to me to offer peace and
friendship, if I would only go away and tell the Pacha
that I had nothing to complain of.   I explained to
them with infinite suavity, that this was out of the
question.   How could I say that I had nothing to
complain of? beside this, my letter must be already

in Cairo, and having said in it that I should wait for an answer, I could not, of course, go away till it came. I also reminded them of their own frequent protestations, that they had no authority over the people, and asked what security they could offer me that I should not be attacked, as once intended, on the journey. Negotiation proving ineffectual, they tried a new dodge. Yusuf was cited before the Mejlis to answer for harbouring a Christian, and men were posted in the narrow dark streets of the town to kill him as he went, but the Mufti again sent him warning of the plot, which Yusuf the more readily gave credence to, as his father had been killed in this way.

Then again a fresh attack with arms was planned for the evening, and this seemed so menacing that Yusuf put garrisons into the largest houses in my neighbourhood, and came himself, with ten men, to aid in defending mine. I was luckily well provided with arms, and disposed everything to make what would probably have been a successful resistance. At the advice of one of the principal men of the place, and to prevent the chance of firing on our own friends in the dark, the garrison was withdrawn from the surrounding houses; their presence there, in case of a *melée*, would, I confess, have been more alarming to me than the attack from below, and being marched to the foot of the Garah, with much screaming but fortunately no bloodshed, they repulsed the Lifayah, who turned backwards when they found preparations made to receive them.   After this night there was a regular patrol established in this part of the town.

One evening, just before sunset, when seated with Yusuf on the roof of my dwelling, four men, with guns, were seen on the rock which overhangs the house.   They were observed just as they were creeping round a corner, by a servant who was bringing a chibouque, our backs being turned to them ; a cry was immediately raised, people were dispatched to arrest them, and two were secured, the others escaping. Yusuf had no power to do anything with them, he being, in fact, as much a prisoner as myself; and was fain to accept their explanation, that they had come to shoot crows, in order to obtain their galls, with which to anoint the eyes of some one who had an ophthalmia.

Other trivial annoyances, many of them so childish as to be merely amusing, were with great ingenuity resorted to.   The little children used to assemble round my house, calling out, " Oh, Consul, there is no God but God ! " and singing songs which I suspect were not altogether complimentary.   Nosrani and Consul were the names I was known by among the people when they spoke of me to one another.   I had declined the latter title, to which I had no pretension ;

and would not be called Hawadjah, which is the polite
name generally given to Franks in Egypt, even by
the Government, in its correspondence with the foreign Consuls, and which means a small trader or
pedlar; Yusuf, therefore, gave me the title of El
Senhor, which I have retained to this day.   The
people were forbidden to sell me anything, and it was
with no small difficulty that Yusuf procured for me
the very meagre fare with which I was fain to be satisfied ; a couple of tame fowls, some rice or lentils,
butter and dates, were the provision for four persons;
and this scanty supply cost, on an average, more than
a guinea a-day.   One of the wealthier people sold me
a goose one day, for which he was cited before the
Mejlis, and beaten, though his brother was one of the
sheikhs.

Time wore on, and the twentieth day, on which I
expected an answer to my letter would arrive, had
come and gone.   Some Arabs from the west brought
a report that the Viceroy had been murdered, and
some of the sheikhs did not fail to come to me the
next day to see how I took the news.   Of course, I
made light of it, telling them that if Abbas were dead,
Said would be Viceroy, and that the English Government, which does not die, would take as good care of
me under the one as under the other.   When, however, a second report to the same effect arrived, a few

days afterwards, I acknowledge that I felt less un-
concern than I cared to show, for such an event, if
true, would have probably prolonged my detention, if
it did not endanger my life and that of my protector
Yusuf, and my servants.

The time which I had calculated would bring an
answer to my letters (for I had found means to send a
second letter on the chance of the first having mis-
carried) had long past; and I had no easy task to
keep Yusuf and his friends in good spirits.   They
were becoming very uneasy, for they had committed
themselves both to the Egyptian government and the
Sewiyah; the first would render them responsible for
my safety, the second would never forgive the protection afforded to the Christian.   At length, one day,
a hot south wind arose, and blew with great violence
during that and the three following days; hereon a
hundred and forty of the men, who felt themselves
most guilty, left Siwah for the Arab encampments on
the Okbah; for now they believed, most of them for
the first time, that something would come of my complaint, as a hot south wind in Siwah, such as this, is
regarded by them as the unfailing signal of some
coming calamity.   One is almost tempted to think
they must be a remnant of the Psylli, who had
escaped the general destruction of their nation, and
still dread their old enemy.   Yusuf's adjurations and

threats had had no effect in persuading them that they would rue their inhospitable conduct to a stranger, but this day of hot wind convinced them that what he said was true.

From this time forward there were constant applications from the sheikhs and principal people of the Lifayah, to see the Nosrani; and those whom I admitted, came to protest that they had taken no part in anything that had befallen me, charitably throwing the blame on the others. Each, in fact, was the only innocent man in the place; and all felt the tenderest affection for my person. Such evidences of esteem and consideration were, of course, most gratifying to my feelings, and made me the more regret that they had put it out of my power to be serviceable to them; having applied to the English Consul-General, and he, of course, to the Viceroy, any decision in the matter now depended, not on me, but on them.

Such scenes were not, however, my only amusements. During the day I picked up some scraps of information about the manners and superstitions of the country from my various visitors. From a Fezyan Fikhi I got some quaint lessons in theological lore; and from a Moghrabi treasure-seeker I heard a good deal of the excavations which he had at different times made, not, however, to seek the antiquities which he seems to have found, but the hidden wealth,

which, judging from his appearance, I should say had
escaped him. Every evening after dinner, Sheikh Yusuf
and a dozen of his friends used to come, and sit with
me for two or three hours. Their favourite conversation turned upon the wickedness of the Lifayah,
whom they seemed to regard as the greatest monsters
in the world; my guests would tell how they had
beaten their last governor, and killed Yusuf's father,
and how they fired upon travellers. Then they would
expatiate with monkey-like chuckling on the exaspe-
ration which their conduct would produce in the
Pacha; what he would do to this one, what to that—
all subjects which my friends wore threadbare, without ever seeming to tire of them. Sometimes the
entertainment was varied by stories which Yusuf told
with great native humour; or we killed time and tried
to satisfy our impatience by practising the method of
divination called Derb-er-raml.

The stories I will spare the reader, who has had
enough of Arab tales in every shape, though I am
sadly tempted to tell how the two little donkeys were
welded into a big one, or how the ass stuck in the
mud, and the hyæna ate him, notwithstanding his
long horns.

The inhabitants of Siwah speak a dialect of the
Berbery, and only a very few of them know any word

of Arabic; they are unquestionably an Aboriginal people, probably the descendants of one of the No-mad tribes, who inhabited the interior of Libya, and who may have succeeded to the possession of the Oasis of Ammon, after the extinction of the Roman power in this country. The entire population con-sists of the inhabitants of Siwah Proper, which is divided into east and west, and those of Agharmy, a small town about two miles to the east, in all little more than four thousand souls. The inhabitants of the eastern part of the town, my enemies, are called Sharkyin, or Lifayah, and these are again subdivided into three clans. The Westerns or Gharbyin are, in the same way, composed of three clans, and each clan has two sheikhs; these, with the Mufti and Cadi, form the Mejlis, presided over until his deposition by Yusuf as Sheikh-el-Beled. Their own account of their ori-gin is, that, excepting three families of the old race, whose genealogy goes back to the remotest times, the whole of them are Arabs, Moghrabin, or Fellahs; none of whom have been settled here for more than four generations. Judging from their features, I should think that there must be a much greater mix-ture of the blood of an older race; nor is it likely, if Arabic had been the original language of the im-mense majority, that it should be now only known to

so few persons, after this short lapse of time.   Of the
women there is hardly one who understands anything
but the Siwy Berbery.

They are a singularly ugly race, with dark-brown
complexion, and a truly bestial expression, but with
no trace of the negro type, while they are still further removed from the Arab and Copt.   Their fierce
disposition makes them dreaded by the Arabs, who
come to Siwah to buy dates, and who are subjected
during their stay there to a most rigorous police.
Those of the women whom I saw through my telescope on the roofs of the houses, were not more
agreeable in appearance than the men; and even
childhood is here devoid of the engaging graces of
its age.

The dress of the men is a long shirt with drawers;
a skull-cap of cotton, to which a milaya, such as is
worn by the Egyptian women, is added.   The head-
dress of the women is curious.   The front hair is
plaited into twelve small braids, which hang straight
over the forehead; on each side is a similar short
bunch, looking like nothing but the cords of a mop,
and round the head are wound two long plaits brought
from behind.   Over this the milaya is thrown, and a
dark blue shirt completes the costume.   They are
kept very strictly confined to the house, which the
wealthier never leave, and no respectable woman goes

out excepting at night. These precautions of the
Siwy are said to be as efficacious as those of the Djin,
who kept his lady-love in a box ; and the moral character of the Siwah fair is such, that had he reigned
here, Pheron would probably never have recovered his
eye-sight.

The men are notoriously bad, at the same time that
they are among the most fanatical Moslemin in Africa.
In fact, I had good reason to believe correct what was
said to me of them :—" Every vice and every indul-
gence is lawful (Hellal) to the Siwy.   Nothing is forbidden to them (Haram), but the presence of a Christian."   They are divided into two schools, the followers of the Sunūsy, of whom I shall have to speak
later, and the Dirkawy, the ranters of Islam, who derive their origin from a celebrated sheikh of Masrata,
who died a hundred years ago.   Between the two
orders the same affection seems to exist as fable attri-
butes to the Jesuits and Dominicans in Christendom.

The Siwy are superstitious, though, perhaps, not
more so than the ignorant masses in all countries ;
nearly all the men have amulets sewed to their caps,
or hung round their necks ; every house is defended
from the evil eye by an earthen pot well blackened in
the fire, which is built mouth downwards over the
doorway, or at one corner ; and in addition to this
charm, it is not uncommon to see the leg bones of an

ass projecting from some part of the building: this struck me particularly, as this use of it was once a superstitious practice in England. This and similar practices were forbidden by the Council of London, held about the year 1075.

After saying so much in dispraise of the Siwy, I must add that, compared with the people of Jalo and Angila, they are an industrious race, paying great attention to the cultivation of their palms and olive-trees, which they manure and tend with infinite care. A great part of the soil is capable of producing grain, and they possess extensive corn-fields; these being cultivated entirely with the spade, demand much la-bour; the consequence of which is, that the small population is unable to bring even the near-lying grounds completely under crop. From this cause several fertile oases dependent on Siwah are now abandoned. Interspersed among their palm-groves they have abundance of vines, apricots, and pome-granates, whose sweet though small fruit they pre-serve all the winter. To manure their trees they employ a thorny plant, which grows in great quanti-ties in Maragah, called 'agul. This they collect and bind into large bundles, three of which form a donkey load; then, digging pits round the trees, they bury these bundles in them, after which they water them regularly once in six days. All caravans coming to Siwah are obliged to put up in a particular place, and the manure thus collected, along with the produce of the 'agul grounds, is sold every year by auction for the benefit of the community.

CHAPTER XVIII.

ONE of my first visitors was the Moghrabi from Tan-
giers, already mentioned, called El Gibely, who has
been settled here for many years. He was a perfect
specimen of this class of adventurers; pretending to
have a familiar spirit, a djin who waits upon him, and
tells him the secrets of futurity. He wrote charms to
discover treasures, and to cure all manner of diseases,
and I almost think had ended by believing in them
himself. The day after I was shut up in Yusuf's
house he took an opportunity of vaunting to me highly
the virtues of his amulets, particularly of one which
renders its possessor ball-proof. He fancied, probably,
that this was the moment to effect a profitable sale,
and I asked questions, and listened to him with a
grave attention which must have given him great

hopes. In this he overrated my credulity; but I repaid his communicativeness in kind, by describing to him the wonders of the electric telegraph, which I thought would astonish him; but in this I was in turn disappointed, as he listened to my accounts of instantaneous messages sent over land and sea, without expressing a doubt, or even asking how such wonders were performed. In fact, he already knew all about it —"It was the djin."

I one day sent for him to perform the often-talked-of miracle, or trick of the ink-spot in a child's hand. A young negro, about nine years old, was introduced, and the inscription on his forehead was written with all due ceremony, the seal was drawn in his hand, the coriander seed was burned under his nose, until the poor child's eyes ran with tears, and the fear he was in covered his forehead with big drops of sweat. After some time he saw a person in the ink-spot; he was then told to order him to bring another, whom he was not long in fancying he saw; but he then became quite wild, and neither the muttered surah, nor the repeated orders of the Moghrabi had any further effect. The child could see nothing more. I regarded the experiment with the most incredulous caution; and, though it certainly failed, I was not convinced that so-called animal magnetism would not

give an explanation of the phenomena, such as trust-
worthy Arabs have assured me they had themselves
seen.   Leo Africanus speaks of these conjurors with
the utmost contempt; and, I believe, all later Europeans who have written on the subject regard the proceeding as a gross trick; but in these countries it is
universally believed, even by men who laugh at the
usual apparatus of charms and amulets.   One of my
friends brought me a manuscript, which he had found
among the effects of a moghrabi who died here many
years ago, in which the whole process is explained; it
was essentially the same as that used by El Gibely,
who, probably to enhance the mystery of the proceeding in my eyes, added, besides the two lines which are
written on the forehead, a sort of star over the nose,
and inscriptions on each eyebrow.*

* How to make the Djin descend.

Write in the right palm of a boy or girl, below the age of
puberty, the seal which is here given, and fumigate with coriander
seed, which among the Djin are counted apples, and conjure them
with the Surah "and the Sun" to the end, until they come down.
Then ask them what you desire to know, and they will answer you
with the permission of God (be he exalted!) ; and this is what you
write on the forehead of the child :—

فكشفنا عنك عطاك
فبصرك اليوم صاحي

And then you write the seal, and in the midst of it make a spot of
ink; and when you wish to dismiss the kings, conjure them with

Having spoken at such length of the art of making
" the Djin descend into a child's hand," I may complete
my confession of the black arts which I learned here,
by describing the process of divination called " Derb
er raml," or "Derb el ful," according to the medium
used, whether it is sand or beans; the latter (with the
beans) is the simplest, but both are in principle the
same. Seven beans are held in the palm of the left
hand, which is struck with a smart blow with the right
half-closed fist, so that some of the beans jump into

the verse of the throne, and they will depart by permission of
God. This is the seal as you see it here, and there is no power
and no strength but in God.

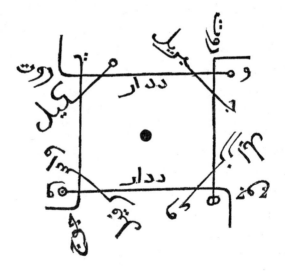

the right hand—if an odd number, one is marked; if even, two. The beans are replaced in the left hand, which is again struck with the right, and the result marked below the first. This being repeated four times gives the first figure, and the operation is performed until there are obtained four figures, which are placed side by side in a square; these are then read vertically and perpendicularly, and also from corner to corner, thus giving in all ten figures. As each may contain four odd or four even numbers, they are capable of sixteen permutations, each of which has a separate signification, and a proper *house* or part of the square in which it should appear. The Derb er-raml is only distinguished from this by being more complicated, fresh combinations being obtained by the addition of every pair of figures. There is a large work on this subject by El-Zenāty, and another called 'Omdat-et-Taleb.

One day the Gibely came to me in all his Friday gaiety of attire, " perfumed like a milliner," his eyes broadly painted with kohl. We had a long discussion on the earth and its form, and the great sea which surrounds it, and jebel kaf which bounds it, and the seven climates, and the seven heavens, for whose existence he quoted the words of Him whose name be exalted! in the Koran. I demurred to some of his theories, and treated jebel kaf and the seven climates

as at least old-fashioned—with the heavens, may they
never be fewer ! I did not interfere ; but even with the
aid of such maps as I had at hand, I could not, of
course, hope to make my very modern notion of the
world's form perfectly intelligible.   From this we
passed, by an easy transition (arising, I think, from
his assertion that Mecca is the centre of the world), to
the subject of natural and supernatural knowledge,
and thence to miracles.   Reason being as much opposed to the mysteries of faith as to a belief in occur-
rences out of the usual course of nature, it is difficult
to prescribe a term to the one without seeming to
doubt the other ; and I therefore, without entering
into explanations, was content to say, " It seems
strange, but God only knows."   He himself pretended
to be able to travel from here to Benghazi and Derna,
in summer, through the parched desert, alone, without
water or wallet, and to want for nothing—an assertion
he has often made to me, as of a thing notorious to
all in Siwah, ascribing the gift at one time to his
attendant djin, at another to the Sheikh Senusi.   To-
day, I suppose because it was Friday, the living saint
had the credit of the prodigy.   The Senusi, of whom
I have had so often occasion to speak, is the founder
of the largest religious brotherhood at present existing
in Africa, its ramifications extending from Morocco to
the Hedjay.   He is a native of Mostaghánem, was

educated in Fez, and now resides in Mecca, where he
has beside his house a large zavia. He is about sixty-
five years old, and from the immense influence which
he has acquired it may fairly be supposed that he is a
man of no ordinary talents. He is a sherif of good
family, and the donations of pious pilgrims have rendered his zavias (convents) very wealthy. The members of these convents, after having completed their
studies, are allowed to marry, and without practising
any great austerities they are very strict Moslemin.
In imitation of the Prophet they say fifty rika'ats in
the twenty-four hours, five of which are said at midnight; they fast, in addition to Ramazan, on certain
days in the months of Sha'aban, Hedjib, and Zil
Hidjih, and abstain from smoking and drinking coffee,
tea being their usual beverage. They seem less fanatical than the general mass of Arabs ; although their
founder is a native of Algiers, he professes, though
perhaps only from policy, a particular esteem for the
English, and I believe I had, very unworthily, the
benefit of this partiality. From one of the disciples
of the sheikh I learned a point in our national history
which was new to me. When the Prophet died, the
English were on the point of becoming true believers,
but, learning his death, they determined to remain as
they were ; they made, however, a treaty with Abou
Behr, by which it was agreed, that though they

continued Christians, there should be perpetual amity
between them and the Caliph.

The Senusi is represented to me as all that an Arab
saint should be—exact in the observances of religion,
gay, and a capital shot; he rides a horse of the purest
breed and of great value, dresses magnificently, paints
his eyes with kohl and his beard with henna.   He is
very hospitable, and if the Gibely may be believed,
has a granary which the large daily drafts he makes
on it never empty; receiving nothing from any one,
he has always money; and a hundred, or even two
hundred, persons eat from his dish of cuscusu, which
miraculously suffices for them all.   The Senusi seems
a man respectable for his talents and probity, though
from the above history of him it may be supposed that
he takes advantage of the veneration of his disciples to
impose on their credulity.   In the eyes of my Moghrabi friend, however, he is not the only living thau-
maturge in Islam; for there are, he asserts, many
individuals in Morocco, some of whom he knows
personally, who pray every day at Mecca, and he told
of one who, no saint himself, owed this favour to the
sheikh he served.   The event happened in Tunis.
The servant wished to go on the pilgrimage, but from
day to day his master dissuaded him, saying, "There
is time, wait yet a little."   Thus passed the months;
the festival was approaching, and still the sheikh an-

swered, " You shall make this year's pilgrimage, but
there is still time." At length the ninth of Til Hidj
came, the very day of the sermon on Mount Arafat,
when, about mid-day, the sheikh called him, and said,
" Shut your eyes," and " now open them." He obeyed,
and found himself with a multitude of people at Mount
Arafat. He performed with them the ceremonies of
the pilgrimage, joining in the processional prayers,
and after this spoke to many of his Tunisian acquaintance. He said he should return before them, and
offered to carry letters, many of which, sealed with
their seals, and referring to their children and family
affairs, were given to him. His master, who was with
him all this time, then said, " Shut your eyes," and in
an instant he found himself again in Tunis, with his
letters. He delivered them the next day; but, notwithstanding the evidence of the seals and the contents,
the people, seeing the date, said, " He is an impostor."
" Wait," was the answer, " till the return of the Hadj."
Meantime, at Arafat, his countrymen looked for him,
and not seeing him, said among themselves, " He is
gone back before us to Mecca;" but when after months
they returned home, and each recognising his own
letter asserted that he had sent it from Arafat, and had
seen the bearer there, the people were convinced of the
miracle.

Miracles performed by mad saints are not less firmly believed by my friend. There is such an one at Damanhur, and I had myself the pleasure of seeing him when there, who, clothed in the costume of Sultan Adam when he left the hands of his Creator, is building a mosque at Tunis. He goes every day to the Nile, and throws stones into it, which are at the same moment conveyed to Tunis, and arrange themselves in proper architectural design. He told of another at Tripoli, whose aid the crew of a ship at sea invoked in a storm, promising him a recompense if saved. He was at that moment in the bazaar; a man riding on a donkey was passing him, when he jumped up, as if possessed, from the stall he was sitting on, knocked the man from his seat, and ——. I should have continued the story in Arabic (my oracular tongue furnishing no terms in which to relate it), but I refrain, as the learned who could decipher the Arabic are probably sufficiently good Oriental scholars to fill up the blank in my narration. At this moment, said the truthful historian, he appeared to the mariners, and when, two days afterwards, the ship entered the port, the saint presented himself to claim his recompense. But the devil was no longer sick, and the sheikh's salvage dues were now denied him. All the people, however, testified that the scene with the donkey in

the market took place at the hour when his aid was
invoked, and, thus convicted, the promised reward was
given.

I might fill a volume with such strange tales, as the
treasure-seeker's visits are frequent; he had a well-
supplied budget, and he freely communicated its contents, in the hope of drawing me out in turn.   He
certainly thought I had private information about the
immense treasures which he believed buried here ; and
whatever the subject we were discussing, he always contrived to introduce in a corner of his talk, *in angulo
sui sermonis,* a question relating to them, or an inquiry as to the process of rendering quicksilver solid.
This was all that he was in need of to discover the
grand arcanum for turning the baser metals into gold
and silver.   Did he know the quicksilver secret he was
master of all the rest, and of acquiring this he did
not at all despair.   I told him that transmutation was a
dream long exploded among the learned ; but I offered
him the receipt how to make rubies and other precious
stones, only premising that the cost was greater than
the value of the newly-formed gem.

Having presented the Gibely to my readers, as a
good specimen of the fortune-seeking Moghrabi who
abound in the East, it would not be fair to omit some
account of Sheikh Yusuf—a much rarer character,
because really an honest man ; though the stories I am

going to tell of him, gathered from his own lips, may not seem to European readers to bear out the fair praise I give him. He is a very remarkable man, full of energy, and has made the best use of the education which an early initiation in affairs gives. He knows the letters of the alphabet, and this is probably the whole amount of his book learning; but his memory is well stored with texts of the Koran, verses of the poets, and those stories which are so pre-eminently an Oriental accomplishment, and which he related with a vivacity remarkable in this country of loutish stupidity. His father was Sheikh el Beled before him, and at thirteen he was also sheikh, giving his opinion freely, even against his father's views. When he was less than seventeen his father was murdered in open day, by some of the discontented Siwy, one of his own servants heading the conspiracy. Yusuf, thereupon, proceeded straight to Cairo, and was by Mohammed Ali appointed Sheikh el Beled in his room. The Pacha had given Siwah and the Little Oasis, with their revenues, as a backshish to one Hassan Bey, who had reduced them to his obedience; and the Sheikh told with gusto some stories of that time, which are too characteristic to be omitted here.

When his father went to the Proprietor-Governor, he used to take Yusuf with him, to make him acquainted with affairs; but only as a listener. One day in the date season, a large number of Arabs, with their camels, had come from the Okbar, or, as it is called here, the Gazelle-land, to purchase dates. Hassan Bey coveted his neighbours' camels, but was perplexed how to become master of them without injury to his purse, or incurring Mohammed Ali's anger. He consulted Sheikh Ali, who would give no advice, but only shook his head, and said, " Tyranny, tyranny." " I'll tell you what you should do," cried Yusuf, eagerly. " What shall I do, my child ? " " You shall buy them for fifteen dollars a-piece, and lose nothing by the transaction." He then explained his plan, which delighted the Bey ; but his father only shook his head the more, and oftener repeated, " Tyranny." " You, Sheikh Ali," said the Bey, " are a graybeard, and do not understand government. Sheikh Yusuf is young and brave, and I will follow his advice." The next day the Arabs were told that the Bey wanted to buy some of their camels, and that they must bring them to the castle in the afternoon. Accordingly, before evening, more than three hundred of the best camels were collected in the court ; and the Bey having ordered several sheep to be killed, invited the owners of the camels to sup with him. After supper, the bargain was struck for fifteen dollars a-piece, the Mufti and Cadi being called to witness the agreement, which was drawn out in writing. All parties affixed their seals, and the money was paid down at once. After this, the Mufti and Cadi rose to leave, and all were going to retire from the castle, when the Bey said to the Arabs, "You are my guests; you must stay here all night, and we will breakfast together in the morning." The bait was tempting to men who love animal food at the cost of their friends; and the foolish Arabs remained after the others had withdrawn. The next morning some more sheep were sacrificed to the genius of hospitality; the Arabs ate with their usual appetite, and took their departure; but, as they passed out of the gates, each was forced to restore the money he had received for his camels. Thus Hassan Bey purchased camels without their costing him anything.

On another occasion, Yusuf helped him to make a not less profitable speculation in oxen and cows. There were many defaulters to the miri; and his father and the Bey were in consultation as to the way to get from them their debt, or its equivalent. There were many cattle in Siwah at that time, and Sheikh Ali proposed to take them in payment, at ten dollars a-head, which was rather less than their value; but Yusuf said, "No; take them at forty dollars a-head, and follow my plan." "What is your plan?" "When the dates are gathered, return their oxen to the owners, making them buy them back at the original price, and take from them the amount of miri

that they owe in money."   At so large a price, every-
body was anxious to give his cows instead of the miri
and the Governor—good-natured soul!—gave them
credit for .forty dollars on each one that was offered ;
but sent the cattle back to their owners, saying he
would take them when wanted.   In October, there was
a plentiful date harvest, and the Bey was chuckling
over his intended finesse, when it occurred to him that
many of the cattle had died during the heats of summer.   He sent for Yusuf, to see if he could help him
out of this dilemma.   "To those whose cows are
alive, return them at the original price ; and as for the
others, it is but just they should refund you the forty
dollars which their oxen cost, as they have never
served you, but remained and died in their keeping."
Thus, by a truly Turkish calculation, the Bey bought
cows without paying for them, and sold them for ready
money to their original owners, who were then made
to pay their arrears of taxes, as if there had been no
question of cattle ; and who do not, perhaps, at this
hour understand how so fair a transaction resulted to
themselves in a clear loss of forty dollars on each of
their beeves.

His own father was once the object of Yusuf's practical pleasantries.   The town had rebelled, and the
ringleaders of the revolt were imprisoned in the castle.
Sheikh Ali received money from two of the worst, on

the promise of obtaining their liberty, and in the afternoon went to the Bey to intercede for them ; and being a favourite with the Governor, he easily procured an assurance that they should be liberated next morning.   Yusuf learned what had passed ; so, after supper, he set off alone for the castle, and asked admittance to the Bey.   " What brings you at this hour, my son ? " said he, after the first salutation.   " My father came here to-day to ask for the liberty of such and such a one.   Do you wish to know the exact truth ? "   " Certainly I do ; speak."   " Well, then, know that, in truth, they are the worst men in Siwah ; but my father has taken a bribe to procure their pardon."   At this the Bey was very angry ; and, calling to the guard, he had the prisoners brought out and beheaded on the spot.   Yusuf returned home ; and, next morning, when he came to release them, his father found their headless bodies lying in the court.   " Of course," said I, " your father returned the money ? "   " To whom ? " said Yusuf.   " The men were dead ; and there was no one could say to my father, ' You took a bribe—return the money ! ' "

After telling these stories of my sheikh, it may seem incredible when I add that, though feared as a most severe man, he was acknowledged by all the Siwy never to have taken a bribe, or committed an act of oppression on his own account.   " If you do not do

such things for yourself," I said, " how can you com-
mit them for others ?" He answered that the Osmanli
only value a man as he serves them as an instrument
of extortion.

My long detention in Siwah must, by this time,
have become as wearisome to my reader as it was to
myself; let me hasten, then, to open my prison-doors,
and pursue my journey to its end.

On the 14th of March, exactly six weeks from my
arrival, about sunset, there came running to my house
some of my Siwy friends, crying " Backshish for good
news !" Two Arabs were to be seen in the distance,
who, soon after, arrived, and announced themselves
as two sheikhs, and very important and big-mouthed
personages they were. They were the avant-couriers
of the detachment of irregular cavalry (Bashi-buzuks),
whom the Viceroy of Egypt had sent to my assistance. One would have thought them the kings of
the world, from the airs they gave themselves, and the
monstrous lies they told ; and had I been less accustomed to the assumption of consequence in which
Arabs, and, indeed, all Easterns, indulge, until they
have received a good lesson, I should have been really
frightened at having to entertain such important gen-
tlemen. They came to demand rations for the men
and horses, which were to be furnished by the town ;

and, as a matter of course, ordered twice as much as was really required ; and, equally as a matter of course, hardly got, I believe, half of what they demanded. This contribution was, at my request, levied on the hostile part of the town, and my friends escaped unmolested. It was not until the 16th, in the morning, that my deliverers arrived, having come from Hhosh ebn Issa, near Damanhur, in nineteen days. They were commanded by a Turcoman, one Hassan Aga, the wahil, or major of the regiment, an easy-natured soul, somewhat sulky withal, as assuming as all Turks are, but only requiring to be held firmly in hand, and an assiduous sayer of his prayers.

Such a commander never was sent in charge of troops ; he had with him twelve or fourteen officers (Buluk-Bashi is their title), and every one of them seemed to think he had a voice in the command. All matters, of whatever nature they might be, were discussed in public, the very soldiers sometimes interfering with advice. Among banditti, such a republican constitution may sometimes exist ; but that the most irregular troops in the world could be kept together with such a system seemed impossible. The first day of their arrival, after having received the Commandant's visit, I went to the castle in which the troops were lodged, and made a formal request that he would seize the Sheikhs of the Lifayah, with the Cadi, and the Imam of one of the mosques, and carry them with him to Cairo, to answer before the Viceroy. He said he could not do so, having no orders, except to bring me away; to which I rejoined, that no doubt he was quite right; and that I had only to beg a written acknowledgment that I had required him to take them with him, but that he, having no orders, was unable to comply with my request. This he absolutely refused, even Turks being afraid of pen and ink; but, after five hours' talk between him and his officers, who were of various minds, on the one part, and Yusuf and myself on the other, he shut them up provisionally, excepting the Mufti, who had accompanied the Sheikhs, and whom I offered to bail. After this, on my giving him a written demand for their arrest, with an order from Yusuf, as Sheikh el Belid, he the next morning determined to carry them to Cairo, and they were consigned to safe-keeping, with orders to prepare for their journey.

Another day had been lost in this way; and it was only on Friday, the 18th, that, accompanied by a soldier and three of Sheikh Yusuf's people, I started early to see the ruins of Omm Beida, and any other antiquities which might be found in the oasis. There was, of course, no longer any opposition on the part of the Siwy, but the Commandant was very anxious to be off, and only with difficulty agreed to give me till Sunday evening—far too short a time to see the many ruins which are met with in the Hattyehs, beyond the immediate territory of Siwah.

CHAPTER XIX.

RIDING due east from the large town of Siwah,
through cultivated fields well covered with green
crops of young wheat, we came to an artesian well,
which for perhaps thousands of years has watered
this part of the plain. The water rises in a circular
basin of ancient workmanship, which is admirably
built with large dressed stones, from whence it flows by
channels running in different directions. It is not
very deep, and the volume of water which it discharges
is so small, that it was emptied in two days, some few
years ago, by persons in search of treasure. All, or
nearly all, the walls of Siwah are of the same description ; they were once more numerous than they now
are ; but the mechanical genius of the present inhabitants is so deficient that some of the wells, even
within the memory of man, have been allowed to get

stopped up by the falling in of their sides—one, for instance, on a hill to the south, to which medicinal virtues were ascribed. A circumstance which seemed to me worth recording is, that after a shock of an earthquake (and shocks occur here at intervals of about twenty years), the supply of water becomes more abundant; and even old wells have been reopened by the convulsion.

After passing this well, we proceeded directly to Agharmy (اغرمى), the modern name of the old acropolis of the Oasis. I had received several visits from the Sheikh of Agharmy, who had shown himself always very friendly; he had, in fact, on the death of his father, become a ward of Yusuf's. He had promised to show me all that his town contained; but the jealousy of prying foreigners is such, that notwithstanding the presence of the soldiers, and the good words of the Sheikh, I should have left Siwah without seeing its most remarkable monument, as all my predecessors had done before me, but for the information given me by the Gibely. He had joined my party as a volunteer, with the secret intention, I believe, of watching my movements, in the hope that he should thus obtain some useful hints concerning the places where the hoards of the unbelievers, which he is firmly persuaded are concealed in all old ruins, ought to be dug for.

Agharmy is built on the platform of a lofty rock,
which rises abruptly from the level of the surrounding
gardens. It is entered only by a single gateway, from
which a very steep winding road leads up into the
town. A guard is stationed at the door to prevent the
admission of any individual of the Lifayah, who,
though only living at a distance of three quarters of an
hour, are never allowed to enter it.   This precaution is
adopted in consequence of an old feud ; the Lifayah
having fifty or sixty years ago seized the town and
expelled its inhabitants, who in turn, after several
years of warfare, surprised the conquerors with the aid
of the Gharbyin, and having recovered possession, they
established sentinels, who still, day and night, guard
the gate. A shed is built just without it, in which
any of the Lifayah who wish to see inhabitants of
Agharmy must wait, while a message is sent to fetch
the person who is inquired for ; and from this rule not
even the Mufti is excepted. The ascent is closed by a
second door, through which I passed, and presently
arrived at a deep well, which I was assured is all that
the town has to show in the way of antiquity. It is
circular, built of regular layers of masonry, with stairs
descending on the north side. Diodorus mentions a
well, lying not far from the oracle, in which the
animals for the sacrifice were washed ; and this is undoubtedly the same, as evidenced by its ancient work-

manship, and its being the only one in the place. It is about fifty feet deep, and is said to be fed by the waters of seven springs, which issue from the base of the rock on which the town is built. A few large stones, remains of ancient building, are imbedded in some of the modern cabins near this. When I had visited these, the Sheikh assured me that there was nothing more to be seen in the place; and being unwilling to provoke unnecessary jealousy, I was satisfied to return. Proceeding ten minutes to the south, I reached Omm Beida, that second Ammonium, which is mentioned as lying not far from the town. It is still very much in the condition in which it was found by Hornemann and M. Linaut de Bellefond, the author of the description published under the name of M. Drovetti, to whom he communicated it on his return.

All that remains of this temple are, one lintel of the doorway, and part of what seems to have been the outer chamber which led to the sanctuary. My measures give twenty-three feet eight inches for the height of the remaining walls, and the inside width is fifteen feet nine inches. The roof is formed by blocks of stone, stretching from wall to wall, on each of which are two royal vultures, displayed side by side, holding swords or feathers in their claws, with bands of stars along the edges. The walls, of a limestone filled with shells, quarried in a neighbouring hill, are covered with sculptures, stuccoed and painted blue and green. These sculptures are in six bands, the fourth from the ground being filled with perpendicular lines of hiero- glyphics. The others are rows of figures, the gods of the Egyptian mythology, who occupy the three lower bands, diminishing in size in each successive band from the ground. The only seated figure is the ram- headed Ammon, in the third row. Above this, is a procession of figures bearing offerings; and over this, a line of hawks, each bearing the jackal-headed stick, and above its head the globe, with the serpent issuing from it. The edifice is raised on a platform of rock; some of the walls which surrounded the inner inclosure can still be traced; but I could find no certain indi- cation of the outer wall, which was formerly visible in the north-east corner. At the end of the platform, im- mediately in a line with the existing building, is a subterraneous passage, which probably marks the posi- tion of the sanctuary, as it would serve for the oracle. Some large masses of alabaster are scattered about this part of the ruins, which have been dug up in all directions by those most persevering of antiquarians the treasure-seekers.

Some visitor of ancient or modern times has left his name on the walls; and as I thought the vanity of seeking such a doubtful notoriety excusable in this place, I copied it. In large roman letters it is written

—" AMIRO." Who, or of what age, Mr. Amiro
was, nothing indicated. A few yards to the south-by-
south-west of Omm Beida is the celebrated fountain of
the sun, a large pond, in several parts of which the
water bubbles up, as if boiling. It has a saltish taste,
and the thermometer in it marked 85°, that of the external atmosphere being 78°, affording thus a very
appreciable degree of warmth in the cold nights of the
desert. At a short distance, eastward from the ruins,
is a place where, not many years ago, extensive excavations were made by a Turkish Governor, as usual, in
search of treasure; his labour was rewarded by finding
a bronze lion and three statues of the same metal,
though called, by my native informants, gold. Returning from Omm Beida to Agharmy, I found, in a
garden to the left, ruins of a temple-like building, consisting of two chambers; the first of which was twenty-
two feet by seventeen, the second twelve feet by
seventeen. They are built of very large stones, and on
one side are fragments of fluted columns, but no capitals, nor anything which, as far as we saw, without
digging, would indicate whether or not they belonged
to a portico.

I was now able to examine the town, as seen from
the exterior, occupying its lofty table-rock. I was
astonished, as well as pleased, to perceive in its outer
wall, on the north side, a large piece of ancient build-

ing in perfect condition.   This, as far as I am aware,
has not been remarked by any previous traveller, and
I eagerly inquired if there were any appearance of
buildings connected with this within the town.   I was
assured that nothing was visible in the interior, houses
being built against it; but information which I derived from the Gibely induced me to return to the
town a few days later, and I now proceed to describe
the results of my second visit.

After passing the wall, a steep street to the right
leads round a large group of houses, in some of which
I remarked ancient foundations, and thence one reaches
a very massive wall, built of large stones.   A doorway
has been broken in this leading into the court of a
house.   At my request this door was opened, and I
found myself in the forecourt of a temple or palace,
now divided in its breadth by a modern wall.   On
entering, to the right and left are two immense door-
ways, now walled up, with a pure Egyptian outline
and well-cut cornice, but unadorned with hieroglyphics.
This court now measures sixteen feet by ten feet, but
in its original state it must have been nearly twenty
feet wide.   After much parley, the door to the right
was opened, and to my astonishment I found myself
in an apartment very low and dark, but whose sides
were covered with hieroglyphics.   A modern wall
divides it in length into two chambers, and a flooring

seemed to have been added to make a second story. Having penetrated so far, and being told there were no women in the house, I went up-stairs, where I found the sculptures continued on the wall up to a heavy projecting cornice, above which the wall is undecorated. A window in the end of the second chamber on this floor enabled me to see that it was the wall of this building which I had seen from below. This chamber, in its original dimensions, is about twenty-four feet long by fourteen broad, and twenty-one high, and from its cornice, which seems calculated to support a ceiling, I presume it consisted of two stories. In the upper and further room, as it at present exists, I found on the right a passage, made in the thickness of the walls, eight feet in length by two in width, which may have served as a place of concealment, there being no egress from it. In the lower room, on the left, is also a small chamber, about six feet by four feet, which seems to have formed a cupboard or some such repository.

Here, as at Omm Beida, I could see no appearance of a cartouche among the sculptures on the walls; but I might have overlooked them, if any such exist, as only a cursory examination was reluctantly granted me by my guides; the walls, moreover, were perfectly blackened by smoke, and the only light we had was that of a flaring palm-branch. Leaving this

building by the door by which I had entered, and
turning round its exterior, I found the remaining part
of the wall of the court, with another large doorway,
similar to those I had already seen. Proceeding southwards from this I came upon indications of walls, and
from the edge of a hill of rubbish to which I had
advanced, I saw the wall just below my feet. I now
turned away, leaving the western door of the old building I had entered behind me, and after a few steps
came to a gigantic gateway (under which the road
passes) of less finished, though good workmanship,
and formed of stones of Cyclopean size. Other antiquities may probably exist among the houses, but
my time was so short, and the unwillingness of the
people to allow me to push my investigations further
was so great, that I was unable to make a more satisfactory examination of the locality.

Agharmy is undoubtedly the ancient Acropolis of
the Oasis, as it is described by Diodorus Siculus.   He
says that it had three walls, the first inclosing the
palace of the kings; the second the women's apart-
ments (the harem) and the oracle; the third containing the habitation of the guards—this is, I believe,
from Quintus Curtius; having no means of examining
the originals, I quote at second-hand or from memory.
I suppose that the building still so well preserved is a
part of the palace of the kings; and if the three walls

are understood as having been not concentric, but the chords of a curve dividing the inclosure into three (the only reading which I think admissible), we have the present town nearly exhibiting the distribution of the old Acropolis. A wall, now principally formed of houses, runs round the edge of the table-rock, and the town can only be entered by a steep ascent on the south-east. At the extremity of this, where the present guard is lodged, I suppose was drawn the first wall, defended by the barracks of the Satellites. In the space beyond this were the palace of the women and the temple, near the well which still exists, separated by a wall (one of whose massive gateways I passed under) from the royal palace.

Outside the town, in the rock on which it is built, and nearly beneath the remains of what I call the palace, is a cave eight feet by six feet, which seems to have been formerly the mouth of a passage cut in the rock, a postern from the Acropolis. The abruptness of the sides of the rock, the fragments scattered round its base, the springs which flow from beneath, the apricots and pomegranate trees with their lively shade around it, render the exterior view of Agharmy a most picturesque desert scene.

I spent an afternoon on the Gara el Musaberin, the hill of mummies, which lies to the north-east of the town. Its surface is literally, in every part, cut into caves, all of which seem to have been violated by the Siwy, those ransackers of tombs. In many there are still heaps of bones, in general bleached by the sun; and in two I found fragments of well-preserved remains, wrapt in a coarse cotton cloth, with stripes of bright red and blue. Several of these tombs exhibit great care in their execution, not a few, towards the summit, have decorated portals, and many are plastered with a fine stucco, on which are traces of painting in blue or red. The Ammonians seem to have interred their dead without coffins, as there are no remnants of wood scattered among the graves; and those who told me of their discoveries here and in once cultivated tracts to the west (though they had found many mummies), never seem to have met with them in coffins.*

To the south of Siwah is a curious hill called Gibel el Beyruh, formed of five cones. It contains several excavations, which have been used as tombs, but which seem to have been originally the quarries whence the stone for building the temple was taken. There was

---

* I am inclined to suppose that after the dead had undergone the process of mummifying, and had been wrapped in their case-ments, they were covered with a coating of stucco : I have a piece of fine white plaster which I picked in one of the tombs, one-third of an inch thick, in which are the impression of a limb and fragments of cloth.

formerly a spring here, celebrated for its medicinal virtues, but now sanded up, called 'Ain el Handa-lieh.

Accompanied by the brother of the Mufti, the only one of the Sheikhs of the Lifayah whom I could trust, I went to see the town proper of Siwah. We first went to the date yards (mestahh, مُسْتَاح), in which the dates are piled up in great heaps, the ground being divided by stones, which distinguish each individual's property. These stone places are three in number, and lie in the plain to the north of the town; they are surrounded by a wall, with a gate to each, one belonging to the Gharbyin, one to the Lifayah, and the centre one to members of both communities. They said that thus left exposed to the sun and air the dates will keep for a long time, neither subject to decay nor to the attacks of insects.

Crossing the open space which separates the mestahh from the foot of the town, we passed the chapel of Sidi Suleiman, who is the most venerated Marābut of this place; he seems, indeed, to have succeeded, in the estimation of the surrounding Arabs, to the old sanctity of Ammon. All disputes and lawsuits, which in Moslem jurisprudence are decided by the oaths of the parties, are adjourned to Sidi Suleiman for decision; and many who fear not to swear falsely by God and his Prophet will speak the truth here, as the Sheikh is said never to have left a false oath sworn in his name unpunished.

From this place, entering by a flight of steps one of the fourteen doors, I was introduced into the interior of the town. A servant carried a lamp, which I soon found quite necessary, for without a light no one unacquainted with the locality could find his way through the dark lanes which run through the town. The principal street, some ten feet wide by seven or eight feet high, runs round the rock which forms the nucleus of this agglomeration of houses; from this branch other streets, seldom more than four feet wide, and so low that one must bend the head to pass through them. There are four wells, two saltish, and two of sweet water; into two of them the light is allowed to enter, the houses being built round, not over them. Excepting here, neither air nor light enter the town from above; it is not, therefore, wonderful that every year Siwah is visited by a typhoid fever, whose virulence is so great that during its continuance no stranger ventures to approach the Oasis.

Having made the round of the place, and tasted the waters of its wells, I was not sorry to return to sunlight, and again to breathe a less stifling atmosphere. We now turned eastward, and crossed a space surrounded by houses and containing some booths for the

market which is held here during the date season ;
the space is called Sebucha (سبوخة).   We then
entered a very pretty grove of palm-trees, dotted with
the summer residences of the wealthier inhabitants,
and thence in five minutes reached the small town of
Menshich (مـنشـية), built on level ground, and for
the most part in ruins.   It was then completely deserted, all the inhabitants having, on the approach of
the soldiers, removed into Siwah.

Excepting the foundations of some of the houses
on the Gara, the western extremity of the town, in
which I was lodged (where a layer or two of masonry
or cuttings in the rock may sometimes be remarked),
I saw no traces of antiquity in any of the buildings,
but, as of old, the houses are built with blocks of rock
salt, sometimes almost pure, cemented together with
mud.   From the dryness of the climate this kind of
wall is perfectly solid, and will even resist artillery,
the ball driving in only so much of the material as
will give it a passage.   The reader must not, however,
imagine that the buildings of Siwah display the glittering appearance which the fairy-like palaces in some
of the German salt-mines present.   To the eye nothing is apparent but the mud with which they are
plastered, and they most prosaically resemble the
rudest village structures in Egypt.

The only excursion in the neighbourhood which I

could make was to Beled er-Roum, of whose ruins,
and the treasures concealed in them, I had heard extraordinary accounts from the natives. It lies nearly
north by north-west from Siwah, the road leading over
a causeway, built, I believe, by a former governor,
across the salt lake which bounds Siwah on this side.
The water is shallow, and from the film of crystallised
salt which covers it to a considerable distance, it has
the appearance of being frozen. Passing through
groves of palms and olives, we came in an hour and a
half to a large mass of shapeless ruins, built of sandstone and salt, called Dāhĭba. An hour further through
hills, all of them containing cave-tombs, brought us to
Beled er-Roum. We first came upon a collection of
small ruins, built of unburnt bricks, in one of which
are two well-turned vaults. In the rocks close to them
are some well-executed tombs, and I am inclined to
ascribe a similar use to these buildings, which may
date from about the second century ; the people call
them the houses of the infidels. A little further on
are the ruins of the temple, which, with a disposition
resembling the Egyptian, is of almost pure Doric
architecture, without a trace of hieroglyphics, and the
stones of which it is built are only two feet six inches
by one foot. The cornice of the sanctuary, or furthest
apartment, is composed of four flutings ; that of the
exterior room is one very large curve, whose outline is

completely Doric. There remain now portions of only
three rooms. The inner one, with two small windows,
is sixteen feet five inches in breadth by fifteen feet six
inches long. The centre room, with the same breadth,
is only eight feet six inches long; and the exterior
one, now in great part ruined, is fifteen feet eight
inches long. Their height is eighteen feet seven
inches. The roof of the inner compartment has fallen,
and its masses encumber the sanctuary; of that of the
second chamber there still remain four immense stones,
stretching from wall to wall, like that of Omm Beida.
The sanctuary is entered by a large doorway with
pilasters, and the space is narrowed by short square
pillars, with very broad capitals, which almost touch,
so that the passage left is only broad enough for one
person, while above there is formed by the summit of
the capitols, a sort of window cut off the height of the
door. In front, and in a line with the remaining
building, extends a long substructure, the foundation
of the remainder of the temple, which seems to have
three times exceeded the fragment which is preserved,
and about thirty yards further on is an extensive
vaulted subterranean, running at right angles to the
line of the temple.

All these buildings undergo continual dilapidations
through the researches of the treasure-seekers; and it
is probable that, at no distant date, this temple will in

this manner be entirely destroyed; for it unfortunately happens that treasure, enclosed in a box of obir-wood, is supposed to exist somewhere within the stones which form the roof. I was shown a Moghraby manuscript, containing detailed directions where to seek for treasures, and stating of what they consisted.

Other antiquities exist in places round Siwah, their distance varying from six hours to two days; but I was kept in such uncertainty as to the time when we were to leave, and I was so unwilling to take the responsibility of detaining the troops, that I gave up my intention of visiting them. Mummies are not unfrequently found in subterranean repositories built in the sand of a Hattyeh five hours distant to the west; and in these graves glass or earthenware vessels are sometimes discovered. There is a place called Dogha (دوغة), a day and a half to the east, never visited by the Siwy, of which I heard from a man who had reached it in tracking some lost camels. He said that there was there a temple like that of Omm Beida, in front of which were rows of warriors on horseback, cut in stone. These may, not impossibly, be sphinxes. He further told me that the earth in this Hattyeh is black, with a strong smell of sulphur when thrown on the fire. I should be inclined to suppose this may be a sulphate of some metal; the more so, that the Gibely told me a man had brought, he knew not from where, a handful of similar earth, which, when exposed to the heat of a furnace, left a button of a white metal in the bottom of the crucible. I think it is Cailland who speaks of sulphur mines in Siwah; but though the hot springs and occasional earthquakes are a proof of volcanic action in this neighbourhood, no one I spoke with had any knowledge of the existence of either yellow or white sulphur.

At Beled er-Roum I spent an hour in the orchard of one of my friends; and in vain attempted to put this time to profit by learning the distinguishing marks of the different kinds of date-trees. It requires a very practised eye to discover the different varieties when not in fruit; the stems and leaves are so similar in all, that my guide was unable to point out the marks by which one is known from the other. The Siwah dates are of four kinds:—the waddy ودّي, used for feeding cattle; the s'aïdy سعيدي, which, with water, are pressed into a cake; the gh'azaly غزالي, a long brown date; and, lastly, the most highly prized, the farechy فَراخي, whose fruit is short, nearly white, and crisp, as if candied.*

---

* The taxes in Siwah are levied on the date and olive trees, at the rate of 2¼ piastres on each tree, yielding an annual revenue of 10,000 dollars. From this tax the waddy date-trees, whose fruit is used for feeding the cattle, and which amount to 90,000, are excepted.

This day there blew a violent chamsin wind, which raised clouds of sand, rendering it almost impossible for any one to see a few yards ahead, and against which spectacles were no protection. Nothing would have tempted me to brave it but the necessity of being ready to start on the following day. On my return, I announced to the Commandant that I had completed my tour of the antiquities ; and would detain him no longer. My eyes and skin were still smarting from exposure to the wind; and I was, perhaps, a little annoyed when he answered that, Inshallah ! we should start the day after to-morrow. But that day was Tuesday, a bad day for starting ; the next, Wednesday, was still more unlucky; therefore, on Thursday, we were positively to go ; and, early in the morning of that day, almost before dawn, came an officer to see if I were ready. By this time, I had learned a lesson in punctuality, and did not hurry myself; but by eight, my camels were being loaded, under the superintendence of one of the Buluk-bashis, who seemed now to think every five minutes of value. I knew that the eighty water-skins had not yet been filled, and looked forward to a departure late in the afternoon as the most that could be hoped for; but when at last, being fairly turned out of my house, I took refuge at the castle, I found there was to be a fresh palaver on the subject of the prisoners. I was

now thoroughly tired of the question; and, like
Falstaff, I was somewhat ashamed of the ragged regiment who were to be carried in my suite, so I told
Hassan Aga he might do as he pleased on his own
responsibility; whereupon, he took from them a
written engagement to present themselves, one and
all, at Cairo on that day month.   I held my peace till
all was done, and they were dismissed; after which I
drily said to him, "I have no hand in the matter;
not one of them will come."   And the event proved
that I was right.

It was now too late in the day to think of starting;
and, having made up my mind to preserve my good-
humour, at least, as far as the Egyptian frontier, I adjourned with Hassan to the front of the castle, where a
carpet was spread, and the officers, old and young,
joined by several of the men, gave us the amusement
of a game of the Jerid.   I had never before seen this
really graceful exercise; but it has been so often described that I refrain from speaking of it.

CHAPTER XX.

GOOD FRIDAY.—*March 25th.*—It was eleven o'clock
the next day before everything was ready. The camels
were loaded and sent on, and then, with loud beating
of the little saddle-drums, the horsemen forming a long
line, their colours in the middle, followed by Hassan
Aga and myself, we rode slowly out of Siwah. The
officers cantered along the line as it advanced, first one
and then another, in no regular order, and with no
other apparent object than that of making a sort of
fantasia, as the Arabs call everything which they think
amusing or gay. A wedding festivity, a gaily-decked
horse, or an embroidered jacket, are all equally fantasia. My servants and the slaves of the officers,
Sheikh Yusuf and his friends, who in considerable
numbers accompanied him, for some hours brought
up the rear. The well-disposed part of the population

had come out to see the show, and to bid me adieu;
among them the Mufti and his brother, but none of
my late prisoners appeared in the crowd, to the great
indignation of Hassan Aga.

An hour out of the town the standard was furled,
and then the line was broken, and every one went as
his fancy led him, excepting myself, who soon found
that I was considered either too suspicious or too
precious a personage to be allowed to stir a step
without Hassan Aga at my side. If I hung back,
he did so too; if I rode to one side, he not only
followed me, but with him the little tin-kettle drum-
mers, and the nucleus of his army. As for dis-
mounting to gather a fossil, or to chip a rock, it
was the signal for a general halt; and I was therefore condemned to stick to my saddle and follow my
leader.

In three hours and a half we reached a Hattyeh
called Wushky Tamoushty, وشكي طموشتي, where we
halted for some little time to allow the camels to
come up. Ponds of bitter water, palm bushes and
minosas, dot this plain, which is infested by myriads of
small, gray, singularly venomous musquitoes. Two
and a half hours further on, we came to some hills
called Gebel Melhiors, ملهيوس, of the same tertiary
limestone as those around Siwah, and here the soldiers
amused themselves by discharging their guns and pis-

tols to enjoy the repeated echoes of one of the rocks.
It was half-past nine, when, after passing Hattyeh el
Kuttef, الكثف, we reached Omm Hoemem هُوَّدَم, a
line of low sand-hills covered with trees; these supplied
materials for making huge bonfires, round which the
soldiers lay themselves to sleep in parties of three and
four.   The next day we were fourteen hours on horseback, riding through a country presenting nothing remarkable; I give, therefore, a mere catalogue of names.
After passing a hill, Ingah Omm Hoemem, we came
to a table-land called Es-sutah, السُوطه, from which,
on the right, rises a rock called Er-Rocheia, الرحيه,
The view was bounded towards the east by low white
hills, destitute of any appearance of vegetation, called,
from their colour, El-abiadh.   Here we halted for the
night; the soldiers were in great discomfort, as the
place affords no means of making fires, and the night
was extremely chilly. Skirting El-abiadh we reached in
three hours a darker-coloured range, called El Ach-
mar, and from this it took us three hours to arrive at
the palm-groves and wells of brackish water, which lie
on this side of the small oasis of El Gara, as it is
usually called, though also known as Omm-es-sog-
haigh, امالسغير.
      This is a miniature Siwah, presenting the same
abundance of water (which is here all bitter), and a

proportionate number of date trees. The town, now almost in ruins, resembles Agharmy in its situation on a table-rock, and is approached by a very steep path, which passes under a gateway. Everything betokens the poverty and misery of the inhabitants, who only number twelve grown men. There is a tradition, that the population of the place can never exceed forty; and whenever, by immigration (which they do not therefore encourage) or by births, this limit is passed, some one is sure to die. The male population seemed very well-disposed, coming at once on our arrival to pay their court to Hassan Aga and Sheikh Yusuf, and showing readiness to make themselves as useful as they could. I never met with twelve such ugly specimens of humanity collected in one place; and their virtues do not atone for their bad looks, as they are said to be drunkards and lazy, taking no other care of their date trees, about 21,000 in number, than drawing *lagby* and gathering the fruit from them. They make no attempt at manuring them, and do not even trim them, so that their produce is very inferior to the dates of Siwah. The interior of the town is even more ruinous than the promise of its external appearance; a circular market-place, surrounded by fallen cabins, occupies its centre, and it has near the entrance a well of drinkable water, 70 feet deep.

The brother of one of the two sheikhs who govern

this important territory acted as my guide to see the
curiosities of the place, and thinking, perhaps, that he
had not sufficiently earned his bachshish, he insisted,
as we came out, on showing the town gate. He closed
the massive door, formed of palm trunks, and, after
drawing some ponderous bolts, linked on an iron cable
chain of the largest dimensions, to show me how
secure it was. I could not help smiling at the precautions taken to close a place which contained nothing of
the smallest value, which drew from him a grave
shake of the head and the triumphant rejoinder, that a
strong door and a big chain are good things. In the
rock on which the town is built are four rudely-exca-
vated sepulchres, and I saw many more in different
parts of the small oasis, but the rudeness of their
fashion leads me to conjecture that even in its most
flourishing times this dependency on the Ammonium
never reached any high degree of prosperity. Either
this, or the lake of El Arachish, to the north-west of
Siwah, must have been the place where Alexander left
his escort in entering on the sacred territory of Ammon. We spent a day and a half here, notwithstanding the badness of the water, from which some of the
horses had suffered in coming to Siwah, as the Aga
had forgotten or neglected to have bread baked for the
soldiers before starting. Leaving El Gara, we took
almost a due northerly direction, and made long days,

as there is no water to be found for four days. The
horses of my escort had the bad habit of drinking
daily, which a thorough desert horse does not require,
and, when possible, the draught is given to them about
midday. Immediately after drinking, their riders
mount them and give them a short gallop, which I can
only suppose is for the purpose of winding them.

The first landmark we reached was Gar-el-lebna,
the milk hill, thirteen hours off, the next six hours
further on, Gar-ed-dih, the cock's hill. Many of the
horses fell, as if struck with apoplexy, on the second
day, and on this day and the two following ones we
lost eleven. I ascribe the casualty to the water of the
Gara, which, stopping digestion, blew them up like a
well-inflated foot-ball, and after a few hours in this
state, if injections, fomentations, and bleeding had no
effect, they dropped as if shot, with all the appearance
of a *coup de sang*. As ten of his horses had died
with the same symptoms on arriving in Siwah, I suggested to Hassan Aga that as short a route might be
found leaving the Gara to the east, which would, perhaps, avoid any risk there might be from a recurrence
of illness among the horses. He made no account of
this ; and now that one would have thought his eyes
must be opened to the results of his stupidity, he and
Sheikh Yusuf agreed in ascribing the misfortune to
the Evil Eye, while Yusuf looked grave, and said no

soldiers had ever approached Siwah without being struck by the Eye in leaving it.   Of course there was no veterinary with the detachment ; but what was stranger, not one of the party seemed to have an idea of what to do ; they had no physic, nor even a fleam. The horses which recovered, as well as, I acknowledge, some of those which died, were doctored by my servant and myself, their owners seeming to have no resource but to sit down and thank God that the Eye was on the horses, not on the men.

We had made thirteen hours this day, but on the next, the Commandant being anxious to arrive at water, as the skins were rapidly decreasing under the charge of the Arabs, the camels made seventeen hours' journey, and the next day, in three hours, we reached a well called Caldeh ; it, however, contained so small a supply that we literally drank it dry.   From Omm Es-soghair to this well the distance is forty-six hours. Though every day their loads, principally water and corn, were growing lighter, a great many of the camels were so exhausted that they dropped down, unable to proceed.   When no application of the stick would induce the poor beasts to rise, their loads were distributed to others, and they sometimes were able to continue the journey.   But if they had been driven too far before falling this was useless, and after a few steps they would again lie down, when the camel drivers would at once despatch them, and then stripping off the hide, they cut all the flesh from the bones to make a feast in the evening, so that within half an hour a pool of blood and a skeleton were all that remained of their long-suffering companion. I was unlucky enough to come up just as one large white camel fell. It lay motionless, while its brutal master, with heavy blows, endeavoured to force it to rise. In vain. The escort stopped to look on, and I was so fascinated with the expression of the dying beast's head, that, though anxious to turn away, I was an involuntary witness of its death. As all efforts to make it rise were unavailing, a man threw it over on its side and slowly cut through its long neck, from which an immense stream of blood flowed, while he pronounced the words, " In the name of God the Merciful, the Compassionate." The camel made no resistance; but, turning its head towards its butcher, uttered two or three loud, heart-rending moans, which sounded in my ears for the remainder of the day. I have seldom witnessed a more pitiable sight.

Five hours beyond Caldeh is another and very remarkable well, being a subterranean chamber hollowed in the rock, 72 feet square, in the floor of which are nine wells, one in each corner, in the centre of each side, and in the middle. Two are now sanded up, but the others afford an abundance of water. The cham-

ber is eight feet high, and presents every appearance
of great antiquity; but there are no ruins apparent in
the vicinity, nor any town named in the ancient geo-
graphies which could have occupied this place; perhaps, in its origin, it served, as at the present day, as a
reservoir for the caravans from the south and west.
We encamped here for the night, as a strong wind,
which had been blowing all day, had increased to such
violence that it was impossible to proceed. The air
was filled with sand of a dark orange colour, while the
sun, an hour and a half before setting, was of a pale
blue, and could be gazed at with the naked eye. Had
we been in July instead of April, this wind, which
blew from the south-west, might have been attended
with serious consequences. In the night a great deal
of rain fell, which moderated its violence, and the next
morning it had entirely ceased. We were now leaving
the region of sand, the ground being dotted with a
spare vegetation, which, in three hours from Bu Bat-
tah, gave the country a general green tone, till on
approaching the sea this was succeeded by a strong,
healthy growth of herbs and grass, affording excellent
pasturage. In eight hours we reached the edge of the
great platform we had been traversing, and by a steep
descent, of not more than 120 feet in perpendicular,
we reached the level of the sea, encamping, at the end
of the ninth hour, in a meadow of rank grass, sepa-

rated from the sea by a ridge of sand. A point to the west forms here a small bay, and Baretoun, the ancient Panetorium, lies a little beyond this. The name given to the place we encamped in is Berbetat-el-mudar. We here passed the following day to rest the horses, and to endeavour to obtain some supplies from the Arabs who are usually stationed here, but who now, at the instigation, I believe, of one of the sheikhs who were with us, had run away. They were probably within a few miles of our encampment, but so well concealed that every effort to discover their retreat was useless; and thus the visions of sheep and milk in which we had all been indulging were rendered illusory. From this place our course turned to the east, riding over a plain raised above the sea, of which we frequently caught a sight. Four hours eastwards is a place called, by the Arabs, Fuhah; and half an hour further on we came to the ruins of a small town whose walls are still to be traced. Nothing that remains indicates the name by which it may have been designated by Ptolemy, whose nomenclature is here, though so near Alexandria, singularly defective. In six hours more we encamped in a valley, surrounded by low hills, called Bu Jerabeh, containing several wells of bitter water, one only of which was drinkable. Here we found Sonagrah Arabs, whom their sheikh, Ḥaj Chalil, prevented from running away, so that we were well supplied with fresh butter, sour and sweet milk, and sheep, paying, of course, for all that we took.

I ought already to have presented the Haj Chalil to my reader, as he was the best of the Aoulad Ali whom I saw, and I exchanged with him on the road many a friendly joke. A day or two after my escort's arrival in Siwah, a tall, stout man, of some fifty years, entered my room, with a certain mysteriously solemn and consequential air. When he had taken his place, he said to me, in a low voice, that he had something very secret to communicate to me. Of course, after learning that he was Sheikh Haj Chalil, I ordered that no one should be admitted during the conference. He told me, as if it had been a matter of life and death, that he was my cousin, there being only seven grandfathers between him and me. The relationship, thus precisely defined, tickled my fancy, and though I supposed he must refer to descent from Spanish Moors, I begged he would enlighten me on his pedigree. It seems that his ancestor, whom he called Songor (hence the name of the Sonagra Arabs), was a Frank boy, who had been washed on shore from a wreck near Sallum. He was seized by the Bedawin, made the property of the Sheikh of Aoulad Hharsuf, and in the end married his daughter, and became the patriarch of a new tribe. The Arabs have no idea that one Christian is not cousin to another; hence the

claim of relationship, which I acknowledged ever afterwards, calling him son of my uncle.   It was not, however, only to have the pleasure of claiming relationship
with me that he came so mysteriously ; it was to beg
that, in consideration of this, I would speak well of
him to the Viceroy, so as to obtain his nomination as
Great Sheikh of the Aoulad Ali, under which name
are comprised the three tribes, Hharsuf, Sonagra, and
Sinnĭna.   I could not promise to interfere in a matter
in which I could have no right to interest myself, and
no power to be useful if I had done so ; but when the
occasion afterwards presented itself, in the course of
conversation, I was not forgetful of my uncle's son,
though my good offices were unavailing, as his Highness had already decided on naming a sheikh from
the Aoulad Hharsuf.   And a lucky escape it was, too,
for Haj Chalil, as the possessor of the coveted honour,
within three months followed his predecessor on the
road to Fazoughla—a sort of penal hell upon earth—
where, if he have good luck, he will arrive, instead of
being murdered, as the other is said to have been, at
Girgeh ; for, I suppose, one must call murder the
condemning a man to one punishment, and secretly
inflicting upon him a heavier one—the loss of his
head.

From Bu Jerabah we travelled over a slightly-
undulating country, covered with a short, wiry grass,

called by the Arabs wild barley, which affords excellent pasture for horses, till we reached Turbiat, in
five hours and a half. This was again a short day,
as the camels and horses were too tired to proceed.
Here, after much scolding and threatening of the
Courbadj, we obtained a small supply of corn for the
horses—a necessity which was not agreeable to Hassan
Aga, as he had to pay here for what he required, while
the corn he took in Siwah was levied as a contribution
on the town. The Siwy persuaded the Arabs, who
were glad to save their camels the extra weight, to
assure the Commandant that corn was to be had in
any quantity after the eighth day ; but these same
Arabs now took care to send on before us during the
night, to warn all their fellows out of our way. As
everything taken from the Arabs was fairly paid for, it
seemed mere spite on the part of the sheikhs who
were with us thus to increase the inconveniences of
the journey, and I acknowledge I was not sorry to
hear that one of the most troublesome among them
had received from the Commandant's own hands a
rather severe drubbing. Twenty-five hours were employed the two following days in reaching the wells
called El Hammam. We had now left the coast line,
but the next day, an hour and a half after starting,
having the Arabs' Tower, or Abou Sir, the old Tapo-

siris, in sight, we passed through extensive ruins, marking, perhaps, the site of Antiphræ, so famous for its wine—it was so bad. At a considerable distance to the right rise the flat hills of Hoshm el'Aish, which may be said to bound the district of Mariout. We only made nine hours this day, stopping at Caraya, where are five wells of ancient construction, the largest built with very solid masonry, having an orifice of twelve feet by three. The old Lake Mareotis is now an extensive plain, covered with dark shrubs, and dotted with low, yellow mounds.

Two thousand female dromedaries belonging to the Viceroy were stationed here for the pasturage, the best camel-browsing ground in Egypt. I wondered to what purpose these were applied, and admired his Highness's tender solicitude for his stud of Arab horses, when I learned that, immediately after the mares foal, the dromedaries are sent up the country to supply them with milk. His horses are decidedly the best lodged, best fed, and best cared for of the present Pacha's subjects. After passing two Marābut chapels, Abu Hadidj and Sheikh Masa'udi, which lay to the right, we came to the first village in Egypt, Gheitá, and stopped, eight hours from Caraya, at El Hamra. The next day was the last of our weary journey: in two hours we came to El Hhosh (Hhosh Ebro 'Isa),

which is celebrated for its breed of falcons ; and in six
hours more we pitched our tents outside the flourishing
town of Damanhour.

Here ended my desert journey, and it was not without feelings of pleasure that I found myself once more
within the circuit of Eastern civilisation.   But it must
not be supposed that I left the desert without some
feelings of regret.   A prolonged sojourn in those vast
plains of sand,—condemned to a perpetual sterility—a
voyage over those waterless seas, is less devoid of interest than at first sight one might be led to expect.
They offer, indeed, little variety, and they promise
less ; but this very monotony renders the traveller
more attentive to the varied aspects which Nature
even here presents, and awakens his attention to many
an object which in more-favoured climes he would
pass unobserved.   The only variety of general feature
is the passing from loose sand to more compact gravel,
or from boundless plains, which the wearied eye ranges
over without meeting an object on which to fix the
gaze, to equally desert hills, whose sandy solitudes are
undisturbed even by an echo.   Sometimes, more awful
still, one comes upon vast tracts covered with small,
dark, loose fragments, giving a chocolate colour to the
ground, which there seems to absorb the rays of the
mid-day sun, but without reposing the eye from its
glare.   The camel here leaves no traces of his path,

so that the solitary traveller must strain his sight to
keep in view the distant caravan ; the dry tramp of his
horse alone disturbs the mournful silence ; the sun is
darting on him his most burning rays ; and, from the
colour of the ground, he seems to have lost even the
companionship of his own shadow.

But this very silence, this monotonous absence of
animation, are of themselves impressive, and soon acquire a peculiar charm for the imagination. The earth
seems boundless as the ocean, not less cheerlessly
uniform than a sea becalmed, and not less dangerously
wild than it when roused by the strife of elements.
The sky is pale in the glare of mid-day, but glows
with the brightest tints as evening closes in ; after
sunset, it is again illuminated by the zodiacal light,
which fades to disclose a surface of the deepest purple,
spangled with thousands of stars, whose twinkling
brightness surpasses anything that our northern climates can show. The desert, where no howling of wild
beasts alarms the ear, no watch-fire proclaims the
vicinity of fellow-men, affects one less with a sense of
solitude than of vastness, and, like the sea, awakens
feelings rather of the moral greatness with which man
is endowed, than of the physical weakness which is
his lot.   Man, alone, can traverse the broad desert ; I
have been days without meeting the trace of a quad-
ruped, or seeing a bird in the air ; the wind-worn rocks

bear no nourishment for the former, the restless sand-waves afford no prey to the latter.

When, in this sea of sand, one approaches the rare islands with which it is dotted, the eye is first attracted to the tracks worn by the jackals and gazelles, which, making their abodes during the day among the shrub-less rocks, often twenty or thirty miles from water, at night go to drink and feed in the oasis.   Then the sand is dotted with clumps of the zumaran, and other thick-leaved plants, whose roots, stretching along the surface, draw sufficient moisture for their existence from the air ; round these may be marked the tiny footprints left by the nightly gambols of the gerboa. A clump of palm-trees, or a few mimosas, are at last seen on the horizon, and welcomed with joy by the thirsty caravan ; the camels now increase their pace, the Arab's step becomes more elastic, though it will be hours before the wished-for spring is reached. Round this are the blackened fire-places of former travellers, the deep claw-marks of the vultures, the tracks of the fox, the jackal, and the gazelle, the trail of the land tortoise, even the black, rough-backed beetle, patiently rolling its load towards its hole, each and all are welcome, as telling of the living world from which the traveller has been separated.

Desert travel has its pleasures as well as its tribulations. Of the former I have said but little in the preceding narrative, for hours of contemplation find no place in a note-book; of the latter I have said, perhaps, more than enough, for annoyances which in the retrospect are insignificant, seem proportionably great while one is suffering from them.

The time of actual travelling from Siwah to Daman-hour was 155 hours, a fair journey of thirteen days, which is the time the caravans usually employ, while Alexandria is a day nearer. There is another road which is easier for the camels, following the coast line (in going *to* Siwah) from Berbetat el Mudar to Kasr Adjubah, one day and a half. Thence to Jarjub, the same distance; to Esh-Shamar, half a day; to Sallum, three days. Thence, turning northwards, to Bir el Hhamza, two days, and thence to Siwah, three days. The direct road to Siwah from Cairo is by Tervaneh and the Natron lakes, but by this route of eleven days there are four without water. From Siwah to Derna is a journey of fifteen days, and to Benghazi twenty days.

I will not detain the reader by an account of my adventures after reaching Damanhour. How the Turk-ish colonel of the Bashbuzuks came to meet me, and then was inclined to treat me somewhat cavalierly; how I recalled him to his senses, and how it ended in our kissing and being friends; and my then spending a night with him at Rachmania, from which place I embarked for Cairo.

This narration of a nine months' journey, in countries little known, however uninterestingly told, is at least faithful. I believe, indeed, that the traveller who simply records what he sees with his eyes and hears with his ears, and indulges in none of the pleasures of the imagination, rarely meets with those stirring scenes which, beheld by the fancy and treated with the pen of an artist, so frequently charm the reader. My tale is true, and it relates to what may still be called unknown countries; and this is my reason for offering it to the public.

I am bound to express my obligations for the ready aid afforded me by Her Majesty's Consul in Cairo, during the absence or leave of the accomplished Consul-General, whose departure, a few weeks after my arrival, was a subject of regret both to Turk and Frank. It would be unjust also to omit stating, that the Viceroy, within twenty-four hours of the arrival of my letter, despatched orders for the march of 150 soldiers to my relief; and, after my presentation to him in Cairo, ordered another party of 200 to be sent to disarm the town, and to bring forty-nine of the Siwy to Cairo to answer for their conduct.

Sheikh Yusuf is reinstated, in more than his

former authority, with a garrison of twenty soldiers under his orders ; so I flatter myself that my prophecy to the Shiekhs of Siwah, that I should be the last European they would ill-treat, is now fulfilled. I can now have the satisfaction of feeling, that my successors in the exploration of the antiquities of that country will meet with no obstacles to their researches.

FINIS.